Supervision and Administration:
Programs, Positions, Perspectives

E. Andrew Mills,

Editor

National Art Education Association
1916 Association Drive
Reston, Virginia 22091-1590

1991

About NAEA . . .

Founded in 1947, the National Art Education Association is the largest professional art education association in the world. Membership includes elementary and secondary teachers, art administrators, museum educators, arts council staff, and university professors from throughout the United States and 66 foreign countries. NAEA's mission is to advance art education through professional development, service, advancement of knowledge, and leadership.

I would like to thank the First National Bank of Chicago Art Program, John H. Neff, Director, for providing the Miyoko Ito painting for the cover of this publication. The First Chicago art collection consists of nearly 6,000 objects, ranging from the sixth century BC to contemporary, from virtually all points of the globe, in all static media. Primarily installed throughout the bank's headquarters in Chicago and the metropolitan area, the collection is also on display in branch offices in more than twenty cities worldwide. A special thank you to Dan Mills, Associate Curator, for his efforts in making this venture possible. EAM

Cover: *Season of Separations*, 1982. Miyoko Ito (American 1918 - 1983). Oil on canvas, 39" x 28". Collection: The First National Bank of Chicago.

ISBN 0-937652-56-3

Contents

3

Foreword

This anthology is a collection of articles by educators who have found their place in, and dedicated their lives to, arts supervision and administration. Each author selected a topic to develop and share with others in the field of art(s) education. Of the 17 essays, 10 are written by district art or arts supervisors, including six supervisors of large city school systems. Three are contributed by state supervisors or consultants, and the remainder are written by individuals involved in various aspects of education and the arts.

Several of the authors provide a complete description of their supervisory role, their constituency, and all that their supervision entails. Several have written about supervision in general, while others have written in detail about specific aspects of their art(s) education programs. These specific topics include staff development, evaluation of art learning, integrating community cultural resources, establishing elementary art specialists, coordinating multiple arts programs, inner city programming, developing management skills, and art education from the state viewpoint.

A short biographical sketch of each author is contained in the section entitled Contributors. After reading this section, the reader may more fully understand the essays and the point of view of each author.

The anthology was edited by E. Andrew Mills, former Chief, Bureau of Arts, Music, and Humanities Education, New York State Education Department and NAEA Board Member. Drew is now retired to another life as arts consultant, exhibiting artist, studio and gallery proprietor, and musician.

This publication should become a valuable resource for all in art(s) education because of the wide range of programs, positions, and perspectives that are presented.

JAMES M. CLARKE, President
National Art Education Association

Art Consultant
Aldine Independent Schools
Houston, Texas

Introduction

E. ANDREW MILLS,
Editor

The Need And The Purpose

Supervision and Administration: Programs, Positions, and Perspectives affords an opportunity for the Supervision and Administration Division of the National Art Education Association (NAEA) to present a wide variety of topics relating to various aspects of art and arts programs as well as the administration of these programs. While other divisions of NAEA are basically concerned with one specific level or area of art education, the art supervisor is involved in each of these levels and areas as part of a districtwide or statewide art(s) program.

The need for literature in the field of arts(s) supervision has been discussed for years. No single volume could possibly include "everything you need to know about art(s) supervision, step-by-step." The diversity among art(s) supervision positions has, perhaps, provided the greatest hindrance. When the National Association of State Directors of Art Education (NASDAE) was founded in the late 1960s, it was immediately apparent that no two "state directors" had identical job descriptions or responsibilities. This diversity is even more apparent when one considers districtwide supervision. Rather than lament this diversity, I chose to become an advocate — *viva la difference!*

When the invitation to write for this anthology was publicized, Gene Wenner, Ronald Topping, Larry Peeno, Paul Patterson, and Katherine O'Donnell were among the first to respond. With this first group of articles, the framework began to fall into place. During the next 12 months the invitation was repeated in the *NAEA News*, and authors were enlisted through announcements and personal discussions at the Division sessions at the Washington and Kansas City NAEA conventions. As time went on, it became apparent to me that those in supervision are not well represented as authors of NAEA publications. As I read and review articles for *Art Education*, it is also obvious that those in supervision are not frequent contributors. My sense is that those in supervision are organized, efficient, literate, innovative, dedicated, and on the leading edge in art education — but that they do not "make the time" in their busy schedules to write, and to let others know about their programs and what each of them is doing so well!

The Scope and Sequence

With this in mind, no strict guidelines were set regarding the content of the various essays. The original call for authors listed supervision as it relates to elementary, secondary , district, state, and higher education, as well as community resources and multiple arts, as possible topics. The articles included are placed in an order that makes sense to me as the editor. I suggest that the reader *start at the beginning and read through chapter 5*. From that point on, the reader might continue through the volume or pick and choose by topic.

In the opening chapter I discuss the need for a supervisor and describe the various administrative titles that exist, then I set forth the responsibilities of the districtwide arts supervisor. Gene C. Wenner presents arts education from a broad national perspective, including funding, advocacy, use of artistic resources of the community, and steps that can be taken in setting forth a case for the importance of arts in our schools.

Gretchen A. Boyer, as fine arts specialist for visual arts, Arizona Department of Education, describes what is happening in the visual arts in the Arizona schools. This essay illustrates how the state art consultant can "bring all of the pieces together" to promote quality art education.

In Laura Magee's essay, we are presented with a comprehensive description of administering the arts in the schools of Pittsburgh, Pennsylvania. While the primary emphasis is on the visual arts, Laura also describes such areas as staffing, budget management, instruction, curriculum revision, and community resources as they relate to media arts, music, dance, and theatre.

Robert Eaker was a major presenter at the NAEA Supervision and Administration Leadership Workshop held just prior to the 1990 NAEA convention. Larry Peeno, who coordinated the workshop, suggested that we invite Dr. Eaker to expand his presentation into an article for this anthology. Dr. Eaker, together with Mary Ann Ranells, describes "Art Education and the Effective Schools Research: Practical Strategies for Including Art in School Improvement Efforts." Presenting the Research, District-Level Leadership, Building -Level Development Efforts, and Creating Winners and Celebrating Success are among the topics set forth in his essay.

Thus, the first five topics deal with art(s) education and the need for leadership, art(s) education on the national scene, a state viewpoint, art(s) education in a large city school system, and how art(s) education relates to the effective schools research.

Nan Yoshida sets forth her role as the elementary art supervisor in Los Angeles, while Ronald Topping of White Plains, New York, presents the dilemma of supervision of art education by an art specialist versus supervision by a generalist. Katherine O'Donnell and Gary Crow of Bank Street College of Education, New York City, discuss the role change from art teacher to art supervisor and the implications for individuals, preparation programs, and the profession at large.

Billie McKindra Phillips gives us a very personal view of her role as districtwide art supervisor in St. Louis, Missouri, in her essay "Uniquely Inner City." The specific topic of implementing and evaluating elementary art specialist services has been set forth in great detail by Richard R. Doornek, curriculum specialist in art for the Milwaukee Public Schools.

Martin Rayala tackles the problem of "Supervising Art Education at the State Level" as he presents his philosophy, responsibilities, successes, and hindrances as state art consultant for the Wisconsin Department of Public Instruction. Larry Peeno, who has a rich background in both teaching and supervision, discusses the changing secondary art curriculum and how technology can ease the burden of the art supervisor. Carolyn White Travanti, an art supervisor with the Milwaukee Public Schools, presents the vital isue of staff development and describes a number of unique options that have proven successful.

Mac Arthur Goodwin discusses the executive management survival skills that he has found essential in his position as arts consultant for the South Carolina State Department of Education. "Coordinating the Fine Arts" in a large suburban school district provides many challenges, trials, and tribulations. Paul Patterson, whose

9

professional background was in music education, describes his role as coordinator of fine arts for the U-46 School District in Elgin, Illinois.

Sandra Finlayson lends her considerable expertise to trends, research, and issues germane to evaluation of art students' learning. Myrna Clark presents a detailed evaluation of the art program of the Anchorage, Alaska, School District, where she is art supervisor. In addition to the findings and recommendations, a complete rationale for the evaluation as part of long-range planning is provided.

While 17 educators have written essays on at least 12 different topics in this volume, there are several subjects that still need to be explored. Among these are the relationship of art education to preschool and kindergarten programs, adult education programs, teacher education programs, and vocational education programs.

I would like to thank the many authors who contributed to this volume and offer a special thanks to Richard R. Doornek, director of the NAEA Supervision and Administration Division, for his support. James M. Clarke, art consultant for Aldine Independent Schools in Houston, Texas, and NAEA president-elect provided wisdom and advice as the anthology developed. I would also like to thank Thomas Hatfield, executive director of the National Art Education Association, for his vision as he encouraged the development of this anthology. It is with satisfaction and gratitude that I present the authors and their topics.

1

The Need for a Supervisor

E. ANDREW MILLS

New York State Education Department (Retired)

Introduction

During my 23 years in arts supervision with the New York State Education Department, I was frequently asked to identify school districts and individual schools with outstanding visual arts programs. There are certainly many individual schools with outstanding programs, primarily because of the efforts of art teachers and the rapport they build with students, parents, classroom teachers, and the principal. In identifying a school district with an outstanding art program, there are, however, several elements to be considered. First, there must be districtwide art program leadership, a districtwide philosophy and goals statement, and a K-12 art curriculum. Another essential element is equity. If a family were to move into a given school district, it should not matter where or if they rent or purchase a house,

This level of quality is reflected in every aspect of a districtwide program — in the curriculum, instruction, classroom environment, quality and quantity of supplies, equipment and facilities, art resources, safety standards, identification of the which school the children attend, or who the art teacher is. At every grade level within any given school district, the art program should be of the same level of quality. *The art education program, therefore, must be equitable!*
gifted, ratio of teachers to students, scheduling, availability of high school electives, provision for students with special needs, and professional staff development.

I maintain, then, that there must be districtwide leadership if there is to be a quality districtwide art program!

What's in a Title?

Many different titles are assigned to those individuals involved in state, regional and schoool district arts supervision. Many are involved in both supervision and administration. Generally, one who supervises also administers; one who administers does not necessarily supervise. A *supervisor* is (a) one who directs and inspects (workers or the operation of an organization), (b) a superintendent or a manager, or (c) in certain school systems, an official who is in charge of the course of study and the teachers of that subject. A *director* is one who supervises or manages. An *administrator* is one who administers, who manages or conducts public or business affairs (*Oxford American Dictionary*, 1980).

In a national survey (Mills & Thomson, 1986), professionals employed in arts and humanities in state education departments listed 37 different position titles. This variety of titles is also reflected in our nation's schools. Among those listed were the following: director of fine arts, supervisor of visual and performing arts, arts and humanities supervisor, fine arts coordinator, arts education consultant, music and art education consultant, and specialist in fine arts. People bearing these titles deal with *multiple arts supervision*. The following titles deal only with *visual arts*: supervisor of art education, associate supervisor of art education, art education consultant, art education specialist, and art education coordinator. In addition to director, supervisor, and administrator, the titles specialist, consultant, and coordinator also have been added to this overall list in arts supervision. A *specialist* is a person who is an expert in a special branch of a subject. A *consultant* is a person qualified to give professional advice. A *coordinator* is one who coordinates, one who brings into proper order or relation, one who brings about harmonious functioning (*Oxford American Dictionary*, 1980).

Through the above definitions and through my experience in working with those in arts supervision, it is apparent to me that the only all-inclusive titles are those of director and supervisor. The other titles generally relate to various aspects of supervision, but often do not include direct or even partial responsibility for such important areas as recruitment, selection and evaluation of teachers, and districtwide scheduling. There are, of course, instances where the title suggests one type of responsibility and the job description another. If the job description honestly reflects the title, then the strongest positions are those of *art supervisor* and *art director*.

Who is the Supervisor?

In large school districts, the art supervisor occupies a full-time position, and the supervisor and the supervisory staff work through the district office of curriculum and instruction. In smaller school districts, the person providing districtwide leadership may spend a portion of the school day teaching, and will probably share a secretary. In other school districts, an administrator such as a principal or curriculum director may be assigned the responsibility for coordinating the arts; in still others, a supervisor of *one of the arts* may be assigned as supervisor of *all the arts*. Each arts supervisory position and its circumstances (title, job description, staff, school district) seem to be unique. Supervision, then, is a case of apples, oranges, pears, and plums.

Whether a school district has full-time leadership, part-time leadership, art leadership, arts leadership, or an administrator as arts leader, the bottom line is that a school system will only have a quality, districtwide arts program when districtwide leadership is provided.

The ideal scenario would be to have a full-time supervisor with an art education background in every school district. However, this concept is neither practical nor possible, since the supervisory hierarchy is developed by each school district. In institutions where supervisory positions have been in existence for years, a title and job description may have been developed to fit each area of the K-12 curriculum. Art, in those cases, is frequently aligned with music, physical education, dance, theatre, reading, the school library, health, psychology, and so on. If those in any form of supervision are to have a position of strength within the system, it is also important that the leadership for every area of the curriculum work together for the common good. There is strength in numbers.

In cases where a new position in art supervision is being developed or an existing position redefined, there is a real opportunity for art teachers to participate in the process and help guarantee that districtwide art program leadership will be effective. There are, of course, teachers who want to work in "their own private world" and do not wish to use a written curriculum or interact with their peers; others "wouldn't mind having a supervisor — if I am it!" These personal notions must be put aside for the good of the students as well as for the art program.

Looking to NAEA

In most states and provinces it is very difficult for those in arts supervision to identify others in supervision to meet with them to discuss trends, directions, and common goals. However, those in art supervision can continue to learn and grow through opportunities provided by the Supervision and Administration Division of NAEA. Through sessions at conventions and leadership workshops and, most important, through informal discussion and interaction, a useful network of support can be maintained.

As one reads the *NAEA Goals for Quality Art Education* and the NAEA brochure, *The Role of the Art Supervisor*, the linkage is immediately apparent. In the *NAEA Goals, supervision and administration is the bottom line!* Goal 5 states: "Every state and school system shall have a supervisor or administrator to coordinate and direct the visual arts program." It is only through state, regional, and district supervision that Goals 1 (sequential art program) and 2 (high school graduation credit) can be attained.

The information below has been taken from the NAEA brochure, *Quality Art Education: The Role of the Art Supervisor*. This information should assist those in supervision as they plan and strengthen their positions.

Districtwide Art Program Leadership

To ensure a districtwide quality art education program, the staff of the central office should include a director or supervisor of art education. The supervisor or director must not only possess a broad understanding of the community and its schools, but also detailed knowledge of philosophies, theories, current trends, methodologies, and materials essential to continually develop, support, and maintain a quality K-12 art education program.

The art supervisor is responsible for directing the overall program and facilitating the articulation of the value of this program to administrators, teachers, parents, students, and citizens of the community.

Major responsibilities and functions of the art supervisor/director include:

• Providing districtwide leadership to maintain and/or improve instruction in the visual arts, pre-K through 12, commensurate with district goals and objectives.

• Meeting regularly with the art staff and teachers to develop and implement philosophy, goals, and objectives for the art program that are consonant with those of the state and the National Art Education Association.

• Developing and implementing an equitable system for providing art supplies and equipment for all schools of the district.

• Developing and implementing an equitable system for providing art resources such as art prints, slides, films, books, and periodicals to all schools.

• Providing information on current research in art education to teachers of art and administrators.

• Developing a policy concerning potential health hazards and procedures to ensure a safe environment for students and teachers of art.

• Developing and implementing a method to identify and encourage gifted students at all grade levels.

• Providing a special program of experiences that will challenge and encourage those gifted in art at all grade levels.

• Encouraging the exchange of ideas, concerns, and talent among staff.

Curriculum

• Working with the teachers to ensure that there is a written K-12 curriculum that includes art history, aesthetic judgment, art criticism, and the contribution of various cultures as well as the making of art.

• Working with teachers to ensure that the cultural resources of the community are an integral part of the school program.

• Ensuring that art teachers meet on a regular basis to review, revise, and broaden the art curriculum.

• Developing a program that ensures that a broad variety of art electives are available to all at the senior high school level.

• Working toward an arts/graduation requirement for all students if one is not already in place in the state or district.

Professional Development

• Working with district administrators to provide ongoing staff development for all art teachers in all areas of the curriculum and methodology and ensuring that funds are provided for this purpose.

• Encouraging art teachers to continually widen their horizons as active members of their local, state, and national art education associations.

• Encouraging art teachers to pursue advanced course work and degrees by publicizing the many opportunities available.

• Arranging for art teachers to visit outstanding art classroom situations of the appropriate level.

Scheduling, Facilities, and Financial Support

• Serving as the resource person in all matters concerning art facilities, equipment, and supplies needed to improve instruction.
• Assisting principals in maintaining a current inventory of equipment, textbooks, and other related materials.
• Working with administrators and teachers to ensure that art class sizes are consistent with the staffing ratio in other content areas.
• Ascertaining that all art rooms are furnished with the specialized equipment required for instruction.
• Ensuring that the budget contains funds for repair and replacement of materials and equipment.
• Working with administrators and teachers to ensure that the district budget supports the established curriculum and that funds are distributed equitably to schools at each level.

Instruction

• Assisting administrators in the recruitment and selection of new staff members.
• Emphasizing and developing a rationale for hiring certified art teachers throughout the district.
• Making classroom observations of teachers in cooperation with the administrator to evaluate classroom instruction.
• Working with art teachers to ensure that instruction reflects the philosophy, goals, objectives, and curriculum content of the district.
• Working with art teachers to ensure that accurate records of student progress are maintained.
• Working cooperatively with district library personnel to ensure that resources in the art activities of aesthetics, art history, criticism, and the creation of art are adequate and available.
• Ensuring that art magazines and journals are available through the library as well as in the classroom.

Public Relations

• Fostering community awareness and support for the value of the school art program through individual school and districtwide exhibitions.

• Developing news releases concerning outstanding facets of the art program as well as special events and opportunities.

• Preparing literature outlining the philosophy, goals, objectives, and basic elements of the district art curriculum for the community as well as the school staff.

• Presenting the purpose and results of the school art program, through visual presentations as well as demonstrations of the program in action, at public forums such as meetings of parent and community organizations.

What Can You Do?

• Make your staff aware that you believe a quality art education program is essential for all students.

• Make your school board aware that the staff of the office of curriculum and instruction should include a visual arts supervisor or director of education in the methodologies, theories, and materials of the visual arts.

• Make your school board aware of the need for a certified art teacher in every school.

• Work with your superintendent's professional association to write a statement recognizing the need for a quality art program.

• Make your PTA and/or PTO and community aware of the importance of a quality education art program.

• Contact the state education agency and state board members to share your interest in supporting and improving art education in your state.

References

Mills, E. A. & Thomson, D. R. (1986). *A national survey of art(s) education*, 1984-85, Reston, VA: National Art Education Association.

Mills, E. A. (1985). *Quality art education: The role of the art supervisor* (brochure) Reston, VA: National Art Education Association.

Oxford American dictionary (1980). New York: Oxford University Press.

2

Arts Beyond the School Walls

GENE C. WENNER
Arts and Education Consultants, Inc.

Background

There should be no doubt in anyone's mind that the arts in the United States have expanded and improved dramatically in the past 20 years, probably more than any other area of public concern and participation.

Although it is often hard for some to believe, the arts, both classical and popular, outdraw professional sports in attendance and in financial support. Rock stars, conductors, and film stars, to name a few, equal the salaries of football, baseball, and basketball players. Arts organizations, symphony orchestras, dance companies, theaters, and performing arts centers have sprung up not just in large cities, but in small and even rural areas. Unfortunately, the arts are not on prime-time television; however, real estate agents tell businesses looking at relocation about the arts or the cultural activities in the area.

In spite of all of this, there still are many "starving artists" who make but a meager living off their art or wait on tables waiting for the "big break." But for most, it is both a living and a comfortable way of life.

Existing Walls

However, arts education has not kept pace. In some schools, 97% of the students receive no arts instruction at all. Why has this happened? It seems that walls have been built between the arts community and the schools, between the arts and the administration, and even between arts areas themselves. I am convinced that the obstacle that prevents artists and educators from joining forces is a lack of understanding, particularly about how the institutions that support arts education and the arts institutions have vastly different governances and achieve their goals in different ways —even though both are involved in the arts. This has tended to build walls between the two.

The same state legislature that provides funds and guidelines for spending for both the state arts agency (SAA) and the schools usually makes no link between the two. Funds are granted to the state arts agency from one legislature committee, while education, which includes arts education, is granted by still another.

The state arts agency gets the money for its programs directly from the legislature. Arts education funds, which account for only a small portion of the money that goes to the school districts, do not support arts education programs directly, only as a per-student allocation for all educational programs. Some states have instituted separate legislation for arts education that provides additional funds for arts education programs or projects. The state of North Carolina has gone one step further and mandated arts instruction for all students. In addition, it has provided money for arts staffing, including dance and theater.

The National Conference of State Legislators (NCSL) publication *The Arts and the States, 1984* indicates that 22 states at that time had passed legislation that defines basic education to include arts education. That is nice, but it does not provide funding to support arts teachers. Lip service is easy.

According to the NCSL report, 14 states passed legislation that requires arts education training for teacher certification for elementary classroom teachers and 10 passed legislation that provides in-service training for arts education. In-service training, although not widespread, is a more important trend if it continues to expand.

Why haven't the schools done more in arts education? Many reasons can be advanced — declining school populations, emphasis on special education and

20

vocational education, desegregation, and many others, including "back to basics." Years ago, schools had art and music teachers in most schools and supervisors in each area. In the past 10 to 15 years, most school districts have eliminated two major elements that isolate arts programs from the mainstream of education. (a) the district-wide supervisor and (b) in-service or teacher meetings district-wide in a single area or in the arts together. This has the effect of relegating arts teachers to the supervision of the building principal, who may or may not support the arts program. The overall effect is that the arts program becomes disjointed, at best, not really producing a coordinated K-12 effort. The lack of teacher meetings causes a lack of sequential teaching in each art area from one level to the next and, worse, from one building to another, if indeed it exists at all. More important, there grew an assumption at the elementary level that the classroom teachers would be able to teach all subjects. This is not as popular today, but few classroom teachers had the inclination or the training to teach the arts.

On the other hand, in the arts world, the major impetus for the massive development and expansion of arts organizations — symphony orchestras, opera companies, dance companies, theater companies, museums, galleries — was the establishment of the National Endowment for the Arts (NEA) in 1965 by Congress.

In turn, the National Endowment for the Arts provided the money and encouragement for the formation of state arts councils, which have sponsored the creation of local arts councils. State and local agencies provide support and technical assistance to arts organizations.

States legislatures were required to match, dollar for dollar, the amounts granted their state arts agencies by the NEA. Most states have passed more funds on to their SAA than they receive from Washington, some as much as three times. There are no restrictions on how that money is spent, except for special programs like Arts in Education, formerly the Artists-in-Schools Program. The state arts agencies were most effective in lobbying for support and often cited education as one of the reasons why the legislature should increase their funds. On the other hand, decisions about what happens in the schools are, for the most part, in the hands of the local community. There are intrusions and infusions of funds from the federal or state government, but they represent only a small part of the funds for educational programs. The federal and state governments tend to preach about what schools *ought* to do but provide little support with which to accomplish objectives. In the past, most of the decisions in the schools were made by the superintendent and staff, then passed down to the school building.

This is not what occurs today in educational decision making. Most decisions are reached through some kind of mediation or accommodation process involving the school board, the teachers' union, special interest groups, parents, principals, and, sometimes, antischool groups only interested in lowering their taxes.

In other words, the community broke down the school walls and took part in the

21

education process, often in spite of the schools. So, in order to make a case for arts education it is not enough to have the superintendent on your side — it has become necessary to influence the other groups mentioned above as well. School administrators who have to deal with parents and the public may not believe the schools should support arts education at all. They believe that parents ought to pay for arts instruction outside of school — let them take art and music lessons at home.

In a nutshell, the arts world was developed as a top-down support system, whereas education has always been bottom-up since education, according to the Constitution, is a local responsibility, with help from the state and on occasion, the federal government. In the arts world, the state arts agencies have become increasingly more powerful and have been successful in obtaining increases from their state legislatures that more often than not, doubles or triples the money from the NEA.

Breaking Down The Walls

I am happy to say that the number of individuals — administrators, teachers other than in the arts, parents, and artists in the community — who are rallying to support arts education is growing. So how can the schools counteract the forces that have built walls around their arts programs? First of all, a cooperative effort from both the school and community is critical, an effort that will allow all students to have the opportunity to learn about artists, their universe, their environment, and, above all, what the arts are and how they can both participate in and enjoy them. Performance of the arts has often been overemphasized, with little time for creation and understanding of that art form. Musical composition, choreography, play-writing, and visual arts should be as important as playing, dancing, or acting. Marching bands, musicals, and art shows are traditionally the expressions shown to the public as an arts program. The marching band on the football field, and the concerts and plays that only the parents of those involved attend, tend to be thought of as *entertainment*.

Schools can make more effective use of artistic resources in the community. However, these activities must be part of a larger concern for a broad, vital arts program in all of the schools. This clearly means building a program on what exists and using community resources to expand and change that program. Changing attitudes toward the arts and changes in existing programs — not by adding another performance, visiting artist, or set of courses but by a sequential K-12 program in each of the art areas — can be the result of long-term cooperative planning involving the arts community and the schools.

A word that is being used increasingly in arts education is advocacy. It is used to describe what "outsiders" ought to do to aid "insiders." In other words, it involves artists, arts organizations, and interested spokespersons who are not a part of the school system advocating more arts in the schools.

On the surface, advocacy makes a great deal of sense in the mediation-accommodation climate of school management and decision making since an outside voice can be very helpful in convincing the unconvinced school administrator or board member. It is a polite word for lobbying, but that is often what is required to influence the decision making processes in schools. Direct involvement in the school's political process is a necessary ingredient.

The problem as it sometimes exists today is that what the outsiders or advocates tend to advocate is not always what the insiders think is necessary. That is, arts agencies often only advocate more artists in schools, not more arts teachers. What advocacy needs to be effective is the close cooperation of the schools.

A more serious problem is that the arts community may merely keep a proper distance when the school board meets on critical decisions about the arts education program or when the state legislature is passing legislation damaging to the arts.

On the other hand, educators have been woefully inadequate in the organization and careful orchestration of efforts to encourage the arts community to be effective advocates. They need to be sure that advocates are always present to be heard when the time is right. Some caution and skill is necessary not to have the efforts seem self-serving for the arts staff but to be in the best interests of students.

The other requirement for success in this process of mediation and accommodation is *persistence*. It is not enough to attend one board meeting or talk with the superintendent or principal once or twice. It is necessary to constantly be present and visible in the arena of educational decision making for developing the support necessary to have a good arts education program.

Wails are not easily broken down; sometimes they come down a brick or stone at a time.

Isolation Of The Arts

Another problem in the past for arts educators was that they were isolated from other teachers, from curriculum or school meetings, and from parent groups and groups other than those directly involved in the arts.

The schedule of classes breeds isolation, since many arts teachers cover so many different classes, some in different schools. This causes problems with attending schoolwide meetings, district meetings, and the like and leaves them unknowledgeable about important school issues. The schedule is often too demanding, and arts teachers are too tired to get involved with the unions or representative groups, let alone arts in the community. In some schools, years go by without the entire arts staff — music and art — meeting together to share and to map out joint strategies. They meet once or twice a year to talk about performance or exhibit schedules but not to plan a coordinated curriculum. There always seems to be some reason why arts teachers cannot deal with these issues. Sometimes the administration is to blame, sometimes the arts teachers themselves. This situation greatly weakens their position for support of districtwide comprehensive arts programs because administrators do not see a complete program, only bits and pieces here and there. Secondary programs are the most visible, while elementary programs are dispensable or assumed to be taught by classroom teachers without assistance or training.

As mentioned above, lack of district-wide supervision positions also contributes to isolation and the building of walls.

What Can Be Done?

What kind of program in the arts should this cooperative effort produce? How can you sell it? First, there should be a well-articulated, sequential, K-12 instructional program in each of the following arts areas: dance, music, theater, visual arts, and creative writing.

Second, the arts should be involved in interdisciplinary studies with subjects such as English, social studies, science, and mathematics, to mention a few. Some arts teachers are reluctant to participate, since they fear that these courses will become a substitute for the sequential arts program. This is not the case at all; however, these courses are often taught without the full-time involvement of arts teachers. Arts teachers are not comfortable with this mode of instruction and are not trained in interdisciplinary approaches. Thus, teacher training is necessary if interdisciplinary studies are to effectively include the arts.

Third, the arts should also be a part of studies for special students, handicapped students, gifted (academically) students. The gifted and talented program was to include the artistically talented; however, without any protest, they were eliminated from most gifted programs.

Fourth, there should be encouragement for the artistically talented student to pursue a career in the arts. There are growing numbers of magnet schools — centers for the instruction of the artistically talented. But beyond that, more arts programs need to provide opportunities for the growth and encouragement of the individual artist, not just the large performing organization.

Unfortunately, most arts programs do not have all of the above, but with the support of parents, the arts community, and others, these are goals that should provide something to attain over time.

There is undoubtedly more interest in arts education today across a broad front than ever before, but it is up to all of us to capitalize on this potential support and direct the flow toward improving, expanding, and strengthening arts education. The arts are a legitimate area of study; all can learn, some can and will excel, and some can "make a living in the arts."

What must schools do to attain these goals for the arts education program? They must enlist the aid of the arts community and others to complete some of the following objectives:

1. Conduct a thorough examination of the current arts program to determine what is taught, how it is taught, and by whom it is taught. For the most part neither administrators nor the community have much of an idea of what already takes place.

2. Determine how the status quo is successful but is lacking in sequential learning, integration, and special populations.

3. Provide a plan for in-service programs for arts teachers and classroom teachers.

4. Develop staff needs and profiles for the future that include districtwide supervision in each of the arts areas.

5. Explore methods of involving artists and the arts community in these plans for the future, not just to employ artists but to improve instructional programs.

What Can You Do?

More specifically, you might try some of the following suggestions to enlist community support for comprehensive arts programs:

1. Invite the community into the school to see what you are teaching and what the students are learning. Your teaching and your students are your best "sales tools."

2. Ask members of the community to do something specific for you or for your students, perhaps sharing an experience, a particular resource, or a piece of equipment that you need.

3. Ask the community to support your program by appearing at a school board meeting when a critical decision is debated or by alerting you to possible problems.

4. Ask community members to write letters on behalf of the arts program and what the students are gaining from their classes to the administration, school board, state legislators, and particularly the education committee.

5. Search out individuals and organizations that might be able and willing to talk about an area of the arts in which you have no expertise or necessary equipment.

6. Schedule performances or master classes that allow members of the community to participate or simply watch.

7. Take your classroom, not just your performing groups or exhibits, into the

community. Find opportunities for showing examples of classroom activities or rehearsals to the school board or the boards of local arts organizations so that they may view firsthand what actually happens in schools.

8. Ask your students to talk or demonstrate what they are learning to civic organizations (Chamber of Commerce, Lions, Elks) and local government agencies.

If you want outsiders to appreciate, understand, and support the comprehensive program in the arts you are providing to students, you must find more effective ways of conveying that program with means other than *performances, shows,* or *exhibitions.*

You must also be interested in what the community is doing if you expect them to return the interest. You must scale the walls of the community groups.

You must be active in school and community politics and activities. Testify on behalf of your local or state arts agency when possible. Become a board member of a community or state arts agency.

Finally, the arts beyond the school walls must become an integral part of the arts within the school walls, so integral that your students will have the maximum opportunity to learn, to participate, to perform, and to create in all of the arts. *Your students deserve nothing less!*

3

Building Relationships: Quality Visual Arts Education in the 1990s

GRETCHEN A. BOYER

Arizona Department of Education

Introduction

How do good art teachers or arts administrators orchestrate and achieve a quality visual arts education program? Their primary responsibility is, of course, teaching art to children. How do they also manage to achieve growth and prosperity for their art programs?

The most obvious key to successful, quality art education programs is people: people who teach art to children, people who administrate and/or legislate programs, people who govern district policy, people who send their children to school. A key mission for art educators may well be to constantly work on improving their abilities to both actively listen to and speak the language of each of these different people.

In building professional relationships, it may also be necessary to educate these important *others* with regard to the value and need for visual arts education programs so that they are willing to do whatever it takes to support and provide program continuity.

Several programs were developed by the fine arts specialist for visual arts in the Arizona Department of Education as a result of studying the actions of successful leaders of art education programs and assessing the needs of the local school districts throughout Arizona. These programs address program and curriculum development, strategic planning, event planning, staff development, and in-service programs for visual art education. These strategies were promoted through four major events either sponsored or cosponsored by the Arizona Department of Education: (a) Building Relationships: Symposium in Arts Education Management; (b) the Visual Arts Model School District Program; (c) the Mountain States Art Education Consortium, (d) the Arizona Fine Art Teacher Cadre.

The Building Relationships Concept

Where did the "building relationships" concept get its beginning? How did it move from an idea to a reality? It happened by *building relationships*, by responding to the needs of the art educators of Arizona. During visits to local school districts across Arizona, and through interaction and involvement with the Arizona Art Education Association, it became evident that there was a need for art educators to become more aware of not only their own roles, but also the expanding roles of others who could assist in promoting visual art education programs.

Six major steps guided the implementation of the buiding relationships concept:

1. Define the needs.

2. Fulfill the needs.

3. Form an advisory committee or select several individuals to be guiding lights — people who are trustworthy and honest and who represent a particular area of expertise and a cross section of constituents. Some might be mentors. Some might represent geographic concerns. These individuals might help to brainstorm implementation ideas or assist in fine tuning a concept.

4. Brainstorm ideas for implementation.

5. Refine the idea.

6. Implement the idea.

7. Evaluate and assess the results.

These steps will undoubtedly recur with any program that is developed.

As ideas were formulated, a symposium structure was suggested that centered on a keynote presentation and responses to that presentation, followed by panels, roundtables, or facilitated discussion groups. Building Relationships: Symposium in Arts Education Management was the result.

The first symposium, in June 1988, brought together art educators, administrators, and leaders of all sorts and all levels of office at the Northern Arizona University campus in Flagstaff. A major goal of this first symposium was to take the first steps necessary to build communication networks with our professional colleagues in educational leadership positions throughout Arizona.

Thomas Hatfield, former state director of art with the South Carolina Department of Education and Executive Director, National Art Education Association, was the keynote speaker. Dr. Hatfield spoke about how South Carolina was able to increase the number of art educators and art programs throughout that state. He shared the strategies he reported in his book, *An Art Teacher in Every School* (Hatfield, 1983). Six other speakers responded to Hatfield's remarks. Each of these speakers represented a different constituency beneficial to art educators, and each spoke of different strategies art educators could develop with them to work to achieve quality visual arts programs. The speakers included the president-elect of the Arizona Parent-Teacher Association, a local school board member, a state school board member, a principal, an art educator, a local school district superintendent, and a county superintendent. These presentations were followed by roundtable discussions where speakers and audience members could interact in small groups and share ideas.

During the symposium, special meetings were held for members of the Visual Arts Model School District Program. These districts had already agreed to establish short- and long-term goals for their visual arts program and carry them out to the best of their abilities. This working session focused on the development of management planning strategies. Closing remarks were delivered by a state board of education member.

The response to this event was so positive that it has continued for a third year. It has grown from a 1.5-day event to a 4-day event. Each year, the program focus has included a new audience with which art educators need to develop professional relationships if their programs are to grow and prosper.

The second symposium addressed the relationships needed to build outside the educational community. Dr. Charles Fowler delivered the keynote address, which promoted a pragmatic approach to quality arts education (Fowler, 1988). In a format similar to that of the first symposium, speakers responded to Fowler's remarks. Representatives from Arizona's various arts and arts education organizations, the radio media, the business community, local governments, and the Arizona legislature were given the opportunity to interact with each other in panel discussions and to respond to questions from the audience. Aspects of leadership and management planning were also addressed.

In another segment of the program, various model school districts described introductory skills they used in developing action plans for their goals, while others shared the experiences of their first year.

In the third year, the structure was maintained and expanded, but the number of keynote speakers was increased. An in-depth look at leadership development and changing paradigms was keynoted by speaker Chuck Farnsworth, president of the Farnsworth and Associates consulting firm. Professional images were discussed by Janet Elsea, author of *First Impression, Best Impression* (Elsea, 1984), and the workings of state government were revealed by MacArthur Goodwin, director of art education, South Carolina Department of Education. Responses to these keynote presentations were made by an artist, arts administrators, a public relations director, a school board member, and the state school board president.

For this symposium, special invitations were sent to encourage the participation of elementary classroom teachers. Afternoons were structured to allow for building relationships and understanding the roles of specialists and classroom teachers and how they can work together to promote quality arts education. Every year, the proceedings of the symposium have been published (Arizona Department of Education, 1988/1989) so that others who were unable to attend the event can benefit from the knowledge gained. The 1990 symposium expanded to become the Building Relationships Symposium in Arts Education Management and included the performing arts. A week-long event is being considered, as well as regional events throughout the school year.

The Visual Arts Model School District Program

The Visual Arts Model School District Program is a recognition program that assists in developing strategic management plans for districtwide visual arts programs. The strategic plan addresses such categories as securing a commitment, developing an art task force, considerations for assessment, and an estimated time line. Issues addressed under the considerations for assessment category might include curriculum, program staffing, instructional time and scheduling, resources, materials and equipment, facilities, financial support, staff development, administrative support, parental support, and relationships with other teachers. This framework allows each of the locally controlled school districts to adapt the program to meet its needs as a quality visual art program is developed.

The function of the visual art model school district program is simple but effective. If policy is to change, attitudes and behaviors must be changed. Information influences attitude, which changes behavior, which will, in effect, change the policy. This is a slow, growing, nourishing process. The visual arts model school district program provides the vehicle to achieve these results.

The elements of the Visual Arts Model School District Program are similar to several of the elements found in the effective schools research of the 1980s (Arizona Department of Education, 1984). The following characteristics are illustrated throughout the program:

1. District plans are developed collaboratively and involve administrators, teachers, parents, and communities.

2. Regular interaction occurs naturally between the educational and noneducational communities.

3. Programmatic goals are clearly stated.

4. A districtwide curriculum is implemented.

5. Meaningful staff development and technical assistance programs are available.

6. A realistic assessment/evaluation of the program is in place.

7. Schools set high expectations for quality education programs.

If the program is to be successful, local school districts must be committed to it. There are many benefits to the school districts involved: In terms of securing a commitment and developing a task force, there is a higher credibility with various publics when the local school district participates in a state program recognized by the state superintendent of public instruction. Resources and assistance are more readily available through both the local and state levels, and opportunities for in-service programs and staff development are available. Districts receive recognition from the state department of education. The program supports administrative district goals and builds awareness and involvement of the community in the school visual art program. Most important, however, it brings together arts teachers, classroom teachers, administrators (both central and building level), and the community (both parents and business) to work together to promote quality arts education in a school district. Ideas are explored, existing programs are reviewed, new programs are speculated and developed, and knowledge, skills, practices, and beliefs are shared. All of these activities promote ownership in the visual arts education program. Ownership may be translated into strong support for art programs.

The model schools program is a school district improvement program (Arizona Department of Education, 1990). The Arizona Department of Education provides assistance to local school district personnel who have agreed to make quality visual arts education a districtwide priority by setting short- and long-range goals as well as strategic action plans. Assistance from the department of education may come in the form of a fine arts specialist, a fine arts teacher cadre, or participation in the

31

department's summer arts education events and regional events. The amount of support is left to the discretion of each individual model school district. The Arizona Department of Education is currently working on a program of recognition for exemplary districts that have achieved all of the components of a quality program.

Mountain States Art Education Consortium

The consortium concept provides the curricular, programmatic, or content component to the overall program. Distinguished national and regional art educators, authors, and publishers provide the basis for the structure of the program. These individuals define the theoretical philosophy of their particular area of expertise and make suggestions for practical application and experiences for the classroom. The program also provides opportunities for participants to work in a variety of studio experiences.

The first Mountain States Art Education Consortium was sponsored by Southern Utah State College and the Arizona Department of Education. Art educators and others interested in current trends of art education were invited to attend. The first consortium, designed around the needs of art educators, focused on a variety of approaches to art education, including (a) a history-based approach, as presented by Jon Sharer, professor of art education at Arizona State University; (b) a studio-based approach, presented by Larry Schultz, Red Rock Community College, Lakewood, Colorado; (c) a discipline-based approach, presented by Michael Day, professor of art education at Brigham Young University; (d) a visual/perceptual-based approach, presented by Ron Piotrowski, art education professor at Northern Arizona University; (e) an integrated arts approach, presented by Thelma Hahn, art educator and then NAEA elementary division director from New Mexico. Jack Taylor, a retired art education professor from Arizona State University, delivered motivational closing remarks that inspired participants to accept the challenge to promote the total visual arts education program.

The second Mountain States Art Education Consortium was a partnership between the departments of education in Arizona, Colorado, New Mexico, and Utah and Southern Utah State College. The program was designed to provide participants with the opportunity to meet, exchange ideas, and interact with experts on a variety of issues related to the effective teaching of art and to combine educational theory with studio practice in various media. Previous participants requested that information be geared to implementation in the school district or art classroom. Marcy Warner and Rosie Herman, from the Scottsdale School District, provided an overview, implementation, and studio experience of their art program. The same format, including the Arts Propel program, was duplicated by Julianne Agar,

Beverly Bates, and Teresa Rozewski from the Pittsburgh School District. In addition, presentations were made on the Wilton Series by Gretchen O'Reilly of Reading and O'Reilly Publications; *Art is Elementary* (Cornia, Stubbs, & Winteers, 1983) by Charles Stubbs, Utah Department of Education; and *Understanding and Creating Art* (Goldstein, Katz, Kowalchuk, & Saunders, 1986) by author Ernest Goldstein of the Garrard Publishing Company. Kelvin Yazzie, a Native American artist, provided inspirational words and a studio demonstration and experience in clay.

Virginia Brouch, an art educator with Palo Verde Research Associates, delivered the summation and encouraged the participants to take back the information gained in this consortium and apply it to their individual work situations.

A special segment of both programs was devoted to the integration of art education and the Utah Shakespearean Festival. Consortium participants took part in seminars on costume design and attended a Renaissance feast, a Shakespearean play, a backstage tour, and a greenshow.

Unfortunately, the third consortium was not conducted because of financial constraints. It was planned that this consortium would focus on practical applications of the components of a quality art program in the mountain states area. Exploration of new art textbooks and programs would have featured several nationally known authors who would have provided insight on the use of their materials. Opportunities for studio experiences and effective integration of visual art and Shakespeare would have continued. A new site is being considered for the 1991 consortium.

Fine Arts Teacher Cadre

The Arizona Fine Arts Teacher Cadre is designed to give Arizona educators special assistance through workshops or in-service programs of at least 3 hours in duration. These workshops and programs are specifically designed to provide teachers with concepts they can use in their teaching, program development, or curriculum development.

The primary purpose of the teacher cadre is to assist Arizona's school districts in the development of quality arts education programs. The cadre includes teachers in dance, dramatic arts, music, and the visual arts. Cadre members visit school districts that request assistance in
  • implementing the essential skills
  • selecting a sequential arts curriculum
  • writing their own curriculum for district adoption
  • developing strategies for achieving a quality arts education program
  • developing assessment/evaluation instruments in the arts

These services, as well as individual requests and technical assistance, are available to the local school districts of Arizona. Preferences are given to the small and rural school districts and the model school districts. Services may also be used for regional in-service or arts education events such as meetings or conferences. The Fine Arts Teacher Cadre was begun as a joint project among the National Endowment for the Arts, the Arizona Commission on the Arts, and the Arizona Department of Education to serve the small and/or rural school districts. The Arizona Department of Education coordinated the Fine Arts Teacher Cadre.

Because the program was so well received by the local school districts, the Arizona Department of Education has continued to fund it. Thus far, the kinds of service that have been rendered include Curriculum Planning and Development, Techniques for Teaching Aesthetics, Techniques for Teaching Art History, Seminar in Elementary Art Education, Scheduling and Equipping Visual Arts Programs, Assessment/Evaluation of Student Progress in Visual Arts, Organization of a Visual Arts Gallery in Your School, Integration of Visual Arts into Other Subject Areas, Strategic Planning, Organization of Parent Support Groups, and others.

Conclusion

Several key issues involved in promoting quality art education have been addressed. These include building professional relationships with those who can influence the growth and prosperity of art programs and learning to actively listen and speak their languages as well as educate them about the value of and need for art education programs. In addition, several strategies and events that promote these relationships have been discussed. By using similar processes, specific needs would be identified and individual planning strategies implemented in any state, region within a state, or school district. In times of school district budget cutbacks and staff reductions as well as in times of prosperity and expansion, it is important for art educators to capitalize on every strategy available to promote quality art education.

References

[1] Arizona Department of Education. (1984). *Arizona's best bet*. Phoenix: Author.
[2] Arizona Department of Education. (1988). *Arizona fine arts teacher cadre brochure*. Phoenix: Author.
[3] Arizona Department of Education. (1988/1989). *Building relationships: A symposium in art education management* (Final Reports). Phoenix: Author.
[4] Arizona Department of Education. (1990). *Visual art model school district program brochure*. Phoenix: Author.

[5] Cornia, I., Stubbs, C., & Winteers, N. B. (1983). *Art is elementary.* Gibbs M. Smith Inc. Salt Lake City, Utah.

[6] Elsea, J., (1984). *First impression, best impression.* New York: Simon & Schuster.

[7] Fowler, C. (1988). *Can we rescue the arts for America's children? Coming to our senses — Ten years later.* New York: American Council for the Arts.

[8] Goldstein, E., Katz, T. H., Kowalchuk, J. D., Saunders, R. (1986). *Understanding and creating art.* Dallas: Garrard Publishing Company.

[9] Hatfield, T. (1983). *An art teacher in every school.* Whitehall Publishers. Reston, Virginia.

35

4

Arts Administration in a City System: Pittsburgh, Pennsylvania

LAURA J. MAGEE

Pittsburgh Public Schools

Simply stated, the Division of Arts Education of the Pittsburgh Public Schools has two major functions: *education* and *show business*. In the best of times, these functions support each other; in the worst of times, they are contradictory. This chapter explains the organization, the responsibilities, and the goals of the division. Five of the myriad responsibilities are described in detail: budget management, personnel selection, supervision of instruction, curriculum revision, and facilities renovation. Visual arts programs are specified; other arts programs are summarized. However, to better understand these responsibilities and programs, it is necessary to understand something about the city, the people, and the school system.

The City and the People. Pittsburgh is built on steep hills and deep ravines at the confluence of the Allegheny, Monongahela, and Ohio Rivers. Although the city is over 200 years old, the downtown area is a concentration of glistening skyscrapers. When one first sees it after driving through the Fort Pitt tunnel, it looks like the Emerald City. Viewing the distant houses hanging on hills across any of the rivers, it looks like a Gramdma Moses painting.

Natural barriers helped form ethnic and social barriers. Europeans left their villages; African-Americans left the South. They came to work in the coal mines and the steel mills, and they settled with others who spoke their language. Many families have lived within the same few blocks for three or more generations. To this day, Pittsburghers identify themselves by neighborhood, and ethnic clubs abound. Some examples are African-American, Bulgarian, Carpatho-Rusyn, Chinese, Croatian, Filipino, German, Greek, Hungarian, Indian, Irish, Israeli, Italian, Lebanese, Lithuanian, Polish, Slovak, Slovenian, Ukranian, and Vietnamese (Pittsburgh Folk Festival, 1990, p. #1). These groups sponsor festivals from May through October that carry on traditions through folk art, music, dance, and food.

Community arts organizations range from large to quite small and from old to new, and they offer a wide variety of arts opportunities. A selected issue of *Pittsburgh Magazine* (Events, 1990) listed 39 music events, 35 live theatre productions, and 30 art exhibitions. Winter is the season for dance concerts, which include folk, modern, jazz, tap, and classical ballet. Most of the community arts organizations are interested in audience development; many are interested in reaching young people.

Foundations support the arts, education, and arts education. Pittsburgh Friends of Art for Pittsburgh Public Schools is quite specific in its mission; it purchases works by local artists and places them in the public schools so that students can view them. The Pittsburgh Foundation/Howard Heinz Endowment funds a wide range of civic, education, and arts initiatives and published a recent report called *Expanding Our Vision in the Arts: Building Multi-Cultural Programming and Multi-Cultural Audiences* (Shepard & Goines, 1990).

The School System. An elected but unpaid nine-member board of education establishes policy and levies taxes for the public schools. It is significant that the board has this independent taxing authority that allows it to be responsive to financial needs. The 1990 operating budget was $313.6 million (Pittsburgh Board of Education [PBE], 1989, p. S-5), or approximately $7,979 per pupil, somewhat higher than the national average.

Each board member represents a specific geographic section of the city that includes a variety of neighborhoods. The system is successful because board members work to improve the school district as a whole while ensuring that their own neighborhoods receive an equitable amount of attention in all respects.

Since the arrival in 1981 of Richard C. Wallace, Jr., the current superintendent, one of the major thrusts of the board of education has been testing and evaluation. Monitoring Achievement in Pittsburgh (MAP) tests are given from three to five times per year in English, mathematics, social studies, and science.

In the Pittsburgh system there are 12 secondary schools, including one arts magnet and one alternative school; 15 middle schools with one arts magnet; 53 elementary schools; and 2 special education facilities. Elementary schools house kindergarten through Grade 5, middle schools Grades 6 through 8, and secondary schools Grades 9 through 12.

From the peak of the baby boom in 1966, when 76,000 students were enrolled, the total pupil enrollment decreased to 39,308 in 1990 (PBE, 1989, p.xii). Although the closing of the steel mills prompted a mass exodus, the population has been generally consistent since 1984 (PBE, 1989, p. xi). Secondary schools range in enrollment from approximately 200 to over 1,500. Middle schools range from 250 to no more than 1,000 pupils, while the largest elementary school contains less than 600 and the smallest barely over 100 pupils.

The Division of Arts Education is one of 12 divisions in the Department of Curriculum and Program Management. The other divisions are foreign language, health and physical education, library and media services, mathematics, reading and literature, science, social studies, staff development, writing and speaking, vocational education, and exceptional children.

Together the divisions have three major responsibilities: to administer and supervise the program of instruction for kindergarten through grade 12; to revise curriculum courses of study and select textbooks; and to evaluate new instructional programs which meet the priorities and needs of the district. The quality of instruction, along with the coordination, articulation, and implementation of all phases of instruction has as the main objective the improvement of instruction and achievement levels of the students. (PBE, 1989, p. #48)

To fulfill their responsibilities, the divisions continually vie with each other for money, building space, students, and recognition.

The Division of Arts Education

Organization
The director and staff of the Division of Arts Education are responsible for visual arts, music, theatre, dance, and media arts. The staff includes three visual arts supervisors, three music supervisors, one half-time media arts coordinator, one

half-time theatre coordinator, one half-time dance coordinator, one half-time teacher project leader in Art Propel, one half-time teacher project leader in Music Propel, one arts resource assistant, and three secretaries. All staff members report to the director. The director of arts education reports directly to the associate superintendent in charge of curriculum and program management, who reports directly to the superintendent.

The director works 250 days (12 months) per year; supervisors work 200 days, approximately 11 months per year. The work schedule of coordinators, teacher project leaders, and the resource assistant follows the school calendar, which is 183 days long and begins the day after Labor Day and ends in late June. The secretaries work 12 months per year.

Responsibilities
"Show business," or showcasing student arts events, is the most visible responsibility of the Division of Arts Education. The Pittsburgh Board of Education and the community expect, if not demand, to see and hear student art, music, theatre, and dance. They want to see it in their schools, neighborhoods, city, state, and nation, and they especially want to see it in their own neighborhoods and city.

While *education* may be less visible than show business to the public, supervision of arts instruction is equally visible to administrators and teachers. It is primarily the responsibility of the art and music supervisors. The coordinators of media arts, theatre, and dance, as well as the teacher project leaders, do not technically supervise instruction, but they offer advice and constructive criticism to teachers. Closely related to supervision are the in-service workshops conducted for teachers. Supervisors, coordinators, and teacher project leaders design and implement these workshops.

Directing the writing and revision of sequentially planned curricula is a continual process in each of the arts areas. Contiguous to curricula revision are the review and selection of textbooks.

Initiation, implementation, and evaluation of arts programs are important functions and vary greatly. Some arts programs are designed for a particular group of students or a specific location or time; other arts programs are districtwide and annual.

To ensure that instruction moves smoothly, the division has a variety of administrative responsibilities, some within the division and some in collaboration with others. Internal administration includes participation in budgetary decisions, ordering of supplies and equipment, and close watch over maintenance of equipment in arts classrooms. Decisions concerning personnel selection and facilities revision are made by the Department of Personnel and Employee Relations and the Division of Facilities, respectively, with recommendations from arts education staff. Although grants are written by the Office of Development, the director,

40

supervisors, and coordinators meet with development staff for joint planning sessions. Each staff member is expected to represent the school district at various city, state, and national arts events and in a variety of arts organizations.

Goals

As a result of the systemwide thrust for monitoring achievement, the cultural diversity of the city, and the interest that community arts organizations have in young people and the schools, the Division of Arts Education has three basic goals:

1. Help students assume responsibility for learning and self-assessment and help teachers monitor students' artistic development by production, perception, and reflection in the arts.

2. Help students develop an awareness and understanding of the artistic contributions of peoples throughout the world and across time periods through a multicultural, multiracial, multiethnic approach.

3. Ensure that community arts resources are an integral part of the program for all students by bringing artists into the schools and taking students to concert halls, theatres, museums, and art galleries.

Together these responsibilities and goals determine the Division of Arts Education's long-range and short-range planning in addition to day-to-day activities.

Budget Management:

The director of arts education is responsible for eight district budgets within the school system and a varying number of others depending on the grants from outside sources. The school district budgets include elementary visual arts, elementary music, middle visual arts, middle music, secondary visual arts, secondary music, center for the musically talented, and the Division of Arts Education general fund (PBE, 1989). Not only must eight separate budgets be calculated, but eight accompanying budget narratives must be written that include goals and/or responsibilities, accomplishments for the past year, objectives for the coming year, and innovations. Each is approximately 600 words long.

The elementary, middle, and secondary schools' visual arts budgets include two lines: general supplies, designated specifically for purchase of art supplies, and books and periodicals, established to purchase art books, magazines, and periodicals for resource use (PBE, 1989, pp. 92, 111, 131). Textbooks come from a different budget in the Department of Curriculum and Program Management.

The Pittsburgh Public Schools fiscal year follows the calendar year, January 1 through December 31. In May the budget process begins for the following year. Each director is informed of the percentage increase or decrease in relation to the preceding year and is instructed to plan accordingly. Occasionally, a plea for additional funds is heeded if it finds a series of sympathetic readers as it makes its way through the bureaucracy to the board for final approval in December. Attempt-

41

ing to increase money for art supplies is almost fruitless because after the money is allocated for art or any other supplies, it is distributed to the schools on the basis of pupil enrollment. Once it is in the schools, the principal has total discretion concerning allocation of funds.

The Division of Arts Education budget is divided into three major areas: regular programs, instruction and curriculum development services, and school-sponsored student activities (PBE, 1989, p. 50). These are divided among programs in visual arts, music, theatre, dance, and media arts.

Regular programs include budget lines that are used for the purchase and repair of musical instruments, risers, computers for classrooms, kilns, cameras, enlargers, pug mills, and so forth. (The Pittsburgh Public Schools System furnishes approximately 10,000 musical instruments to students and has 3 full-time music repair people on staff.)

Instruction and curriculum development services pay for the daily functions of the Division of Arts Education. Salaries and employee benefits are the major items. Also included are funds for consultants to come into the schools and to broaden the range of arts experiences for students and teachers through a multicultural approach to arts education. Travel for staff, printing, postage, and general supplies are part of this section.

The school-sponsored student activities budget covers a wide range of services, from cleaning band uniforms and choir robes to overtime pay for music teachers rehearsing and directing student performances. Several years ago, music teachers succeeded in having up to 100 hours of overtime written into their contract (PBE, 1988, p. 173). Art teachers have not been persuasive enough with union leaders to be considered for extra pay for preparing and hanging shows and exhibitions. Student transportation is a large item because it covers the expense of taking bands, choruses, and orchestras to citywide adjudication festivals, football games, parades, concerts, and district and state competitions. It also includes the costs of taking pupils at all levels to visual arts, theatre, and dance events throughout the city. Each arts area is allocated a specific amount of funds annually from various budget lines. However, there must be flexibility because unanticipated expenses always occur, and one area has to borrow from another. If possible, the borrowing occurs with the cooperation of the supervisors involved. If not, the director decides.

Personnel Selection

Although the Department of Personnel and Employee Relations is primarily responsible for hiring and placing arts teachers, the director and supervisors of the Division of Arts Education often assist. Following Pennsylvania commonwealth law, Pittsburgh Public Schools hire strictly from an eligibility list (Title 24, Purdon's PA Statutes, 1949).

In the past, placement on the eligibility list depended on credential folders and panel interviews. However, there was increasing concern that teacher applicants could look good on paper and interview well but might not have expertise in their subject area. Also, they could exhibit bias toward students based on race, gender, or socioeconomic status. Pittsburgh visual arts and music supervisors have been giving technical tests to prospective teachers for several years to gauge candidates' musical or artistic ability. Much to the consternation of the Division of Arts Education staff, the technical tests were not officially a part of the score for determining teacher eligibility.

Beginning in spring 1990, placement on the eligibility list was broadened to include four factors: credential folder, panel interview, technical test in the specific subject area, and videotape quiz of generic teaching practices.

The credential folder contains an application form, transcripts, scores of the Pennsylvania Department of Education teachers test, and recommendations. This folder can be evaluated by individuals in the personnel department, supervisors in visual arts or music supervisors, or possibly the director of arts education. This evaluation is scored according to specific guidelines, and points are awarded on the basis of a variety of criteria.

Panel interviews are conducted by three administrators and may include principals, vice principals, directors, or supervisors. In most instances, one or more arts supervisors and the arts director are on the panel. Interviews consist of a series of structured questions that deal with educational philosophy, teaching, classroom management, and a brief overview of the candidates' academic backgrounds. Each interview lasts about 30 minutes; usually, six to eight interviews are scheduled for one day. Scoring is done by each interviewer on a standardized form that is machine graded. The final score is an average of the three scores.

The purpose of the arts technical test is to determine whether the prospective teacher can actually play a musical instrument or create works of art. This test is always given by a supervisor, vice principal, or director who is certified in that content area. These tests are designed to last about 20 minutes. The music test and the visual arts test were developed by music and visual arts supervisors, respectively, with advice from staff members of the Division of Research, Evaluation, and Test Development.

For the technical test in music, the music teacher candidate performs a selection of his or her choice for the evaluator, sight reads, claps or taps a rhythm, and then creates and plays a keyboard harmony from a written melody (Pittsburgh Public Schools, 1989a).

In visual arts the art teacher candidate is asked to bring at least five examples of his or her artwork, either slides or original art, and possibly examples of student work. The personal artwork is evaluated on the basis of technical ability, variety of media, presentation of work, and artistic ability. The candidate is also asked to

43

create a line drawing containing a few figures. This drawing is evaluated on human form, geometric and organic forms, understanding of space and spatial relationships, use of page, use of line, and design (Pittsburgh Public Schools, 1989b).

The videoquiz was developed and is administered by staff from the Division of Research, Evaluation, and Test Development. First, the candidate views a classroom teacher who demonstrates a variety of teaching practices. Then the candidate completes a quiz about the videotape that is machine graded.

The candidate's name is placed on the eligibility list once the credential folder contains all the necessary information and the candidate has completed the panel interview, the technical test, and the videotape quiz. As openings in the subject area occur, candidates are interviewed for specific positions.

Supervision of Instruction

There are approximately 100 full-time visual arts teachers and 110 full-time music teachers located in 83 schools. Responsibility for supervising the content of their instruction is divided among three visual arts supervisors and three music supervisors. Each supervisor has K-12 assignments to ensure sequential programs from elementary through secondary school. Because computer literacy programs (LOGO at the elementary level and CLIPS at the middle and secondary levels) are part of the visual arts program, visual arts supervisors are responsible for supervising them.

In 1981 the Pittsburgh Research-based Instructional Supervisory Model (PRISM) was developed. In this model, based on Madeline Hunter's method of teaching effectiveness, specific steps of instruction involve teacher questions and student responses (Staff Development [SD], 1985). Because administrators and teachers have been tutored in its usage, there is a common language that describes teaching in Pittsburgh. Although final authority for supervision and annual rating of teachers rests with the principals, supervisors are assigned to assist them in improving instruction in the classroom (Herman, 1985).

Each supervisor is required to make at least six PRISM observations per month and take anecdotal notes. This is followed by a supervisor/teacher conference to discuss teacher effectiveness. At these conferences, the supervisor may recommend strategies for improvement or arrange for the teacher to observe a peer in order to expand the teacher's repertoire of techniques. Occasionally, the supervisor may teach a demonstration lesson or show the teacher a method of organizing materials (SD, 1985).

All supervisors, directors, and building administrators have been taught a variety of conference styles ranging from high praise to letting the teacher know that there are major problems. When there are problems, the supervisor and teacher cooperatively develop a plan of action for improvement. There may be collaborative observations of teachers by supervisor and principal, supervisor and director, or director and principal (SD, 1985). Supervision of classroom instruction is especially

44

important in the arts, where few principals have extensive academic preparation or professional expertise.

Facilities Renovation

Because Pittsburgh is built on steep hills, most of the school buildings are multistory with many steps, few ramps, and few elevators. School grounds are limited in size; in many instances, there is little outdoor space for play, practice for marching bands, or use for athletics.

In the last 4 years, additions and renovations have been completed at three secondary schools, and construction is scheduled for addition and renovation of one other school. Because of a baby boomlet, four elementary schools have reopened and planning has begun to enlarge a middle school (PBE, 1989, pp. xv-xvii). Each major construction is preceded by several lengthy meetings at which visual arts and music supervisors assigned to that building and the director of arts education discuss their curricular needs with architects and representatives from the Division of Facilities. All divisions are constantly competing for more space for their programs. Each time, arts education staff produce guidelines of the National Art Education Association, Music Educators National Conference, and National Theatre Education Project for teaching, exhibition, practice, and performing spaces. The arts staff states what it needs; the facilities staff supplies existing blueprints; the arts staff argues for more space and rearrangement of current space. The blueprints are brought back to the next meeting; the arts staff attempts to place the necessary equipment in the revised spaces, then argues for more or different space again. Window and door placement, ventilation, acoustics, and location of electrical outlets are among the many considerations. After the construction is completed, the arts staff devotes continued attention to getting the old and new equipment installed properly.

Curriculum Revision

Curriculum revision, textbook selection, and implementation of a new course are parts of an ongoing process. The master schedule and budget for these activities are controlled by the associate superintendent for curriculum and program management. The Division of Arts Education competes with other divisions for use of these limited funds. Although it takes 3 or more years from beginning to end, the process provides opportunities for participation among teachers, board members, parents, and citizens.

Arts education curriculum revision is designed to meet the changing needs of the students by incorporating new trends in the arts as well as findings from recent research in education. Once a course has been placed on the master schedule and funding approved, the process begins:

1. The director assigns a supervisor or coordinator to direct the project.
2. Teachers are informed about the curriculum writing opportunity, and they

45

apply because of their interest in the topic and/or the amount they will be paid.

3. The director and the supervisor select 3 to 10 teachers for the curriculum committee, depending on whether it is a course for one magnet school or for the entire district.

4. The committee meets, develops specific strategies, reads pertinent material, discusses, and writes.

5. A limited number of curriculum drafts are printed.

6. Two or more teachers pilot the course over a few weeks, a semester, or two semesters. Usually, everyone who helps in writing wants to be involved in piloting.

7. The original curriculum reassembles and revises the curriculum based on the piloting process.

8. School district editors edit the curriculum and return it to the director and supervisor for final approval.

9. A limited number of copies are printed and sent to the school board for approval.

10. After board approval, copies are printed for the teachers, supervisors, and administrators who will use them.

11. Simultaneously, a committee of parents, citizens, and teachers are selected to review and select textbooks and resource materials for the new course. Parents and citizens are paid, while substitutes are provided for the teachers who are away from their classrooms.

12. The texts and resource materials selected by the committee are displayed by the Pittsburgh Board of Education for 1 month at each of 11 branches of city public libraries to give board members and citizens an opportunity to peruse them.

13. After board approval, books are purchased.

14. The supervisor organizes and plans in-service workshops for teachers assigned to teach the course. Often the same teachers who piloted the course conduct these workshops.

The following are three examples of curricula that are in the process of being written or revised, piloted, or implemented: *Arts Propel* (Art and Music, Grades 6-12); *Pennsylvania Arts History* (Grade 3) and *Art Moves* (Grade 4).

Arts Propel is not a new course. Rather, it is an approach to learning and assessment in the arts based on collaborative research by the Pittsburgh Public Schools, Harvard Project Zero, and the Educational Testing Service. Over half the teachers in art and music in Grades 6-12 are implementing some or all of these processes that emphasize student production, perception, and reflection in the arts.

Pennsylvania Arts History, Grade 3, is a new course designed to provide a balance in children's understanding of the state through art, music, dance, and theatre experiences. The visual arts portion is limited to the study of six painters and sculptors: Romare Bearden, Selma Burke, Alexander Calder, Mary Cassatt, Edward Hicks, and Andy Warhol. The visual arts portion was piloted in Fall 1990. One element of the music portion, the Manchester Craftsmen's Guild Jazz Concert, was implemented in spring 1990.

Art Moves (Multicultural Objects from Various Ethnic Societies), provides girls and boys with the opportunity to hold three-dimensional art objects from around the world. These objects were created for both utilitarian and aesthetic purposes by both female and male artists and are the resource texts for the course. This course was implemented in 53 elementary schools in fall 1990.

Visual Arts Programs

In addition to the functions described above, there are approximately 28 visual arts responsibilities that are anticipated annually. Because these responsibilities are anticipated, planning, organization, arranging of schedules, and allocation of resources can occur. However, there are other programs or events that are not anticipated, and thus allow little time for planning and organization. Schedules are turned upside down and resources are juggled.

Visual arts responsibilities are divided more or less equally among three *art supervisors* who are assisted by the *media arts coordinator*, the *director*, and the *teacher project leader*. At every opportunity, teachers are involved in each of these programs, not only to have a sense of ownership but also because their ideas and participation are invaluable. The anticipated programs can be loosely categorized as follows: art exhibits, community organizations, museum programs, and equipment and resource management.

The Division of Arts Education makes a valuable contribution to the cultural life of Pittsburgh by sponsoring art exhibits and showcasing student art throughout the city in art galleries, in office buildings, and at community arts events. Through these exhibits, people can see the quality of art produced by students in the schools; also, budding young artists can gain confidence by seeing their work exhibited in a professional manner. Although the division staff also occasionally arranges for an international exchange of student art, the annual anticipated art exhibits include the following:

- All-City Elementary School Art Exhibit, May
- All-City Middle School Art Exhibit, May
- All-City Secondary School Art Exhibit, February
- Black History Art and Essay Contest, January
- Board of Education Lobby Display, Continuous
- Board President Office Display, Continuous
- Elementary/Middle School Office Display, Continuous
- Youth Arts Month Displays, March
- Pennsylvania Governor's School for the Arts, Pittsburgh Intermediate Unit, January
- Pittsburgh Public School Week Displays, May

- Scholastic Art Awards, Allegheny County, February
- Western Pennsylvania Very Special Art Exhibit, May

Community organizations involve Pittsburgh Public School visual arts teachers or students in a variety of art experiences, including:

- Carlow College Art Student Teacher Placement
- The Carnegie Art Express
- The Carnegie Museum of Art Saturday Creative Art Classes
- Generations Together
- The Manchester Craftsmen's Guild
- The Pittsburgh Center for the Arts
- The Pittsburgh Foundation for Arts Education
- The Society for Arts and Crafts

Museum programs have as their basic purpose the viewing of art, and include the following:

- The Carnegie Art Tours for Fourth Grade
- The Carnegie Art Tours for Art and Nonart
- Classes
- The Children's Museum
- Friends of Art for Pittsburgh Public Schools

Equipment and resource management includes the almost invisible activities that are most necessary for the smooth operation of the more visible ones:

- Consumable art supplies preprinted list
- Equipment inventory
- Kiln exhaust and repair survey
- New equipment requests
- Replacement equipment requests
- Resource book bibliography
- Review of books, videos, and films

Music Programs

The three music supervisors handle several music showcasing functions. Students from across the district are included in the following All-City programs: Bell-Aires, middle school band, honors orchestra, middle school chorus, junior strings, senior chorus, Marching Band Festival, and senior honors band.

Public School Week features elementary, middle, and secondary student music concerts from 11:00 a.m. until 1:30 p.m. held at the City County Building, the Station Square Shopping Center, and other locations in the city. Music supervisors are responsible for arranging for the draying of risers, microphones, and speakers as well as serving as master of ceremonies for these events.

Adjudication festivals are held every spring for choral and instrumental music students in secondary and middle schools. These are not competitions, but concerts where judges develop written critiques and audiotapes that show students and teachers what they have done well and how and where they can improve. Another benefit of these adjudications is that students have the opportunity to hear similar groups perform.

The Pittsburgh Symphony Schooltime Concerts are a gift from the symphony to the public schools. Each year, there are three concerts for the all-day kindergarten classes and one concert each for all second-, fourth-, and sixth-grade students. Symphony personnel and Division of Arts Education music staff meet during the summer to plan. The division prepares a booklet containing information, activities, and evaluation procedures; the symphony prepares an audiotape. Copies of both are sent to all elementary and middle school music teachers in the district. The concert and its evaluation are part of the music curriculum.

The Manchester Craftsmen's Guild Third Grade Jazz Concert is an annual event complete with preconcert activities and postconcert evaluation for all students. It is part of the music portion of the Third Grade Pennsylvania Arts History curriculum.

The Center for the Musically Talented program provides additional instruction for students with exceptional music potential or capability. Students are selected by audition each spring and fall. From September through May, approximately 180 young musicians meet to study through private lessons, small ensembles, and classes in musicianship, conducting, and solfeggio. Instructors are musicians from the Pittsburgh Symphony, the Pittsburgh Opera, the Mendelssohn Choir, local university music departments, and the Pittsburgh Public Schools. The center is managed by one music supervisor and two teacher/coordinators.

There are 10 itinerant instrumental teachers who teach small-group lessons to interested students in Grades 3-5. These 10 teachers are primarily supervised by a music supervisor with support from elementary principals.

Managing the transportation budget and schedule is a massive assignment for one music supervisor. The division continually buses students throughout the city to perform, view a performance, or view an art exhibit.

Each year a number of student teachers in music from local universities must be assigned to a cooperating teacher. Other music education majors who need to complete weekly observations in music classrooms need to be placed as well.

A music supervisor is assigned these tasks.

Other Arts Responsibilities
In addition to the visual arts programs and the general responsibilities described above, there are a wide range of division assignments.

The division staff is continually involved in many cooperative activities conducted by committees. The director, supervisors, coordinators, teacher project leaders, and arts resource assistant all serve on numerous committees — division, department, school district, city, and state. These meetings consume time and occasionally resources; however, the value in working with others for mutually beneficial goals is invaluable.

The *media arts coordinator* provides leadership, plans, and conducts workshops and identifies specific high-tech equipment in the areas of computer graphics, photography, film, and video for division staff, teachers, and students.

The *dance coordinator* conducts workshops for teachers and students and advises teachers on dance. Directing the African Dance Festival and coordinating the student presentation of the Pittsburgh Dance Council are additional responsibilities.

The *theatre coordinator* conducts workshops on the use of drama in the academic classroom, arranges for other theatre workshops, and advises teachers on directing concerns. Other duties include distributing stage makeup kits and lending costumes and theatre equipment to drama teachers and directors of shows.

The *Teacher Project Leaders* in Art Propel and Music Propel assist in planning Propel activities with teachers, researchers, and visitors. They plan and conduct workshops and represent the school district at regional and national conferences on assessment in the arts.

The *arts resource assistant* is responsible for the two artists-in-residence programs, Gateway to Music and ARTSHARE. These programs place at least one artist in each school building annually, with the objective of broadening the base of arts experiences for students and teachers by providing multicultural role models. Another responsibility is the division calendar, which is printed monthly, September through May, and distributed to all central office administrators, to principals, and to art, music, theatre, and dance teachers. The calendar lists all the arts events of the month sponsored by the division, along with many individual school arts activities.

Summary

In the Pittsburgh Public Schools the organization, responsibilities, and goals of the Division of Arts Education are largely determined by the support and expectations of the board of education and the community. The board supports *education*; the board and the community expect *show business*. The Division does both by administering and supervising programs in visual arts, music, theatre, dance, and media arts for students from kindergarten through Grade 12.

The five responsibilities described in detail here, in addition to other visual arts and other arts programs, support arts education and arts showcasing. Budget management is the organized planning that ties allocation of funds to responsibilities and goals. As a result of the recently refined personnel selection process, the best possible new teachers for the system are hired. Supervision of instruction improves the teaching strategies of new teachers and those who have been in the system for several years. Curriculum revision incorporates recent research findings and new trends in arts, education, and arts education to meet the changing needs of students. The process of renovating facilities results in older buildings being remodeled and improved to fit curriculum and teaching changes.

While the Division of Arts Education is primarily in the business of educating students in the arts, it is through *show business* that the division showcases student progress in the arts.

References

Events. (1990, June). *Pittsburgh Magazine*, pp. 18-22.
Herman, S. J. (1985, November 1). *Procedures for supervisor visits* (Memorandum to All Principals). (Available from Department of Curriculum and Program Management, Pittsburgh Public Schools, 341 S. Bellefield, Pittsburgh, PA 15213)
Pittsburgh Board of Education. (1988). Article 116, Music Department Activities: *Collective bargaining agreement for teachers and other professional employees between the Pittsburgh Board of Public Education, Pittsburgh Pennsylvania, and the Pittsburgh Federation of Teachers, Local 400, American Federation of Teachers, AFL-CIO, September 5, 1988, through September 6, 1992.* (Available from Pittsburgh Board of Education, 341 S. Bellefield, Pittsburgh, PA 15213)
Pittsburgh Board of Education. (1989). *1990 final general fund budget, 1990 major maintenance program: Setting the pace for the challenges of the new decade.* Pittsburgh: Author.
Pittsburgh Folk Festival. (1990). *Thirty-fourth annual program, May 25-27, David L. Lawrence Convention Center.* Pittsburgh: Author.
Pittsburgh Public Schools. (1989a). *Musical technical score sheet.* (Available from Division of Arts Education, Pittsburgh Public Schools, 850 Boggs Avenue, Pittsburgh, PA 15211)
Pittsburgh Public Schools. (1989b). *Visual arts technical score sheet.* (Available from Division of Arts Education, Pittsburgh Public Schools, 850 Boggs Avenue, Pittsburgh, PA 15211)
Purdon's PA Statutes Ann., Sect. 21-2110. Eligible lists of persons qualified to teach (1949).
Shepard, M., & Goines, L. (1990). *Expanding our vision in the arts: Building multi-cultural programming and multi-cultural audiences.* Pittsburgh: The Pittsburgh Foundation/Howard Heinz Endowment.
Staff Development, the Board of Public Education. (1985). *PRISM manual.* Pittsburgh: Author.

5

Art Education and the Effective Schools Research: Practical Strategies for Including Art in School Improvement Efforts

ROBERT EAKER

Middle Tennessee State University

MARY ANN RANELLS

Nampa, Idaho, School District

In the decade of the 1990s schools will be influenced, in part, by two trends. One will be the continued emphasis on school improvement. School improvement efforts in the 1980s were greatly influenced by the effective schools movement, and we believe this trend is likely to continue. Second, we believe the coming decade will be characterized by an increased awareness and emphasis in the arts. John Naisbitt and Patricia Aburdene, in their book *Megatrends 2000* (1985), observe:

> *Time was you prayed your child would not become an artist, a musician, or an actor. But the arts boom has opened up a wealth of new career opportunities. Between regional orchestras and local acting troupes, young people have a better chance to make a living (albeit modest) doing what they love.*
>
> *"The number of painters, authors, and dancers increased some 80 percent over the past decade — three times faster than the growth rate for all occupations and well above the growth rate for other professionals," writes University of Maryland sociologist, John P. Robinson, in* American Demographics.
>
> *Between 1960 and 1980 the U.S. work force increased 43 percent, while the number of artists, writers, and entertainers shot up 144 percent.*
>
> *Even during the 1980's, when the United States created new jobs at an unparalled pace — 16 million between 1983 and 1988 — jobs in artistic careers outpaced overall job growth.*

At first glance, these trends are seemingly contradictory. Some observers believe that the effective schools research is "too narrow" and places an undue emphasis on the "basic skills." They believe that the flip side of the increased test scores that result from the effective schools programs is a decreased emphasis in the arts as well as other areas of the curriculum.

We do not believe this has to be the case. We can find no evidence whatsoever to support the idea that effective schools proponents favor a decreased emphasis in the arts. What we do find is this: As school districts and individual schools set out to create better and more effective schools, the role that the arts will play in this effort must be addressed squarely and up front. Otherwise, other curricular areas will take precedent and the arts will, indeed, suffer. We believe the arts can flourish in schools where the effective schools research is viewed as the basis for school improvement efforts. We concur with Ernest Boyer (1988, p. 2) who made the following observation in *Toward Civilization*, a report on arts education published by the National Endowment for the Arts:

> *Art is humanity's most essential, most universal language. It is not a frill, but a necessary part of communication. The quality of civilization can be measured through its music, dance, drama, architecture, visual art and literature. We must give our children knowledge and understanding of civilization's most profound works.*

The Effective Schools Movement

In 1979 Michael Rutter and others published results that directly challenged the assumption that schools make very little difference in student achievement. Although a few studies done as early as 1974 had examined school practices and academic achievement, Rutter's *Fifteen Thousand Hours: Secondary Schools and Their Effects on Children* (1979) brought the issue of effective schooling practices to the forefront. Additional studies by Brookover and Lezotte (1979) and Phi Delta Kappa (1980) supported Rutter's findings. Ron Edmonds's (1979) research on school effectiveness may have contributed more than any other study to the widespread recognition that what schools do affects the achievement of students.

Edmonds identified five variables that correlate positively with student achievement: (a) strong leadership by the principal, particularly in instructional matters; (b) high expectations of students; (c) an emphasis on basic skills; (d) a safe and orderly environment; and (e) the frequent, systematic monitoring of student achievement.

Since the first school effects studies were published, there has been a flurry of research activity regarding effective schooling practices. According to the Northwest Regional Educational Laboratory, their updated synthesis of effective schooling practices (1990) is documented and supported by more than 800 research studies and summaries.

As impressive as the sheer number of studies may be, even more impressive is the consistency with which the findings describe effective schooling practices. In the last decade the effective schools research has become the basis for a nationwide approach to school improvement. School districts and individual schools across the nation have developed school improvement plans based on this body of research.

Implementing the Research: Some Basic Assumptions

Although the interest in the effective schools research is impressive, implementing the research findings in a workable school improvement program is a complicated endeavor. One of the major problems facing those who are being asked to improve schools — superintendents, principals, and teachers — is that they are often unsure of exactly how to proceed. Since those who are charged with the responsibility for school improvement are having to not only learn the research but also develop a framework for translating the research into practice, it is critical that those who teach or supervise arts programs be actively involved from the very beginning in the school improvement process. If not, there is a very good chance that art will become merely an "afterthought" once the important decisions regarding the school program have been made.

As one begins to develop a conceptual framework for planning school improvement programs, it is important to think about the assumptions that will guide the process. The basic beliefs one has about the nature of planning, decisionmaking, working with groups, and the role of the arts will have a major impact on the directions ultimately taken. As an example, the following are a few beliefs we have about school improvement that have formed the framework for our work with school districts:

• School improvement efforts should emphasize building from within rather than importing from the outside.

• School improvement efforts should offer options rather than prescriptions.

• School improvement efforts should recognize that practitioners have a knowledge base that is valuable.

• School improvement efforts should avoid useless busywork and meaningless paperwork at all costs.

• School improvement efforts should result in a realistic, attainable dream for the future for each school.

• School improvement must be viewed as a process, not an event.

One particular school district that has been involved in highly successful improvement efforts developed its plan on the basis of these asssumptions:

• The educability of all children.

• A common curriculum content by grade and subject.

• The school exists first and foremost for an academic purpose.

• If children are not learning, it is the fault of the school system — not the children.

• Certain educator behaviors elicit more student learning than other behaviors.

• Behavior changes can occur without attitudinal changes.

• Program requirements can create behavior changes.

Frank Hodsoll, chairman of the National Endowment for the Arts, makes these assumptions about arts education in the foreword to *Toward Civilization* (1988):

Arts education can help elementary and secondary school students to reach out "beyond prime time" and understand the unchanging elements in the human condition. It can teach them to see and hear as well as read and write. It can help them understand what civilization is so that as adults they can contribute to it. In a culturally diverse society, it can generate understanding of both the core and multiplicity of America's culture. In an age of television, it can teach our children how the arts can be, and have been, used. In a world made smaller by modern communication and travel, it can teach them how the cultures and civilizations of other countries affect attitudes, beliefs, and behavior. It can help our children develop the skills for creativity

56

and problem-solving and acquire the tools of communication. It can help them develop the capacity for making wise choices among the products of the arts which so affect our environment and daily lives.

Time and again throughout the improvement process problems and roadblocks will occur and disagreements will emerge. At these times it is critical to refer to the district's basic assumptions about school improvement. Whatever the assumptions are, they should be the basis for decisionmaking and action.

District-Level Leadership: A Prerequisite for Success

While numerous individual schools have successfully implemented effective schools programs without any help or direction from the district office, it is very difficult to convince teachers that school improvement will be the major thrust of the district without the visible and vocal leadership of the school board and the superintendent.

Leadership for arts education is critical at the districtwide level. As major decisions are being made regarding the nature and direction of school improvement, someone must stake out a position for the arts. If there is a leadership void at the district level regarding the arts — if there is no advocate for arts education — there is a good chance that other priorities will take precedence. We are not saying the position should be one of touting the arts as the most important aspect of schooling. However, we are saying this: The role of arts education should be an essential element in any discussion about districtwide school improvement.

What should be the basic nature of district-level leadership? Clearly, district leaders must cultivate a culture for change. The superintendent is in the best position to promote, protect, and defend the district's school improvement efforts. If the superintendent isn't willing to confront those behaviors that weaken the quality, efficiency, and equity of good schools striving to become better, the school improvement process will ultimately end up being another dying fad.

We believe the district-level leadership for effective schools must manifest itself in at least three observable ways: planning, modeling, and monitoring.

Planning

If things are truly valued, plans are made to see that they occur. School improvement efforts will never be taken seriously as long as the efforts are characterized mainly as "just talk." Planning should be viewed as a process for implementing the things that are valued the most.

At the district level it is critical to establish processes and procedures that lead to a shared view of what the entire district should become. In other words, there should be a shared, comprehensive view of the future for the entire district.

As an example, picture a large macrame design hanging on a wall This entire macrame represents the vision of the future for the district. Hanging from the top of the macrame are several strands, each representing a major division of the schooling process: curriculum, instruction, personnel, staff development, and so forth. Since the macrame is large and represents a comprehensive view of the district, there must be widespread collaboration in its creation. How tightly or loosely the strands are woven together, what dominant patterns are incorporated, and whether or not an artistic balance is achieved blend together to form an image of a vision for an entire school system.

In this vision of the future, what would be the role of arts education? Can the district dream into the future and describe an arts education program that will be in place 3 years from now? This critical question must be addressed in the early stages of any districtwide school improvement process. Resource allocation is an essential aspect of planning. While it is true that people plan for the things they value the most, it is also true that people spend their time and money on things that they truly value. The same is true with a school district. If, in fact, improving the schooling practices in a district is a core value, then resources must be provided to ensure the success of improvement efforts.

Likewise, if the district leadership is committed to improving the arts program in the district, resources must be provided. Resource allocation always involves a competition between important areas for limited funds. Hence, it is critical that a well-thought-out, articulate, realistic, and reasonable presentation regarding the resource needs for arts education be developed. It serves little purpose to make a strong case for the importance of the arts, but not receive the resources necessary to make the arts program what it should be.

Modeling

Modeling is the way leaders advertise their values. The *behavior* of district leaders will do as much as anything to convince those in the school district of what is *really* important. Do the school district leaders model the behaviors they expect from others? Are their day-to-day behaviors congruent with their professed values? These are critical questions in any effort to incorporate values within an organization. In *Leaders: The Strategies for Taking Charge*, Warren Bennis and Burt Nanus

(1985) put it this way:

> *The leader is responsible for the set of ethics or norms that govern the*
> *behavior of people in the organization. Leaders can establish a set of ethics*
> *in several ways. One is to demonstrate by their own behavior their commit-*
> *ment to a set of ethics that they are trying to institutionalize.*

Philip Selznick (1957) observed that the essential problem of leadership is the identification of key values and creation of a social structure that embodies them. Modeling is the way leaders advertise their personal values, as well as the central values around which the organization operates.

If arts education is going to be an essential ingredient in school improvement efforts, then district leaders must model an interest in and a commitment to the arts. Otherwise, they simply will not be believed.

Monitoring

Finally, if school improvement is to be viewed as an important goal within the district, a plan for monitoring the school improvement process must be developed. Monitoring is the way leaders pay attention to the things they value the most. And what gets monitored gets done. Not only should the monitoring of the various aspects of the school improvement process be effected (including the arts program), it should be welcomed. This is one way the leadership of the district signals what is important. It is like saying, "We care enough about this program — we think it is so important — that we're checking on it to see if we're doing a good job and seeking ways we can do even better."

Also, monitoring raises expectations. One of the most frequently asked questions regarding the role expectations play in educational outcomes is this: How can we raise expectations within our school district? Part of the answer involves deciding what you value and then paying attention to those key values. If art education is to be improved within a school district, someone must be responsible for paying attention to it.

Building-Level Development Efforts

The effective schools research has had perhaps its biggest impact at the building level. Numerous examples exist of individual schools making a commitment to school improvement based on the effective schools research. Many of these schools have done so with little or no support from the district office.

Perhaps the real hope for school reform lies not with national commissions of state legislatures, but with one building at a time making a genuine commitment to improve the quality of schooling for boys and girls. To accomplish this goal, building principals must not only be committed to school improvement, but must have the ability to organize and plan in such a way as to ensure that dreams become a reality. The leadership skills of the principal are critical. Much has been written about the characteristics, traits, and skills of the ideal instructional leader. Suffice it to say that the principal must be able to communicate, motivate, empower others, keep things in perspective, and do these things with warmth and humor. It isn't enough for the principal to *want* better schools. The principal must turn the dream into a reality. This is typically done by working with a school improvement team.

School Improvement Teams

Most schools attempting to implement the effective schools research begin the process by appointing a school improvement team. The school improvement team becomes the vehicle by which all major decisions regarding the improvement process are made.

The size of the school should determine to some extent the size of the school improvement team. Teams typically range in size from 5 to 15 members.

The composition of the team is critical. Obviously, the team should represent the diverse groups within the school and the community and should include teachers and parents. Depending on the situation, representatives from other groups may also be included. For example, secondary school teams would want to include students and, perhaps, representatives from the business community. A district-level administrator is often viewed as an important person to have on the team.

Team members should be selected on the basis of their ability to influence various subgroups within the school. It is advantageous to involve team members who are highly respected individuals and whose opinions count.

Team members should possess the ability to envision a broad perspective. Remember, the goal of the school improvement team is the improvement of the total educational experience for all students. Individuals who can only see one side of an issue or who are interested in fulfilling their own particular agenda will not provide the kind of leadership needed.

We believe it is important that the principal serve as the leader of the school improvement team. The principal must be able to mold the team into a cohesive group that is based on trust, openness, and consensus decisionmaking. At the same time, the principal must not abdicate the role of instructional leader of the school.

Developing the School Improvement Plan

If the launching of the ship occurs at the district level, raising the anchor and heading out to sea happens when a school improvement plan is developed. Remember: "If you want to sail the big ships, you have to go into deep water."

Although the school improvement team will provide direction for all the various activities associated with school improvement, the team's primary responsibility is to develop a school improvement plan. The goal is simply to cooperatively develop a realistic, meaningful, systematic, and comprehensive school improvement plan that is based primarily, but not exclusively, on the effective schools research. If the school improvement plan is going to become the framework for school improvement efforts, it is critical that those concerned about the arts program be heavily involved in the development of the plan. Nothing will substitute for active participation. Although there is no "correct" way to develop school improvement plans — teams have been successful using a variety of approaches — we believe the following process will result in a plan that is both workable and practical. Several schools have been successful using this approach.

STEP 1: *First, describe the school you seek to become, remembering to focus on specific areas.* Virtually all approaches to planning for school improvement focus on the importance of a "vision" or articulation of a "school mission statement." In their highly regarded study of leadership, Warren Bennis and Burt Nanus (1985, p. 89) observed that a vision "articulates a view of a realistic, credible, attractive future for the organization, a condition that is better in some important ways than what now exists. A vision is a target that beams." It is a view of the school of the future that provides the organization with a sense of purpose and direction. Hockey great Wayne Gretzky notes: "I skate to where the puck is going, not to where it has been." The development of a process that results in both this common vision of the future and widespread support for the vision is where the quest for excellence should begin.

One of the problems many school improvement teams face at this point is that their vision of the school of the future might become too broad. Some teams write about "developing good citizens" or of educating students who can "function effectively in a multicultural, global economy that is characterized by ever-changing technology." These types of statements provide very little direction for individual faculty members or staff personnel.

We believe the school improvement team should be very specific in describing the school they seek to develop. The following is a list of some of the issues successful teams have considered in developing their vision of excellence. (Ob-

61

viously, each team has to develop its own list of areas that should be considered).

- Districtwide goals and plans
- Academic achievement
- Students' feelings, emotions, attitudes, self-concept development, and so forth
- Depth and breadth in the curriculum (i.e., the desired balance of emphasis on basic skills, the arts, physical development, social development, higher order thinking, programs for special children, vocational programs, etc.)
- Faculty involvement, pride, and morale (quality of work life)
- Quality and nature of parental involvement
- A safe, orderly, and drug-free environment
- An atmosphere of mutual respect and trust
- Quality of facilities

The desired role of arts education must be addressed in the development of the vision of the future. We believe it is critical that a consensus be developed regarding not only the visual arts but the performing arts as well. The school improvement team should address the following questions:

How do we define basic arts education? and What do we want our basic arts education program to look like 3 years from now? Without a consensus as to the ideal art education program, it will be next to impossible to gain commitment and support.

Reaching a consensus about the school you seek to become is a time-consuming endeavor. Some school improvement teams spend the better part of an academic year engaged in this process, while others can complete the task in 3 or 4 months. The following process was used by one successful secondary school in developing a school mission statement.

1. The principal reviewed the purpose of the task and described what process and procedure should be considered by the school improvement team.

2. The team and the faculty reviewed the findings of the research on effective schools.

3. Surveys and brainstorming sessions were held with teachers, students, parents, business representatives, and community organizations.

4. The school improvement teams categorized the initial responses into groups and wrote a draft statement.

5. The draft narrative was shared with the various constituents, and feedback was solicited.

6. On the basis of the feedback, the school improvement team revised the draft, and a final draft was ultimately presented to the board of education for their acceptance of and commitment to the statement.

Several benefits accrue as a result of describing the school you seek to become, but the most important one is that it helps establish an agenda for action. As Naisbitt and Aburdene observed (1985, p. 27), "It is easier to get from point A to point B if you know where point B is and how to recognize it when you have arrived."

STEP 2: *Determine the current state of the school in each area that was identified in the school mission statement.* Once the school improvement team has described what kind of school is desired in the future, the current state of the school can be evaluated to identify discrepancies between the reality of the existing school and the characteristics of the ideal school.

Although all areas of the school should be examined, particular attention should be paid to student outcomes. In analyzing student outcomes, the school improvement team should disaggregate achievement data in a number of different ways. The relationship between achievement scores and the socioeconomic levels of students should be examined. Data should also be examined by race/ethnicity and sex.

Student outcome data should include results from teacher-made, criterion-referenced tests as well as nationally normed-referenced tests. The school improvement team will want to analyze correlations between items on these two types of tests.

In examining student outcome performance, some areas of the curriculum such as art, music, drama, and dance, do not lend themselves to "accounting" measures such as standardized test scores. Yet, "quality control" is critical in these areas. Hence, the school improvement team will need to identify *indicators* of achievement other than test scores from these important areas of the curriculum.

This issue is of particular importance for arts educators. Because of the relative difficulty involved in "evaluating" the outcomes of a program such as art or drama, it is tempting to resist evaluative efforts by making the case that since arts outcomes cannot be "measured," student achievement in the arts cannot be analyzed.

We believe arts educators must be at the forefront in developing quality control measures for the various arts courses and activities. If arts educators do not perform this function, outcome measures will probably be developed by someone else, or worse, the arts program will be given such little emphasis that no one will care.

STEP 3: *Develop specific plans for closing the gap between "what exists and where you want to be."* In actuality, the school improvement team in an individual school is responsible for determining a number of improvement plans — one for each area of improvement. These plans are in writing and open to public scrutiny. They constitute the team's ideas for moving the school from where it is to where it should be — rather like dreams with deadlines.

While many different bodies of research should be considered in developing various parts of school improvement plans, the effective schools research should be used to plan for improvement of academic achievement. The plan should include specific ways each of the effective schools correlate will be addressed in the school improvement process.

STEP 4: *Develop a school improvement calendar for a 3-year period at a minimum. Set improvement goals for various aspects of the improvement program for specific years. (It is unreasonable to work on everything every year.)* There is a saying that "the administrator who has too many goals has no goals." The school improvement plan should cover multiple years so that everyone can see the big picture, but should also be detailed enough to include specific goals and activities for specific years. Some critical areas will need attention right away, while others may be addressed during the second or third year. Yet, everyone should know that there is a plan and a timetable for addressing all of the improvement goals that have been identified.

STEP 5: *Develop a monitoring plan.* In many ways this is the most important step in developing a school improvement plan. Unless a monitoring plan is developed and implemented, the school improvement plan will not be viewed as being important. Leaders check on what they value, and keeping touch of the progress that is being made is one way expectations are communicated throughout the school.

Creating Winners and Celebrating Success

Terry Deal and Allen Kennedy (1982, p. 63) observed in their book *Corporate Cultures* that "in the absence of ceremony and ritual, important values have no impact." We believe it is vitally imperative for the school to develop mechanisms throughout the school to create lots of winners (both faculty and students) and celebrate their successes. Those interested in school improvement should make a systematic and sustained effort to celebrate the successes of teachers and students, both within the school and the larger community.

School leaders must recognize people's innate desire to be on a winning team and continually seek to provide evidence of their successes. There is much in education that is quantifiable — achievement test scores, passing rates, attendance rates, levels of student participation in cocurricular activities, and so on. A concerted effort to monitor, report, and extol the gains that occur in such areas will promote

64

a sense of excellence.

Those who dismiss improvements in such areas as insignificant are making a major mistake. The celebrations that recognize the delivery record of Frito-Lay employees or the sales achievements of Mary Kay Cosmetics representatives do not just recognize the delivery of corn chips or the sale of makeup. These corporate celebrations promote specific cultural values, establish norms for others to emulate, and convey a sense of the effectiveness of the organization and its people.

Effective companies use celebrations to promote the attitude that "we will succeed because we are special." As that attitude becomes ingrained in an organization, it is ultimately recognized by those outside of the organization as well. Deal and Kennedy (1982) illustrated this point with the example of the sales representative who says "I'm with IBM" rather than "I peddle typewriters for a living." Because of the outstanding reputation that IBM enjoys, the simple statement "I'm with IBM" serves as a source of personal satisfaction for the sales representative.

Furthermore, it heightens his or her expectations for personal performance. Deal and Kennedy concluded that the attitude "we will succeed because we are special" can be maintained only by continually celebrating achievements that reflect the values of the organization. Thus, those interested in promoting particular values within a school must always be on the lookout for indicators of the presence of those values. Teachers must be given evidence that their efforts are having an impact.

Effective leaders extol the virtues of exemplary employees day in and day out at the slightest sign of successful behavior. If a school is to be excellent, its administrators must recognize that one of their most important responsibilities is to identify and publicize the efforts and achievements of staff members that reflect the values of the school. There are at least three reasons why this responsibility should be given priority.

First, recognition improves the morale of those singled out. Public recognition of exceptional effort is certain to have a positive motivational effect on the recipient of that recognition. In treating someone as a star, we increase the likelihood that the individual will, in fact, act like a star.

Second, recognition affects others on the staff. People tend to assess their own performance not according to some arbitrary standard, but in relationship to the performance of others. As Deal and Kennedy (1982, p. 38) concluded:

People can't aspire to be "good" or "successful" or "smart" or "productive," no matter how much management encourages them in those directions. They can, however, aspire to be like someone: "He's just an ordinary person but look how successful he is. I can be successful like that too."

By recognizing the performance of individual staff members, administrators provide other staff members with a model and motivate them to engage in similar behavior.

Finally, public recognition reinforces the values of the school. Recognition serves as a reminder of what is important.

Two points bear reemphasis. First, in order to be effective, an award program must provide for a wide distribution of awards. A school with only a handful of outstanding teachers will have a difficult time achieving excellence. The reward system should make all teachers feel that they have an opportunity to be recognized as outstanding. Second, an achievement need not be monumental to warrant celebration. It is important to vigilantly seek out the small successes — those teachers whose students performed well on a competitive exam or in a cocurricular contest, who attracted exceptional student enrollment, who modeled their academic discipline by practicing it outside of the classroom, who earned advanced degrees, who contributed to their professional organizations, or who were acknowledged as having made a difference in a student's life. These teachers merit the recognition of the school community.

Students, too, will benefit from the perception that they attend a high-quality school and that they are achieving success and recognition for it. Many of the studies of the effects of positive reinforcement and praise have taken place in educational settings. It is ironic that educators generally have failed to take advantage of the power of positive reinforcement.

The arts program offers one of the best opportunities to lead the way in celebrating the successes of students. If provided a variety of opportunities in the arts, virtually every student at one time or another can enjoy success. The art program can be the example for the rest of the school by demonstrating a belief that every student has a talent and that celebrating the successes of art students can become the basis for feelings of success and accomplishment.

Sustaining the Improvement Process

Those who set out on the quest for school excellence must do so with the clear understanding that they can never permit themselves to feel that they have arrived at their destination. As Peters and Austin (1985) observed, the bad news about the pursuit of excellence is that you'll never finish. Toynbee's (1958, p. 50) description of civilization also applies to the pursuit of excellence: "It is a journey and not a destination, a voyage and not a harbor."

How can school improvement be sustained when the goal is so elusive and timeless? The only answer is persistence. As Admiral Hyman Rickover (1985, p.

415) observed, "Good ideas and innovations must be driven into existence by courageous patience." Naisbitt and Aburdene (1985) contend that people are energized by the vision of an organization when it is not only powerful but persistent. When Bennis and Nanus (1985, pp. 187-199) asked 90 leaders about personal qualities they needed to run their organizations, they found that

> *They never mentioned charisma, or dressing for success, or time management, or any of the other glib formulas that pass for wisdom in the popular press. Instead, they talked about persistence and self-knowledge; about willingness to take risks and accept losses; about commitment, consistency and challenge.*

Perhaps an analogy to farming is appropriate. Educational leaders should become experts in "farming," that is, planting the seeds of school improvement and cultivating, nurturing, and caring for them. We should practice patience and celebrate the unfolding of each blossom. We should believe that the quality of the lives of our families, friends, and neighbors depends on the success of each harvest — because it does. We must realize that one profitable crop will not be grounds for retirement. We will need to continually plan, monitor, and model the best behaviors and practices known.

It is an exciting time for education. More is known about good schooling practices than ever before. The research on effective schools has provided those who are committed to school improvement with a framework for making schools better. Also, we believe the effective schools movement does not have to be an intellectually narrow movement. There is ample evidence that the arts flourish in effective schools. In fact, we believe the interest in school improvement offers a unique opportunity to improve the quality of art education. J. Carter Brown, director of the National Gallery of Art, notes in *Toward Civilization* (1988, p. 2): "This moment of mounting concern about American education is the time to help our dedicated teachers and our schools transmit the significances and common heritage of the arts, so that our young people will not be denied the opportunity to become citizens this nation deserves."

References

Bennis, W., & Nanus, B. (1985). *Leaders: The strategies of taking charge.* New York: Harper and Row.
Brookover, W., & Lezotte, L. (1979). *Changes in school characteristics coincident with changes in student achievement.* East Lansing: Michigan State University, Institute for Research on Teaching.

Deal, T., & Kennedy, A., (1982). *Corporate cultures: The rites and rituals of corporate life*. Reading, MA.: Addison-Wesley.

Edmonds, R. (1979, October). Effective schools for the urban poor. *Educational Leadership*, pp. 15-23.

Naisbitt, J., & Aburdene, P. (1985). *Megatrends 2000*. New York: William Morrow.

National Endowment for the Arts. (1988). Toward civilization: A report on arts education, 1988. Washington, DC.

Rickover, H. (1985). In T. Peters & N. Austin, *A passion for excellence*. New York: Random House.

Rutter, M., Maughan, B., Mortimore, P. Outson, J., & Smith, A. (1979). *Fifteen thousand hours*. Cambridge, MA: Harvard University Press.

Selznick, P. (1957). *Leadership in administration: A sociological interpretation*. New York: Harper and Row.

Toynbee, A. (1958). The Graeco-Roman civilization. *In civilizations on trail*. London: World Publishing.

Additional Resources

ASCD (1982, December). On school improvement: A conversation with Ron Edmonds. *Educational Leadership*, pp. 12-15.

Brookover, W., Beamer, L., Efthim, H., Hathaway, D., Lezotte, L., Miller, S., Passalacuqua, J., & Tornatzky, L. (1982). *Creating effective schools*. Holmes Beach, FL: Learning Publications.

California State Department of Education. (1977). *School effectiveness study: The first year*. Sacramento: California Department of Education, Office of Program Evaluation and Research.

Eaker, R., & DuFour, J. (1988). *Fulfilling the promise of excellence*. Westbury, NY: J. L. Wilkerson.

Educational Research Service. (1983). *Effective schools: A summary of research*. Arlington, VA: Author.

Eisner, J. (1979). Good schools have quality principals. In D. Brundage (Ed.), *The Journalism Research Fellows Report: What Makes an Effective School*. Washington, DC: Institute for Educational Leadership, George Washington University.

Finn, C. (1985). The dilemmas of educational excellence. In *Honor of Excellence*. Reston, VA: National Association of Secondary School Principals.

The five correlates of an effective school. (1983, November). *Effective School Report*, p. 4.

Gardner, J., (1961). *Excellence: Can we be equal and Excellent too?* New York: Harper and Row.

New York State Department of Education. (1974). *Reading achievement related to educational and environmental conditions in 12 New York City elementary schools*. Albany: Division of Educational Evaluation.

Peters, T., & Waterman, R., Jr. (1982). *In search of excellence: Lessons from America's best-run companies*. New York: Harper and Row.

Weber, G. (1971). *Inner city school children can be taught to read: Four successful schools*. Occasional Paper 18. Washington, DC: Council for Basic Education.

6

Elementary Art Supervision in The Los Angeles Unified School District

NAN YOSHIDA

Los Angeles Unified School District

Introduction

Being the elementary art supervisor in a large urban school district larger than the city of Los Angeles is no easy job. To improve art education in 414 elementary schools, the supervisor must play many roles — art education advocate, curriculum writer, program coordinator, workshop presenter, conference organizer, meeting facilitator, and district ombudsman for art. This involves working with staff members of all levels in the school district, as well as communicating with parents and the community at large. Often, the community extends beyond the locale as one responds to questions and requests from other states and countries.

A large urban school district has the advantage of being part of a metropolitan area with many museums, galleries, and cultural institutions. Art instruction can be infinitely enriched through field trips to museums where students and teachers can interact with original works of art previously studied in the classroom. Art prints are a wonderful resource, but there is no substitute for seeing the "real" thing.

Individuals and organizations in the public and private sectors often invite the district to collaborate on experimental programs or pilot projects. The art supervisor evaluates the merits of each proposal relating to elementary art education to determine educational soundness and the ultimate benefits to the instructional program.

Description of the Los Angeles Unified School District

The Los Angeles Unified School District occupies 708 square miles, extending well over the 469 square miles of the city of Los Angeles. Los Angeles County encompasses 4,083 square miles, including the city itself.

It carries on its work in a total of 837 schools and centers. The district is made up of elementary, secondary, continuation, community, adult, special education, magnet, and opportunity schools; also, there are children's magnet, newcomer, primary, opportunity, regional occupational, business and industry, and skills centers. Over 85% of the 610,000 students in the district are minority. According to the statistics of fall 1989, the ethnic breakdown is 14.6% White, 15.8% Black, 5.6% Asian, 0.5% Pacific Islander, 1.9% Filipino, 0.2% Indian/Alaskan Native, and 61.5% Hispanic.

Responsibilities of the Elementary Art Specialist

The elementary art specialist is a member of a work force of 60,000, 30,000 of which are teachers. The job involves 414 elementary schools, as well as additional early childhood programs. The specialist position is considered middle management, and the responsibilities include the following:
- Developing curriculum
- Coordinating programs
- Communicating with all levels of staff, as well as parents and members of the community

• Keeping abreast of current developments and research in art education
• Communicating with colleges and universities in teacher training and other programs
  • Assessing and evaluating art programs and materials
  • Providing staff development
  • Visiting schools to meet special needs
  • Maintaining ties with the county office of education and the California State Department of Education.

Curriculum: An integral part of the district's *Elementary School Course of Study* is the art curriculum. This is correlated to the state *Framework for Visual and Performing Arts* which describes within its goals and objectives the four components of art education:
  • Development of aesthetic perception — visual and tactile
  • Development of creative expression — artistic knowledge and skills
  • Study of visual arts heritage — historical and cultural
  • Development of aesthetic valuing — analysis, interpretation, and judgment
These four components form the basis for art instruction and are amplified in the concepts and skills delineated for kindergarten through Grade 6. To assist teachers in implementation, a sample concept development page is provided for each grade level to demonstrate how activities and skills may be taught to develop the desired outcomes and major concepts.

Instructional Materials. To augment the *Elementary School Course of Study,* a new elementary art guide is currently being written. Until it is completed schools have access to the following district art publications: *Art Education: Activity Experiences for Creative Expression; Arts and Crafts in American Life; Every Day's a Holiday — With Art; Exploring Art: Feeling, Form, Function; Exploring Clay; Let's Start Drawing; and Mark My Word.*

Instructional bulletins or publications designed to enhance teachers' knowledge of timely topics with broad popular appeal are also developed. For example, in anticipation of the 1988 Olympics in Seoul, Korea, *Focusing on Korea and the Summer Olympics in Grades K-6* was developed by the district. This book supplied a brief history of the Olympics and general information about Korea and its cultural achievements, customs, traditions, and holidays. The suggested classroom activities integrated art, language arts, social science, and physical education. Resource pages listed district publications, kits, films, community organizations, museums, and a bibliography of adult and children's books. The text was illustrated with reproductions of Korean children's art, the result of an exchange between this school

71

district and the Pusan City School District in Korea. To further enrich classroom studies, teachers borrowed portfolios of the original artworks made by the children of Pusan.

In addition to district publications, schools are urged to purchase art instructional programs adopted by the California State Board of Education. The current adoptions are *Through Their Eyes*, W. S. Benson; *Discover Art* and *Teaching Art*, Davis Publications; and *Art Works*. Harcourt Brace Jovanovich (Holt, Rinehart, and Winston). These materials are on display at the textbook services section and are available for review throughout the adoption period.

Schools may also purchase supplementary audio/visual materials that have been approved by a district evaluation panel composed of teachers, administrators, and the art specialist. An evaluation of materials in all subject areas, including art, is conducted every year by the audio/visual services section.

Instructional Television Programs. An important resource of the Los Angeles Unified School District is the district-owned and operated television station KLCS, Channel 58. The station has won many Emmy Awards for high-quality educational programming. Instructional programs are aired across all areas of the curriculum, including art programs appropriate for the elementary classroom. Teachers augment their art instruction with such programs as *The Art Maker, The Big A,* and *The Art Chest.*

As the elementary art specialist, I have taken the opportunity to produce and narrate two programs for KLCS. One is called *The All-American Family Mural Project*, a series of 23 classroom murals depicting family and patriotic activities. Putting this project together was quite an education. First, the paintings were individually videotaped at the station. They were grouped into 2-minute segments of five to six murals each. I wrote and narrated the script in what is called a "voice-over," and then selected and located the background music to be added. The viewer sees each mural identified with the credits naming the teacher, school, and principal. The station continues to air the segments, produced in 1987, as public service announcements or fillers between programs. The original 23 murals were a collaborative venture with the Community Development Department of the City of Los Angeles and were hung as welcome banners at the Hollywood Bowl during the city's celebration of the Bicentennial of the United States Constitution. These delightful canvases, painted in acrylic by children in Grades 3-6, were later exhibited for a month at the Los Angeles County Museum of Science and Industry.

Projects such as this one often have a longer life span and serve more purposes than originally planned. Initially intended to help the city with decorative art, the project provided an opportunity to train interested teachers in painting with acrylics on canvas and to teach children composition and mural making. Furthermore, publicity and recognition for the teachers, students, and their schools was most welcome.

The second television program I produced was the *Wonderland Avenue Magnet School Art Exhibit*. The student body of Wonderland Avenue School comprises both neighborhood children and children who are bused in from other areas of the city to attend the magnet program for gifted and high-achieving students. The magnet coordinator teaches art at the magnet school. Each spring, the year's instruction culminates in an impressive exhibit with panels and tables of children's art in a variety of media. These drawings, paintings, collages, and constructions resulted from learning about the work of such artists as Georgia O'Keeffe, Henri Matisse, Frank Lloyd Wright, Red Grooms, and Norman Rockwell. The exhibit also reflects multicultural studies in African masks, Indonesian tie-dye, Eskimo carvings, and American quilts and samplers.

For television, I interviewed the instructor, several students, a parent, and the school principal at the art exhibit. The program emphasizes the importance of art education in the development of the whole child, is approximately 15 minutes in length, and has been aired many times. Videotapes of both the Wonderland exhibit and the All-American Family Mural Project have also been used for staff development.

District In-Service Training and Staff Development

In-Service Credit Classes. The district has a structure for granting teachers salary credit for attending in-service classes. Teachers may earn one salary-point credit for completing 16 hours of attendance and 32 hours of outside assignments. These in-service classes are especially important because in the Los Angeles School District all elementary subjects (including art) are taught by the elementary classroom teacher, who is a generalist. In the area of art education, classes such as drawing, painting, printmaking, design processes, crafts, three-dimensional art, multicultural art, mask making, mural making, art history, and appreciation are offered. In-service leaders are selected for their expertise in subject matter and their ability to communicate this knowledge using effective instructional strategies. For their work, they may receive payment or double salary-point credits, according to their preference.

Staff Development. In contrast to in-service classes (which teachers voluntarily attend to earn salary-point credit), staff development is conducted by the art specialist to meet the specific needs of a particular group. For example, new administrators receive training in supervision of instruction. They learn about art content and methods in order to assess classroom art instruction at their schools. Teacher interns, new to the profession, receive an orientation of the elementary art curriculum as part of their staff development. They must then take in-service or college courses to learn art methods and media. In response to requests from elementary schools, on-site staff development is provided on such topics as room environment, art appreciation, critical thinking through art, integrating art and literature, and implementing the *Framework* and *Course of Study.*

An essential role of the art specialist is to identify teachers who are already doing an excellent job of teaching art in their classrooms and train them to become workshop leaders. These teachers receive in-depth training to familiarize them with current art research and practices and to develop their leadership skills.

Community Partnerships and Collaborations

Evenings for Educators. This a collaboration that the district has enjoyed since 1980 with the Los Angeles County Museum of Art and the Los Angeles County Office of Education. The concept was to open the museum in the evenings with special programs for educators. This was successful from the very beginning when the programs were first attended by 100. Now an average of 800 per evening attend.

Evenings for Educators are held on the second Tuesday of each month from 6 to 10 p.m. Teachers and administrators attend docent tours, workshops, performances, and slide lectures by renowned experts on the topic of the evening. Exhibitions have included "Thomas Hart Benton, an American Original," "Contemporary European Painting," "One Hundred and Fifty Years of Photography," and "Romance of the Taj Mahal." During the reception, participants have an opportunity to visit with colleagues and discuss the evening's events. They visit the museum book and gift shop, which is held open especially for them (often, they acquire posters at the bargain price of one dollar!) They look forward to receiving the teacher resource packet, which contains slides or other visuals, background information on the exhibition, suggested ideas for classroom instruction, and a bibliography/resource list. While enjoying these culturally rich experiences, teachers and administrators may earn in-service or college credits.

With the success of *Evenings for Educators* at the Los Angeles County Museum of Art, other museums now invite our collaboration on similar or other types of outreach programs. The Palos Verdes Art Center, which exhibits work by local contemporary artists, has initiated *Afternoons for Educators* and makes accessible excellent programs for teachers in the southern area of our district.

The Craft and Folk Art Museum worked with the district to design a multicultural mask-making curriculum. Teachers attended an in-service workshop where they learned about the masking traditions of African, Asian, and Hispanic cultures, and they worked with artists in dance, story telling, and mask making. Some were selected to have a museum educator and artist go to their classrooms to teach their students a unit on mask making.

The Getty Center for Education in the Arts began its discipline-based art education program in Los Angeles County with the 1983 Summer Institute. In the first year, two schools from Region E of our district participated, along with schools from other districts in the county. Participation was contingent upon a commitment by the principal and two teachers to attend the 3-week summer institute. Since that first institute, other principals have added their commitment of time, personnel, and resources. There are now approximately 50 schools in our district whose principals and teachers have had training in discipline-based art education.

In 1984, the district was contacted by the Junior League to collaborate with them and the Museum of Contemporary Art (MOCA) on a pilot project to make contemporary art accessible to elementary school children. After almost 2 years of meetings and discussions with different members of the Junior League, we were pleased to hear that sufficient funds had been raised to begin the project.

The Junior League then hired a project coordinator to work with the district to develop and implement a curriculum. The program was named *Contemporary Art Start* and began with the participation of 11 schools and 22 teachers in 1986. It now has a new funding source and has expanded to 74 classrooms. Teachers must attend 1 week of training in the summer and several update sessions during the year for which they receive in-service credit. The curriculum is taught through classroom and gallery experiences. A unique feature of *Contemporary Art Start* is its provision for parent outreach. Toward this end, the museum provides complimentary memberships for participating students and their families, as well as for the 74 teachers.

Art in Our City. This was a short-term outreach program conducted in 60 classrooms. Designed by the Municipal Art Gallery for Grades 4-6, this 5-week sequential unit introduced teachers and their students to the work of artists living in the Los Angeles area. Participants explored works of art for artistic meaning by relating their own life experiences to the artists' diverse attitudes about themselves, the environment, and art. They created art and wrote poetry. Funded by grants from the National Endowment for the Arts, the California Arts Council, and the City of Los Angeles Cultural Affairs Department, this school and gallery collaboration resulted in a handbook composed of participants' ideas for classroom and gallery art activities.

Other museums, galleries, and institutions contribute to the enrichment of the school art programs. Among them are the Getty Museum, the California Afro-American Museum, the Museum of Cultural History and Wight Art Gallery; at the University of California at Los Angeles, The Junior Art Center, The Performing Tree, and the Los Angeles County Music Center/Education Division.

In addition to partnerships with museums and galleries, the staff works with the civic and business communities on art display opportunities, such as calendar art for the Department of Water and Power, HUD fair housing posters, Great Western Agricultural Fair murals, Sierra Club wetlands conservation posters, and the national Binney and Smith "Dream-Makers" traveling exhibition.

Higher Education: Integral to our work in the schools are the universities that provide teacher training programs. Articulation is essential between the school district and the universities in order to graduate teachers who are prepared to teach quality art programs in their classrooms. We have successful collaborations with the California State University campuses at Northridge and Los Angeles in organizing art conferences and workshops that are often cosponsored with the California Art Education Association and the Los Angeles County Office of Education.

Professional Support. Professional organizations such as the California Art Education Association and the National Art Education Association provide vital support for district art supervision. The conferences and seminars sponsored by these associations are lively forums for ideas in art education; their publications and newsletters channel valuable information to their membership. Active participation in art education associations is essential for developing professional growth and collegiality.

Conclusion

The purpose of this chapter has been to share my experiences of elementary art supervision in one large urban school district. I hope that this will inspire an exchange of ideas on effective methods of art supervision.

7

Art Specialist Versus Arts Generalist: Timely Considerations

RONALD J. TOPPING

White Plains, New York, School District

Introduction

The art specialist versus the arts generalist — how does this issue affect the delivery of a quality art program to children? Who can best deliver superior art education through instruction, curriculum, and staff development? What factors affect the role of the art specialist and arts generalist? How can educators compensate for negative factors while emphasizing positive ones?

The main objective of this chapter is to weigh the pros and cons of coordinating *one art program* as opposed to *a number of arts programs*.

Past History

There have been some gradual changes in the coordination of arts programs during the past few decades. At one time most districts employed coordinators of one art form, more recently, however, they have provided coordinators for a number of art disciplines, the most common combination being art and music. The reasons for this change include funding problems, declining enrollments, and a shift in emphasis from supervisors of special subjects (e.g., art, music, and physical education) to coordinators for all subjects, including academics. At the same time, roles have changed dramatically. The traditional authoritarian image of the director has given way to the collegial coordinator who involves teachers in the decision-making process. School districts vary greatly in how they implement art supervision as a result of the organizational structure and philosophy of the district as well as the coordinator's style. They will probably continue to provide art supervision in a variety of ways because of differing philosophical viewpoints, financial situations, and political needs.

Factors Influencing Art Coordination

There are many complex conditions that influence the decision to employ an art specialist versus a generalist. These include (a) the quality of available staff members, (b) the politics involved in a district's line-staff relationships, and (c) the district's preferred style of administration. School systems sometimes trade off the advantages of a specialist in order to employ a multi-arts coordinator with more broad-based coordinating skills.

All arts coordinators — whether specialists or generalists — must operate within the parameters of *time, status-power,* and *content knowledge.* These parameters, in turn, influence a coordinator's style and effectiveness as a change agent. Because of their importance, these factors should be carefully weighed.

Time

Clearly, the more areas a coordinator supervises, the more he or she deals with time management. The coordinator of art (i.e., specialist) has far more time to spend in classrooms than the coordinator of several art forms (i.e. generalist), who devotes more time to meetings and desk work. Relatively speaking, the generalist becomes more of a manager than an instructional leader. The specialist has more time to develop interpersonal staff relationships and can give more time to teachers on an individual basis.

Status-Power

Educators tend to perceive multi-arts coordinators differently than single-focused art coordinators. Principals and other administrators typically value the views of generalists more than specialists because of their perceived ability to understand the "big picture" while coordinating arts programs. The generalist tends to be closer to the power structure and thus can have more influence in helping teachers with budget and scheduling matters. On the other hand, art teachers have greater respect for the art coordinator's in-depth knowledge of the art field and often feel that the specialist can give them more assistance and understanding.

Coordinators, whether specialists or generalists, are usually in a staff rather than line position. Thus, the coordinator's authority and ability to influence comes form factors such as technical mastery, subject-matter knowledge, theoretical insight, persuasiveness, personality, and demonstrated vision. The specialist is more likely to possess the first three of these factors. The last three factors, more general in nature, relate more to innate abilities rather than an individual's knowledge of art and/or art education.

Content Knowledge

The role of change agent also affects the generalist/specialist discussion. A specialist's knowledge of art education is an enabling factor in assisting staff to improve instruction, especially in those areas that require technical mastery and conceptual insight. These skills help in designing and implementing the curriculum and providing staff development activities for art education. On the other hand, generalists may be more receptive to new ideas in unfamiliar art disciplines because they are often more flexible than those involved in a given subject area for a number of years. At times, looking from the outside gives one a clearer vision.

The foundation of any art program depends on the quality of its teaching staff. Therefore, the recruitment and selection of art teachers is of prime importance. The art specialist and generalist would tend to handle recruitment and selection in very different ways. The specialist, by virtue of attending professional conferences and visiting various art programs, has an established network of colleagues at the university level who can help with the recruitment of teachers. This network is also beneficial when evaluating references. The specialist also knows which art schools or universities to use for recruitment. The specialist is better able to evaluate a candidates portfolio as well as student work. If a teaching exam is part of the selection process, the specialist also has greater insight than the generalist into the content aspects of the lesson.

Functions Of Art Coordination

The three principal functions of art coordination are instructional, curriculum, and staff development. How effectively they are carried out depends to a large degree on whether they are delivered by a specialist or a generalist.

Instructional Development

The supervision of the instruction program is one of the prime roles of the coordinator. The task is an intricate one regardless of how many areas one supervises; the process involves different teachers, classes, and school climates. Regardless of the line-staff relationships of a given district, the style of the coordinator is a critical factor.

The specialist has fewer teachers to coordinate, and thus has more time to devote to the tasks of instructional improvement. More observations and conferences per teacher are possible. With a larger staff and more limited time, the generalist must use time more effectively, which means more formal observations (preplanned) and less opportunity for informal drop-ins. There is also less opportunity for the generalist to provide in-depth classroom supervision. Such supervision requires preplanning with the teacher, being in the classroom for extensive periods of quality instructional time, and giving appropriate feedback after each observation. Because of time constraints, a generalist with the best of intentions can only deal with the above activities in a limited manner.

Subject matter knowledge also affects the quality of supervision. The generalist can help art teachers improve their management and general teaching techniques, setting clear objectives, using effective question-answer methods, pacing the lesson, and motivating students. Other areas that may prove more challenging include demonstrating an art technique, explaining a principle of design, helping teachers accomplish their art objectives, and guiding students through the creative process. Nonspecialists often have difficulty discerning the appropriateness of a teaching strategy to use in accomplishing a specific objective.

In order to compensate for lack of art knowledge and time, generalists often need to become "orchestrators of instructional supervision." That is, they need to assign specific tasks of instructional improvement either to outside consultants or to art teachers within the district. The hope is that art teachers will play a larger role in facilitating new art curricula and staff development.

Curriculum Development

Specialists and generalists typically bring different kinds of talents to the area of curriculum development. The specialist is at a distinct advantage because of his or her knowledge of the subject area. This knowledge helps in facilitating sound decisions regarding the philosophy and content of the curriculum; it also helps the specialist focus the limited time schools have available for art education in ways that are rich and appropriate to the students' instruction. Because the specialist knows the scope and sequence of art education, curriculum development becomes a task that can be effectively accomplished. The specialist also tends to be more timely and updated in his or her knowledge of research in the field.

The generalist, on the other hand, is at a disadvantage in the above areas. As a result of not having a strong bias regarding subject-matter content, the generalist may rely more on teacher opinion in curriculum matters. This approach has some attractive possibilities since it gives teachers a more active role in the decision-making process. The generalist can give staff some optional opportunities to share curriculum concerns and successes in a variety of settings. It is also possible that the generalist will bring a fresh approach to the curriculum area. When I assumed responsibility for coordinating the districtwide music program, in addition to my duties as an art educator, the content was primarily vocal. I encouraged teachers to expand the curriculum to six areas, including composition, instrumental, listening, dance, musical drama, and vocal. I also provided staff development activities in composition and dance, areas the staff identified as needing assistance.

The generalist is usually supportive of the holistic approach to education because of his or her involvement with the total school program. This may also lead to a more supportive role for interdisciplinary education.

Staff Development

The goal of staff development is the ongoing professional development of teachers for the ultimate enhancement of student achievement. Staff development flows into both instruction and curriculum development and requires openness to change. The coordinator can play a major role in creating an environment that supports change. Regardless of whether the coordinator is an art specialist or generalist, effectiveness in interpersonal relations and astuteness in employing skills as a change agent are critical.

The art specialist's knowledge of art and time availability are enabling factors in identifying skills teachers need to develop. Comprehension of the art process and what it takes to produce quality art products is critical to providing staff development activities for art teachers. The generalist, on the other hand, relies upon teacher initiative in identifying staff development needs and the experts that are best able to address them. These consultants or teacher mentors can organize and run art workshops and institutes.

After considering the relative advantages and disadvantages of the specialist versus the generalist, I emerged with a clear bias. I favor having specialists as art coordinators whenever feasible. The specialist's technical mastery and conceptual awareness far outweigh the comprehensive vision and political acceptance of the generalist. The specialist also provides the optimal art curriculum, instructional, and staff development because of time availability, greater content knowledge, and more staff acceptance.

If a school district elects to have a coordinator of several arts programs for economic or personnel reasons, art teachers will need to be involved in staff recruitment/selection, peer coaching, and curriculum/staff development. This may be achieved by teacher mentors, interns, and staff developers, with the assistance of the generalist and teacher center personnel. School districts may also accomplish these activities by employing outside consultants with expert knowledge in art education.

We are in a challenging time for art education. School districts need to focus their art education resources in sensitive balance with a variety of educational, political, and economic demands. Although I am partial toward the specialist, the key challenge is for selected art leaders in each school system to draw upon available resources to provide an optimal art program. This is especially critical in this conservative era where the existence of creative self-expression is threatened by an overemphasis on the cognitive aspects of art.

Reference

Oliva, P. F. (1989). *Supervision for today's schools,* White Plains, NY: Longman Inc.

8

From Art Teacher to Art Supervisor: Views of Teacher Collegiality

KATHERINE O'DONNELL

GARY M. CROW

Bank Street College of Education

Although the practice of teaching art has recently received increasing attention, the career and role of the art teacher have seldom been investigated (Chapman, 1982). The role change from art teacher to art supervisor has received even less attention. Yet the unique balance of artist, teacher, and administrator creates a complex role transition that demands greater understanding by the individuals making the transition, the preparation programs that facilitate the transition, and the profession that supports the continued development.

In this chapter, we examine various conceptual issues concerning the role change from art teacher to art supervisor, report on a research project that examines this transition in terms of conceptions of school leadership, and discuss implications for individuals, preparation programs, and the profession at large.

Conceptual Issues of Role Change

Three sources of literature highlight features of role and career transition that inform our examination of the move from art teacher to art supervisor. These sources include studies concerning the initiation into and identification with a role, career stages, and conceptions of school leadership. As we discuss the conceptual issues raised in these bodies of literature, we will identify specific implications for the role transition of art teacher to art supervisor.

Entering a New Role

Literature on initiation into and identification with a role highlights the processes that art teachers undergo in moving into administration. Early classic studies of occupational identification ([1]Becker & Carper, 1956a, 1956b; [2]Becker, Geer, & Hughes, 1968; [3]Becker, Geer, Hughes, & Strauss, 1961) emphasize the importance of graduate training for facilitating and structuring the movement into an occupation. Becker and Carper (1956a) found five mechanisms, typically occurring during academic preparation, that influence the development of identification with an occupation: investment, acquisition of new skills and development of interest, acquisition of ideology, internalization of motives, and sponsorship. The longer one studies for a particular occupational role, the greater the investment in that role and the harder it is to reverse one's decision. The acquisition of new skills and development of interest in the tasks of the role occur typically through informal student groups, informal apprenticeships with faculty, and the formal academic structure of courses and degrees. Students, faculty, and academic structure also aid in the acquisition of an ideology of the occupation and the internalization of the value and norms of the work. Finally, professors act as sponsors of the student into jobs within the occupation. This sponsorship and the obligations it entails also serves to develop a strong identification with the occupation. Becker and Carper found that these mechanisms acted in different degrees for the three occupations they studied: physiologists, engineers, and philosophers. Some of the mechanisms

84

are clearly important for art teachers moving to administration, while others are indirectly relevant because of their absence.

The financial costs and time requirements inherent in graduate study create a powerful investment that art teachers are unlikely to waste. However, individuals moving into art administration already have investments in a prior occupation — teaching — and may also see themselves as artists. These multiple commitments can complicate the development of identification with the new occupation of administration.

Like the engineering students in the Becker and Carper study, (1956a) art teachers begin to develop an interest in the tasks of the occupation of administration and perhaps even acquire some of the skills prior to graduate training. All teachers have experienced some form of "presocialization" by virtue of observing administrators at work. Furthermore, it is not unusual for art teachers considering this move to administration to have been "tapped" by other teachers and administrators for their administrative potential. One possible effect of this prior acquaintance with administration is an identification with the occupation as enacted in a particular setting, namely one's own school. Academic preparation may or may not broaden the scope or content of the identification beyond the school setting.

The current school setting also influences the mechanisms of acquisition of ideology and internalization of motives. The conception of administration as practiced in one's setting is likely to have a strong influence on the individual moving into administration. Furthermore, because most students moving from art teacher to art supervisor attend graduate school part-time, there is little opportunity to be part of informal student "cliques" or to participate in apprenticeships with faculty members where one begins to internalize an ideology of and a set of motives for the occupation. The stronger sources for the acquisition of ideology are more likely to be the role models in one's own setting, that is, other administrators.

The mechanism of sponsorship is also influenced by the setting. Although university faculty may sponsor students in art supervision positions, it is likely that art teachers see their career mobility opportunities as primarily tied to their current school districts and thus their administrators as their most potent sponsors.

While the five mechanisms of Becker and Carper are relevant for the development of identification with art administration, they act in different ways than in the original study. For art teachers, the current school setting becomes a powerful force for identification.

In another study, Becker and Carper (1956b) examine the elements of identification with an occupational role. Three of those elements are especially useful in our study of art teachers moving to administration: occupational title and ideology, commitment to task, and organization and institutional position. Entering an academic program to prepare for art supervision entails specifying the type of role with which one wishes to become identified. Art supervisory roles contrast not only with art teaching, but with general administration of schools (e.g., principalship). By entering art administration, an individual has chosen to maintain an interest in, and even a commitment to, art and the supervision of art programs.

In addition to title, ideology, and tasks, identification with an occupation includes a view of organizational and institutional position. This view, according to Becker and Carper, can involve identification with one organization or many organizations and with one kind of position or a variety of positions. Teachers tend to move into administration within the same district in which they taught, thus limiting the identification to a particular setting and to the kinds of positions available in this setting. However, because art education/supervision is practiced in organizations other than schools (e.g., museums), it is possible for an individual to identify with the occupational role more than with the enactment of the role in a particular setting.

The importance that Becker and Carper place on ideology as a component of identification is reflected in studies that examine the development of a conception of the role. Davis (1968) examines the stages in the subjective experience of developing a conception of an occupational role. These stages occur during the entry into a new role. His stages reflect a "process of doctrinal conversion" in which individuals move from an initial frustration over the incongruity between their original expectations and those of the faculty through a "psyching out" stage of attempting to figure out what the faculty expect to an internalization of a conception of how to enact the role. Davis's stages are useful in understanding the process during the academic preparation. However, we suspect that in a role in which identification is shaped in a major way by the strong forces of the individual's school setting, the conception of the role is also influenced by role models, such as other art supervisors and school administrators. Thus, the original expectations are formed in part by these role models from the individual's setting whose conception of the role may contradict the university faculty's conception. Furthermore, since art teachers moving to art supervision tend to be part-time students who continue to perform jobs in their school settings, the process of internalizing a conception will be complicated by the interaction between school and university factors.

Career Stage Literature

The identification literature considered in the previous section has traditionally emphasized the early or entry career stages (Hall, 1986) in which one moves from a lay to a professional position. Hall claims that

the central assumption of this research on role transitions has been a titled power relationship, with a low-power individual moving into a high-power

86

environment, with a resulting one-way influence process: the organization
socializes the person, but the person does not innovate or otherwise act on the
organization. (1986, p. 121)

However, the move from art teacher to art administrator involves a career change
from one professional role to another. A career stage vantage point involves two
ways of conceiving the transition from art teacher to art supervisor: the career stage
of teaching at which the individual moves to administration and the move to
administration seen as a career stage.

Although rarely applied to the careers of art teachers (May, 1989), the concept
of stages of teacher development has informed our understanding of teachers' career
since the late 1960s. The concept of stages can be used for understanding where
teachers are when they begin the transition from teaching to administration.

Stages of teacher development may be broadly categorized as referring to
external factors (e.g., preservice or inservice teaching and numbers of years spent
teaching) or to internal factors (e.g., level of ego development [Witherell &
Erickson, 1978] and conceptual levels [Harvey, Hunt, & Schroeder, 1959]).

Katz (1977) and Yarger and Mertens (1980) offer career stage theories that
describe the process from the beginning teacher to the retiring professional.
Although these authors differ in their labeling of identified stages, there are
similarities in their formulations. The stages that they identify progress from the
survival stage of the beginning teacher (Katz, 1977) to the professional security and
growth of the experienced teacher. The intervening stages engage the teacher in
various levels of mastery of teaching and various levels of involvements with
teacher colleagues and supervisors.

Career stage literature emphasizes the importance of acknowledging differences
among teachers in how a move to another occupation may be perceived. Moving to
administration in an early teaching stage is likely to present different training needs
for the individual (e.g., developing skills in curriculum supervision). Also, it is
likely that the norms of teaching and the identification with teaching will be
diminished for individuals at this early stage, thereby lessening the conflict involved
in leaving teaching and the eventual identification with administration. In contrast,
the individual moving to administration at a later teacher career stage may
experience greater conflict. Preparation will be affected by different needs depending on the career stage. For example, teachers at an early stage may need help in
developing the knowledge and skills of teaching in order to supervise, whereas
teachers at a later career stage should be more comfortable with these skills but may
need help in developing managerial skills.

Conceiving of the move from art teacher to art supervisor as a career stage is also
a useful vantage point. Two structural features of the transition from art teacher to
art supervisor are especially relevant to our focus. First, there is a major change in

orientation involved in moving from teaching to administration that makes new demands on the role enactment by the individual and influences the image of the role. Thompson, Avery, and Carlson, (1968) refer to this transition as a "disrupted career" in which one moves from a collegially defined occupation (teaching) to an enterprise-defined occupation (administration). Collegially defined occupations are those in which the definition of appropriate professional conduct is determined by colleagues rather than an organization; appropriate professional behavior in enterprise-defined occupations is organizationally determined.

There are also differences in the organizational spheres of the two roles that create a change in orientation. Even if they move among several classrooms, teachers enact their practice by focusing on a group of students and, for some teachers, a single subject — art. The move to administration requires a shift of attention and orientation across multiple classrooms, numerous groups of students, and a variety of subject areas or grade levels.

These features contribute in at least two ways to the complexity of the role change for the art teacher moving to administration. First, balancing the three orientations of artist, teacher, and future administrator is more difficult than balancing the roles of teacher and future administrator. Second, the balance of artist and teacher permits both collegiality and solitude in work. But the move to administration disrupts at balance by running the risk of decreasing collegiality. Administration has been characterized as a "lonely job for the person at the top" (Jackson, 1977).

Conceptions of School Leadership

As Davis (1968) acknowledges, an individual moving into a new role eventually internalizes a conception of the role. A student examining school leadership will soon find that at least four ideal types of the role now exist: charismatic, bureaucratic, human relations, and collegial. All four have historical roots. Charismatic leadership, aptly described by Weber (1946), may have roots in preindustrial society but can be seen reflected in recent discussions of effective leaders. In this perspective, leadership is based on certain traits or qualities of the individual with little or no regard to the influence or followers. Charismatic leadership involves personal qualities that enables the leader to persuade individuals to follow his or her lead and to perform certain tasks.

Bureaucratic leadership has been the traditional model since the advent of the industrial era, and it has endured despite attempts to modify it. This view calls for placing sole decision-making authority in the hands of administrators based on their office and emphasizes the leader's responsibility for the smooth operation of the organization.

One of the attempts to modify this traditional model of leadership arose in the mid-20th century and was based on the work of Mayo (1945), Roethlisberger and Dickson (1939), Barnard (1945), and others. These researchers and theorists acknowledged the role of followers in defining zones of appropriate administrative influence and in withholding or providing their cooperation with administrators. The human relations model of leadership emphasizes the need to obtain input from staff and to focus on the working conditions of staff. However, no attempt is made to enlarge the sphere of decision-making authority, especially in regard to joint efforts of staff.

In the past few years, collegiality has received new attention as a critical attribute of school leadership and an advocated form of educational power (Nyberg, 1982). As a conception of leadership, the collegial model emphasizes the leader as facilitating greater teacher involvement in making decisions about as well as implementing instruction. The Carnegie Commission Forum on Education and the Economy (1986) made one of the more significant calls for greater teacher involvement by suggesting alternative models for organizing schools and the decision-making processes of schools, including the establishment of a committee of lead teachers.

Some educational theorists have linked school improvement with greater teacher collegiality (Liberman, 1988; Little, 1982). Judith Warren Little, studying the characteristics of effective and ineffective schools, identified the effective schools as those with "norms of collegiality" (e.g., schools in whose hallways teachers continuously discussed teaching and planned, taught, and analyzed their teaching). A collegial model of leadership emphasizes the role of the administrator in facilitating interaction among teachers for the purpose of influencing the instructional program of the school.

We have noted that, for art teachers, the conception of the role may be influenced by the school setting as much or more than the graduate school. Thus, any of the four conceptions of leadership may be found among students. If charismatic and bureaucratic forms are primarily enacted in the student's setting, graduate programs that emphasize collegial or human relations conceptions will create conflict for the student and may have difficulty convincing the student that these forms of leadership are "practical." It is important that faculty understand the range of conceptions of leadership that students bring with them to administrative preparation programs.

In the research study reported below, we examine the conceptions of leadership held by a group of students moving to art supervision and their views at various stages of the preparation program regarding collegial leadership.

Moving to Art Supervision: A Research Study

Since teacher collegiality has been identified as an important element in successful schools and collegial leadership an increasingly emphasized model for school leadership, this study examined students' views of collegial leadership as an indicator of one aspect of administrative role perception. The study also broadened the perspective to look at similarities and differences among students in the preparation program as they move from art teacher to art supervisor.

Methodology

The sample for this study included all art instructors enrolled in an administrative preparation program: the Bank Street College/Parsons School of Design Master's Program. The students were divided into three groups depending on the length of time that they had been involved in the program. There were 11 students in the first-year group, 16 in the second-year group, and 20 in the third-year group. The total population was 47, of which 43 were female and 4 were male. Incomplete information was obtained from 6 of the students, resulting in a sample of 41.

The Bank Street/Parsons program is designed for art instructors who wish to obtain administrative and supervisory certification that will enable them to become art supervisors, school principals, or staff developers. At the completion of the program, students receive a master's degree in supervision and administration with a focus on the visual arts. There are two unique features of the program. First, the program involves the combination of coursework in educational administration with studio art courses. This combination is used to prepare future administrators and to encourage continual development in the visual arts.

The second feature involves the centrality of cohorts in organizing much of the students' work. Students progress through the program with the same group of students with whom they entered. All students within a group take the same courses and meet together during the summer in weekly conference groups to integrate theory and practice. In addition, they have weekly individual conferences during the summer and regular telephone conversations during the rest of the year with the same faculty advisor. The process of beginning and ending the program with the same group of students intensifies the impact of the program.

In order to understand students' views of teacher collegiality and their perspectives regarding the role transition from art teacher to art supervisor, we used two sources. First, we used a short case study of a school situation that focuses on a plan for teacher collegiality and asks for the administrator's response to the plan. Students' comments regarding the case provide qualitative evidence of their views of collegiality.

We also examined admission material that provides evidence of the students' definition of effective leadership and their personal resolution of the artist/teacher balance.

Since the sample size was small and our intent was to provide evidence of how the students made sense of this role transition, we concentrated on qualitative methods of analysis, such as content analysis, identification of patterns and themes, and other methods described by Miles and Huberman (1984), rather than quantitative analysis of the frequency of response. Also, since the study was cross sectional in regard to similar and different views of the students, there is no way to discuss changes over the preparation period. Data provide themes, patterns, and questions that should be examined in future longitudinal studies of students in this and other administrative preparation programs.

Demographic Characteristics

The demographic characteristics of this sample are remarkably homogeneous. For example, the age range of the sample was 23-52 years. For the first-year group, the range was 27-52 years, with a mean of 40.8 years; for the second-year group, the range was 23-50 years, with a mean of 35.5 years; and for the third-year group, the range was 25-50 years, with a mean of 35.5 years.

The teaching experience of the sample reflects work in elementary, junior high, and senior high schools, community colleges; and musuems. Students entering this program are likely to have worked at several levels of the public school system as well as in adult education or higher education. Their experience at varied levels of schooling seems reflective of the nature of art teacher preparation and market conditions in art teaching. Art teachers are prepared and certified to teach K-12. Many begin their teaching careers at whatever level at which an appropriate and attractive teaching position is available and then move to teaching positions at the level they would most prefer as positions open. This means that many art teachers may begin teaching at the elementary school level and move to the high school level, and vice versa. Their preparation for teaching and credentialing allow them this flexibility. This breadth of experience may be extremely valuable, though atypical, for teachers moving to administration.

Another atypical characteristic of this sample of students was the amount of administrative experience they had prior to admission to the program. Fifteen of the 41 (over one third of the group) entered this program with administrative experience. Again, this may be, in part, attributable to their work as teachers of art. Much of their administrative experience was obtained in settings not demanding advanced degrees or state certification, for example, museums, art centers, businesses (usually design firms), and community colleges. The visual arts, with their history of emphasis on the quality of the artists' productions as a criterion for recognition rather than credential, may allow a greater range of work roles for people.

As a counterpoint to looking at the experience that students brought to the program, we also looked at their aspirations. Where did they see themselves going? Where did they want to go at the completion of this program? What occupational title most fits their career goal? Many students' aspirations were, as yet, undefined; others had a general desire to work with adults, primarily in a museum or higher education setting. Fifteen in this sample aspired to become school administrators, art coordinators, assistant principals, and principals. Twelve wanted to be in higher education, with four in that group specifying college administration. Two in the sample wanted to remain as teachers. This range of roles seems consistent with and reflective of existing opportunities in the field. While the range has diversity, it lacks innovativeness: The questions of aspirations did not stimulate respondents to seek roles as yet uncreated.

A fourth area of student characteristics that was explored with this sample was the artist-teacher dynamic. Was there a conflict between these two roles and, if so, how had it been resolved? For these men and women, there seemed to be no conflict between these two roles. There were 10 exhibiting artists in the sample, only one of whom identified him- or herself as an artist. All of the others identified themselves as artist and teacher or as art teacher. The emphasis was decidedly on the choice of teaching art, as reflected in the comments of one of the students: "My talents and pleasures found compatible outlets most often when I was in an academic environment in the role of teacher, leader, or advisor." Another statement emphasizes the interpersonal role of the teacher: "My art teacher was so supportive. I felt I would like to do that for others." Clearly, for this group, the folklore of the field that the art teacher is a disappointed artist is not substantiated.

Conceptions of Leadership

The final area of characteristics that students brought to the program was their conceptions of leadership. As part of their admission process, candidates for the program were asked to identify and elaborate on their personal conceptions of effective leadership. The responses to this question reflected a familiarity with three of the forms of leadership mentioned earlier: charismatic, bureaucratic, and human relations. The one unfamiliar form of leadership was collegial. Only three of the students mentioned collegiality as a feature of effective leadership, for example, "current and confident enough to let others make decisions and influence the school." This student's description concluded with human relations qualities — "able to give teachers confidence, knowledgeable, visible, able to support good teachers"; and "makes me feel like an important part of the faculty; I am free to consult with him and am welcome in the educational family and accepted as a contributing member of the team." The following descriptions were included in the comments of the second student mentioning collegial leadership: "sets goals with teacher input; goals are reasonable and measurable; open to new ideas; politician, diplomat, makes decisions on educational need, not politics." The paucity of comments reflecting any degree of collegial leadership is notable in this sample.

What is most typical of the students' conceptualizations of effective leadership was the absence of single categorical definitions of effective leadership. Students drew most frequently from the charismatic, bureaucratic, and human relations forms in giving their definitions.

Upon entering the program, most of the students described effective leadership primarily by identifying traits and specifying aspects of the leader's task. Among the traits identified with an effective leader are those that emphasize charismatic vision and interpersonal qualities. According to the students in this sample, leaders should be "imaginative, innovative, and creative"; they should be "a model of desired actions"; and they should be "inspiring to those [they] work with." The view of effective leadership held by these students also includes a stress on the professional sense of the leader: "dedicated to education as a profession, undertakes lifelong learning, aware of the history of education, concerned with communicating education to the community and the larger society" and "committed to making the arts available to the public."

The following comments a bureaucratic conception of leadership: "efficient in making well thought out decisions" and "has good management skills to assure smooth operation; must establish goals and see the big picture." These or synonyms occur frequently in descriptions of effective leaders.

The human relations conception of leadership is reflected in "guides the school team, values opinions of all, caring and supportive of teachers"; "plans activities that teach teamwork, respect for self and others"; and "dedicated, sensitive in working with people."

Although separated here for emphasis, students' descriptions of effective leadership wove together bureaucratic, charismatic, and human relations conceptions. This is desirable in that good leaders are more likely multidimensional in their actions than rigidly pure. However, it is important to note the virtual absence of the use of the collegial conception by students entering an administration preparation program, especially since the collegial aspects of leadership are receiving attention both in the literature and in preparation programs.

Views of Collegiality

Students' responses to the collegiality case study indicate some interesting diversity. Only half of this group unqualifyingly approved of the teacher collegiality plan. Three students approved but did so with qualifications — all of which involved the administrator's involvement in the plan. One student commented:

I support the idea and along with the support I offer the suggestion that an administrator and/or resource person work with the teachers to plan the development sessions. I also recommend that each session be well planned by the teachers so the sessions are carefully choreographed in terms of time, information given, and method of presentation, so the sessions are as professional as possible.

Another student added that, "the administration would still have authority to select styles, etc., that they would like to develop." The two students who disagreed outright with the collegiality plan did so because of potential conflict among teachers and lack of teacher expertise. One student argued that "[the plan] creates a situation of different teaching methods, positive and negative, conflicting."

First-year students. The comments of the first-year students who supported the collegiality plan provide information as to how collegiality works and what it accomplishes. They said that such a plan works because of the teachers' credibility with each other and because of their commonality, especially in regard to language and experiences. For example:

I believe that teachers have more credibility for other teachers, as opposed to experts from the outside, especially when they share a school setting by virtue of the fact that they are in the trenches and have a common language of problems and dilemmas.

Another reasoned that, "teachers are the ones who have experienced the classroom setting and can offer this experience to their colleagues."

Students' rationales of what teacher collegiality accomplishes fall into three patterns: instructional, interpersonal, and professional growth. Most of the first-year students provided rationales that are mixtures of these three elements. The instructional rationale involves the importance of teachers having ownership of the instructional program and the need for teachers to communicate student expectations with each other. One student justified the collegiality plan in this way: "It leads to a sense of ownership in the school curriculum, leading to a feeling that a teacher has a vested interest in the ongoing improvement of the learning process and educational setting." Another gave two reasons why the teacher collegiality plan helps teachers communicate their expectations of students: "because it would inform the faculty at large as to what students were exposed to during the year [and] because the level of expectation of teacher and their demands on students could be

94

realistically viewed."

Students who said that the collegiality plan has interpersonal justification identified the effect on morale and on improved communication among teachers. One put it concisely: "Interaction will only encourage good morale and commitment to school, staff, and students." First-year students also mentioned professional growth as a reason for approving the collegiality plan: "Asking someone to share their experience can be a very positive reinforcement to their own self-respect and respect for their craft." Another argued that the teacher collegiality plan is a form of learning:

Learning experiences continue to take place through various avenues throughout life. One way is to learn from colleagues, not necessarily in a teacher-student relationship, but in a shared experience context. It's too often ignored in school situations that some of the most valuable resources for in-service are the resident faculty.

Second-year students. When they were asked to consider the collegiality case study, second-year students were more likely than first-year students to give unqualifying approval to the plan (66.7%). Those who qualified their approval were less interested in involving the administrator in the plan and more interested in broadening involvement and ensuring quality. One second-year student's only qualification involved broadening the support for the plan: "I would ask that they go to the faculty in some way, small group, questionnaire, etc., to gain wider acknowledgment and support for the idea." Another said that she "would bring in another source of information so the group wouldn't stagnate over a period of time." One other student was concerned with the qualifications of the staff development providers: "If there were teachers who were qualified to teach others, master teachers, etc., then they should be allowed to do so."

When we examined what these students said that collegiality accomplishes, we found the same three patterns as with the first-year students — instructional, interpersonal, and professional growth — but there was a tendency to identify a single rationale and to emphasize the interpersonal. Students mentioned staff morale, community building, teamwork, and an atmosphere of openness as features of the interpersonal pattern that the collegiality plan would accomplish. One teacher described why this improvement in interpersonal dynamics is crucial: "Teachers lead a very isolated existence and instead of getting strength and support from each other, they work independently and then don't use themselves as their own best source of strength." This isolation has been mentioned by Lortie (1975) and others who describe the work of teachers. Students in this group said that teachers teaching teachers helps to break this isolationism by building a sense of community. "I think this is a good idea to build a good rapport among the staff, to help them see themselves as a team working together to achieve certain goals, rather than competitors."

Those who mentioned instructional reasons for collegiality emphasized the variety and diversity of models that could enrich the instructional program. One student described what could be accomplished and a possible plan:

Although varying disciplines would create different classroom models, the experience of having a variety of methods, styles, etc. would provide an arena for discussion and at the same time allow for new synthesis to occur. A theme might be developed from a certain year of the school's curriculum and different methods be discussed as to the alternative means for reaching that goal.

The students in this group also gave reasons for collegiality that emphasized professional growth. One student used the isolation theme to emphasize a teacher's growth: "We are not isolated instruments who are born with all the information, techniques, etc. We all have different ideas and by interaction we improve ourselves."

Third-year students. Students in the third-year group overwhelmingly favored a collegial stance. Thirteen of these students approved of teachers planning staff development while two approved the plan with qualification. No one in the third-year group disapproved of teachers planning staff development.

The rationale for approval was based on instructional reasons, interpersonal reasons, and a mix of the two. Those students who justified their approval of collegiality with instructional reasons cited the following: "Familiarity with other instructional methods will give teachers new ideas for instruction"; "teachers will be able to help other teachers improve their instructional methods"; "teachers will improve their willingness to change"; and "observing in other teachers' classrooms has made me sit back and analyze my own teaching." Another student, also citing instructional reasons for approval of collegiality, noted:

I would encourage this plan which would emphasize teaching each other in regards to instruction. There are numerous ways in which we teach our classes. This would be an excellent way for teachers to pick up on new techniques and to share what works and what doesn't.

I'd give the superintendent a copy of the Judith Warren Little article on collegiality. I'd stress that an open exchange of ideas must be experimented with. Teachers learn from teachers how to teach.

Those who approved of collegiality for interpersonal reasons listed factors such as increased morale among staff, opportunities for teachers to feel they were making a contribution to the school, and improved communication: "I would support the plan because it provides for idea sharing"; "[It] will create collegiality among staff, improving morale, will create something to identify with, a direction, values, judgments among staff. Teachers will be more empathic and sensitive to the problems of the staff."

One student cited a mixture of reasons for approving collegiality:

First, other teachers are closest to the students, which is why staff is trying to improve their teaching; master teachers can be used to observe and confer with others ... discussions can continue after the formal training sessions are over in informal sessions. The sharing, learning can continue well after the time period is over. Problems or questions that arise can be discussed further. Teachers will share the same kinds of problems, time constraints.

"Teachers will improve their willingness to change their instructional methods because of peer interaction, suggestions, and help."

Teacher Career Stage and Views of Collegiality

We also examined the relationships between different demographic characteristics and the rationale for the collegiality plan. Although we found no relationship among age, sex, administrative experience, and preprogram descriptions of effective leadership and collegiality, we did find a strong relationship between years of experience as a teacher (i.e., teacher stage of development) and rationale for collegiality. We found that teachers with 4 to 12 years of experience were more likely to justify a collegial staff development plan for its interpersonal benefits. Sixty-one percent of those with 4-12 years of teaching experience gave interpersonal reasons as a rationale for collegiality, compared to 41% of those with 0-3 years of experience and 54% with 13-25 years.

If these individuals with 4-12 years of experience perceive that they have achieved basic mastery of teaching practice, they may be more interested in professional relationships with colleagues. This is the stage that Katz (1977) refers to as the renewal stage of teacher development when the teacher is rewarded by meeting peers, formally and informally, rather than developing skills in the mechanics of teaching, as was done in the earlier career stage. This interpretation is reinforced by the reasons these students gave for supporting teacher collegiality. One student in this experience category illustrated the importance of interpersonal reasons for collegiality when she said that, "I think sharing ideas and experiences among teachers helps ... not only the success of the program but also the relationship of staff working as a community. I have always thought that working in groups has better results." Another said: "I think telling about how a teacher teaches is less effective and certainly less exciting than sharing the actual teaching experience. Interaction will only encourage good morale and commitment to the school, staff, and students."

Implications

For Individuals

For art teachers considering the move to administration, the literature and research we have presented suggest at least three implications. First, it appears to be important for artist/teacher/administrator balance to find programs or support systems that help the individual retain the commitment to art at the same time that a new role is being added. The tension between collegiality and solitude in the life and work of an artist who is an educator is complicated by the move to administration. Programs that permit the simultaneous practice of art and leadership would be advantageous to the student. Barring these formal programs, individuals may join or establish informal or formal support groups of art teachers anticipating role transitions.

Second, the importance of viewing the move to administration as part of a larger career suggests the need to find ways to emphasize continuity between parts of the professional work of art teachers moving to administration. Identifying skills developed while teaching (e.g., curriculum development, work on schoolwide projects, and work in communicating art issues to the larger community) facilitates the development of leadership skills and the transition to this role. Furthermore, connections between the practice of art and the practice of administration are useful and necessary for emphasizing the continuity of career. The creative problem solving (e.g., in design) inherent in art has clear connections with the educational leader's role in implementing and facilitating problem solving in schools.

Third, it is important for individuals moving to administration to recognize that the collegiality they developed and enjoyed as teachers need not be sacrificed in enacting an administrative role. The skills inherent in collegiality are consonant with current conceptions of leadership.

For Preparation Programs

The findings of this research and the theoretical issues raised in the literature also have implications for programs designed to prepare art teachers for art supervision roles. First, the findings demonstrate the importance of time in the preparation of administrators and in their view of collegiality. These results suggest that program planners should be sensitive to the effect of time on two dimensions of professional preparation: length of time in the program of study and length of time the program participant has taught prior to entering the program. Furthermore, we found that the stage in the teaching career had a powerful influence on the reasons students gave for approving collegiality. This suggests the need to pay close attention to the career stage of the student entering an administration program.

Second, we need to address the role of the preparation program in the acquisition of a collegial conception of leadership. Unlike other professions, the conceptions of leadership of prospective supervisors have been developing experientially and latently from at least age 5 forward, rather than being formed exclusively during professional preparation. Our sample brought to the preparation program conceptions of leadership that emphasized bureaucratic, charismatic, and human relations elements more than collegial features. Preparation programs that wish to encourage a collegial conception of leadership must pay close attention to presenting information on collegial leadership and its effects, modeling collegiality among faculty and between faculty and students, and establishing structures and climate to support student collegiality.

Finally, our research points to the need for further reflection and examination of how preparation programs support the art teacher in balancing the roles of artist, teacher, and administrator. While we need further evidence, we suspect that programs that address both art training and administrative training facilitate this balance.

For The Art Education Profession

Our research demonstrates that art teaching is a primary professional choice rather than a default for those who cannot make it as an artist. Professional associations must recognize and further define the unique needs of art teachers who wish to practice their art in tandem with art teaching. Opportunities for balancing art courses and education courses that (should) characterize preparation programs should continue to be available throughout one's professional life.

Second, further research should compare this group of art teachers with other groups of teachers who do not practice a specialty to determine differences in regard to collegiality. Are art teachers more likely to support collegiality moves because collegiality offers an antidote to the possible isolation of practicing one's art?

The profession at large should also realize the unique assets that the art teacher brings to administration. The nature of the art teacher's work includes broad contact with other teachers, school building administrators, and district administrators, thereby providing opportunities to grasp the "big picture." The tendency to have had experience working directly with adults provides the art teacher with more opportunities to develop interpersonal skills necessary for effective administration. Art teachers are more likely to have had broad community contacts through such activities as sponsoring art exhibits, judging juried shows, and contributing to community art productions. This community contact broadens and enriches the skills that art teachers bring to administration. Acknowledging these unique and critical skills permits us to move beyond the proverbial coach-to-principal career tracks and encourage art teacher-to-principal career tracks.

References

Barnard, C. I. (1945). *The functions of the executive*. Cambridge, MA: Harvard University Press.
Becker, H., & Carper, J. (1956a). The development of identification with an occupation. *American Journal of Sociology, 61,* 289-298.
Becker, H., & Carper, J. (1956b). The elements of identification with an occupation. *American Sociological Review, 21,* 341-348.
Becker, H., Geer, B., Hughes, E. C., & Strauss, A. (1961). *Boys in white: Student culture in medical school*. Chicago: University of Chicago Press.
Becker, H., Geer, B., & Hughes, E. C., (1968). *Making the grade: The academic side of college life*. New York: Wiley.
Carnegie Forum on Education and the Economy. (1986). *A nation prepared: Teachers for the 21st century*. New York: Carnegie Forum on Education and the Economy.
Chapman, L. (1982). *Instant art: Instant culture*. New York: Teachers College Press.
Crow, G. M. (1989). The perceived opportunity structure of educational administration. *Journal of Research and Development in Education, 22,* 70-78.
Davis, F. (1968). Professional socialization of subjective experience: The process of doctrinal conversion among student nurses. In H. Becker, B. Geer, D. Reisman, & R. Weiss (Eds.), *Institutions and the Person*. Chicago: Aldine.
Edmonds, R. (1979). Effective schools for the urban poor. *Educational Leadership*, pp. 15-23.
Gardner, H. (1973). *The arts and human development*. New York: Wiley.
Hall, D. T. (1986). *Career development in organizations*. San Francisco: Jossey-Bass.
Harvey, O. J., Hunt, D. E., & Schroeder, H. M. (1959). *Conceptual systems and personality organization*. New York:Wiley.
Harvey, O. J., White, B. J., Prather, M., Alter, R., & Hoffmeister, J. (1968). Teacher belief systems and preschool atmosphere. *Journal of Educational Psychology, 57,* 373-381.
Irwin, R. L. (1989, Spring). The fine arts supervisor's practical knowledge: A case study. *Visual Arts Research*, pp. 21-34.
Jackson, P. W. (1977). Lonely at the top: Observations on the genesis of administrative isolation. *School Review, 85,* 425-432.
Joyce, B. R., & Hunt, D. E. (1967). Teacher trainee personality and initial teaching style. *American Educational Research Journal, 4,* 253-259.
Katz, L. (1977). *Talks with teachers*. Washington, DC: National Association for the Education of Young Children.
Liberman, A. (1988). *Building a professional culture in schools*. New York: Teachers College Press.
Lipham, J. (1981). *Effective principal, effective school*. Reston, VA: National Association of Secondary School Principals.

Little, J. (1982). Norms of collegiality and experimentation. Workplace conditions of school success. *American Educational Research Journal, 19,* 325-340.

Lortie, D. C. (1975). *Schoolteacher. A sociological study.* Chicago: University of Chicago Press.

Louis, M. R. (1980). Career transitions: Varieties and commonalities. *Academy of Management Review, 5,* 329-340.

May, W. T. (1989). Teachers, teaching, and the workplace: Omissions in curriculum reform. *Studies in Art Education, 30*

Mayo, E. (1945). *The social problems of an industrial civilization.* Boston: Graduate School of Business Administration, Harvard University.

Miles, M., & Huberman, A. (1984). *Qualitative data analysis: A sourcebook of new methods.* Beverly Hills, CA: Sage.

Nyberg, D. (1982). A concept of power for education. *Teachers College Record, 83*

Roethlisberger, F. J., & Dickson, W. J. (1939). *Management and the worker.* Cambridge, MA: Harvard University Press.

Thompson, J. D., Avery, R. W., & Carlson, R. O. (1968). Occupations, personnel, and careers. *Educational Administration Quarterly, 4,* 6-31.

Weber, M. (1946). *From Max Weber: Essays in sociology* (H. H. Gerth and C. W. Mills, Eds. and Trans.). New York: Oxford University Press.

Witherell, C. S., & Erickson, V. L. (1978). Teacher education as adult development. *Theory Into Practice, 17*

Yarger, S., & Mertens, S. K. (1980). Testing the water of school based teacher education. In Corrigan & Howey (Eds.), *Teaching the teachers of teachers.* Reston, VA: Council for Exceptional Children.

9

Uniquely Inner City:
A Personal Essay

BILLIE MCKINDRA PHILLIPS
St. Louis Public Schools

The St. Louis Public School System has approximately 43,127 students. These students, 135 art specialists, and a multitude of instructors and teachers populate 17 secondary, 26 middle, 71 primary, and 8 special schools within the city. (Note: Art teachers should never be referred to as *ancillary*. Therefore, this document refers to the art staff as *specialists*. They have to be.) Included in these numbers are one visual and performing arts high school that also encompasses an honors art program, two visual and performing arts middle schools, and one visual and performing arts elementary school. The student population is made up of diverse backgrounds and cultures; about 77% are Afro-American, 21% are Caucasian, and 2% are of other backgrounds. The above variations are the beginning of many that influence the K-12 art curriculum.

The word *vary* means to make a partial change in, to make different in some attribute or characteristic. The art program scheduling and/or design *varies* from school to school. Some variations include the following:

1. Students remain in their classrooms, and the specialist comes to them. Some, for many reasons, call it the *Cart Art Plan.*

2. The specialist has his or her own space, and students report to the art room at scheduled times. This arrangement is constant in the middle schools.

3. Generally, the visual and performing arts, as in all high school programs, have art rooms provided for the instructors.

In addition to the regular programs, there is the pull out program called *Honors Art.* Students from the city and surrounding counties attend one-half-day art programs. They return to their regular schools for core curriculum courses.

Now picture *these* variations:

Every one of the 122 schools implements a version of the described program. Each program is financed under the school-based management plan. In brief, this means that the principal manages the budget allotted to his or her school. The art budget is included in this allotment.

Elementary and middle school art time blocks and meetings per week may differ. Students are required to take 60 to 90 minutes of art per week. Class time may encompass 30-45 minutes per period. Class numbers and sizes are governed by the enrollment at the individual sites. Generally, special education students are mainstreamed into these classes. Naturally, there are no 30-minute classes in the middle and high school programs.

Another factor deserves mention because it too influences the individuality of inner-city programs — the interests of the school and the community in the visual arts. The greater the interest, the easier the implementation by the supervisor and specialists. Therefore, "selling the art focus" to the individual school populations is a must. One can readily understand that there have to be varying degrees of interest and enthusiasm for the visual arts. Building interests and enthusiasm is a priority in inner-city programs. This, then, becomes a part of our platform as specialists.

Making connections is a vital part of this platform. As the curriculum is being written, the variations in sites, school emphasis, funds, numbers, and cultural backgrounds remain prime factors. Art specialists must have options while manipulating spaces, places, and ideas within the art curriculum "frame." As the options are selected, it is important that communication lines remain open. The curriculum goals and objectives make up a third part of the platform.

The fourth part involves seminars, in-service programs, demonstrations and previews of techniques, new art materials, and publications. The art specialists expect and receive updated communications concerning meetings and opportunities involving special contests and projects, community invitations, in-service programs, and so forth. Regular and direct printed communications concerning events are received from the St. Louis City Art Museum. The museum is certainly a strong factor in this platform.

Now, gathering all of these variations into one curriculum frame, one can understand the necessity of the "opened-ended" style of our art guide. It is also conceivable that there is need of a strong support system for such a platform. The support system is involved with and nurtured by the community, the business world, arts organizations, parents, and friends of the visual arts. There is one other major support paramount in this uniquely inner-city program: I believe that all of these variations and support systems will produce excellence if the specialist's self-esteem is protected and allowed expansion space.

Therefore, developing and maintaining high visibility is of major importance. The role of the supervisor encompasses providing resources and means that result in this visibility. Specialists must never feel that they are alone in this effort. They must believe that the strength of the program depends on the achievements of all. Art supervisors must do much more than write, implement, and supervise curriculum. They must:

• Provide multiple choices for involvement in and out of the classroom

• Provide and support opportunities for specialists to say: "Hey, look at us! Look at my students!"

• Integrate the *cubistic, impressionistic,* and *realistic* teaching styles of special-ists so that everyone benefits and finds at some point, amid all of the variations, a chance to exclaim with enthusiasm, "Hey, look at me!"

• Offer suggestions for supporting and integrating the core curriculum

• Applaud, encourage, and assist those specialists who "find a way" to get it done

• Find permanent and temporary display space within the community, city, and state so that visibility remains constant

Trusting and understanding each other and believing the power of the visual arts are the adhesives that keep us on target. This mutual support system keeps us laughing, crying, trying, and always believing there is a way — we simply have to discover it. But then someone said, "How can you discover something that was already there?" Specialists *are* here, there, and everywhere within the inner city. We simply must remain visible, for the sake of our students, parents, homes, communities, the city, the state, and the nation. More important, we must remain visible for our own self-esteem. The challenge is *uniquely inner-city.*

These theories are used by art specialists to meet the challenges of creatively connected art and the other disciplines. *Self-esteem* is a driving force in the creative process. It is paramount that specialists experience successes and enjoy high visibility in the *uniquely inner city.*

Glossary of Terms

Inner: More intimate
City: Center of population
These selected definitions best describe our St. Louis City Public Schools community because we *are* the center. Achievements in curriculum writing, planning, and implementation greatly influence the techniques necessary to orchestrate an intimate centralized art program.
Unique: One and only, single, sole, unequaled, highly unusual, common but rejected by some
This term deftly describes abstracts on which the challenges are based that foster inspiration, determination, and creativity in our uniquely inner-city art program.
Cubistic: To separate a subject into geometric forms
Impressionistic: To capture a momentary glimpse
Realistic: To face facts/be practical

10

Art is for Everyone: A Systematic Approach to Implementing and Evaluating Elementary Art Specialist Services

RICHARD R. DOORNEK

Milwaukee Public Schools

Background

Just four years ago the Milwaukee Board of School Directors decided to provide specialist instruction in its 107 elementary schools. In the 4-year period Milwaukee went from 12 art teachers in unique elementary settings to 76 art teachers serving all 107 schools and all classes. In this chapter I will discuss some of the supervision and administration issues that arise when a school board decides to support the concept of specialty teachers in elementary schools.

Creating the Need for the Elementary Art Specialist

The philosophical and educational arguments for the necessity of art instruction by trained specialists are articulately spelled out in many articles and NAEA documents. The real test of educational validity occurs when the special-area teacher is given a chance to work side by side with the classroom teacher and is able to demonstrate the depth and breadth of learning that can occur in the arts. This phenomenon occurred in the Milwaukee district as "magnet schools" were given special staffing allowances to support art, music, and physical education specialists. The classroom teachers in these schools made a remarkable discovery: They found that the schools improved because of the presence of the special-area teachers. *The evidence was so persuasive that the teachers' union made the provision of these services a bargaining item for all of the teachers in all of the schools.*

The board was concerned about the cost. With the help of the teachers' association, the administration was able to convince the board that it was buying a valuable commodity — time: time for planning, time for organizing, and time for effective instruction. At the risk of oversimplification, the board agreed to add specialty instruction if the teachers would agree to an extended day. The teacher/ student day was extended by approximately 20 minutes, and the board agreed to provide specialty time that was equivalent to approximately 45 minutes from each area (art, music, and physical education) per week. By using this approach, the board is really buying more time in school for children, preparation time for elementary teachers, and, incidentally, effective instruction by trained specialists. Using this approach, Milwaukee has not just "added staff," but also has provided a more effective instructional program. In management terms, this is a "win-win" situation.

Who Receives Specialty Instruction?

The Department of Curriculum and Instruction developed a policy in concert with the Division of Exceptional Education and Elementary Education that is educationlly sound but has raised new issues for art specialists and all specialty teachers. Essentially, art is for everyone! That is, every elementary school student should have access to a sequential program of study in art education. The policy states: "Every k-top classroom, including exceptional education and early childhood, will have approximately X minutes of service weekly from each specialist." The number of minutes depends on the staffing formula, which is examined in subsequent paragraphs.

The issues raised here address the preparation of specialty teachers to deal with (a) early childhood students (ages 3-5) and (b) exceptional education students, especially severe and profound and low incidence (hearing impaired, vision impaired, etc.). Staff development becomes a priority. Some staff development needs can be addressed with the help of the exceptional education staff and the support of P.L. 94-142 funding for exceptional education. However, only some of the problems involve information. Attitudes and previous experiences are sometimes more difficult to redirect.

The Milwaukee district has been fortunate to receive funding for five staff members (called adaptive art support staff) who have had extensive training in exceptional education. They are beginning to make a difference with the exceptional population. Fortunately, most of the art specialists are finding the early childhood students a joy to teach and have been very successful in adapting the kindergarten curriculum to the younger children. Staff members with previous early childhood experience have been capitalized upon, and in-service sessions to extend the good practices have been created.

Staff Development Directions

In addition to providing direct student instruction, the adaptive staff participates in extensive staff development activities on a school site and staff development course basis. Art specialists are provided with the opportunity to design staff development courses and to participate in the teaching of needed units. Successful practices in teaching art to early childhood, exceptional education, and upper elementary students are taught/modeled by our successful art teachers.

Another needed development was the New Art Teacher Mentor Program. Experienced art specialists were recruited to provided individual modeling and periodic advice to one assigned new art specialist. The supervisor coordinates school site visits and substitute release time. The program was voluntary but was accepted by both new teachers and "mentors."

Scheduling Policies

What should be considered in developing a scheduling policy? The arts administrators responded to frequent questions from principals and specialists with the following statements and model schedules:

Specialist schedules should be developed to meet the needs of the school. There are several configurations or options available to the principal. Specialists' contact time should not exceed the total of 285 minutes per day.

Because of the developmental characteristics of students in kindergarten and exceptional education early childhood classes, the specialist's time for these classes may need to be adjusted. It is recommended that these classes be scheduled for approximately 35 and 45 minutes for art education. Kindergarten and early childhood teachers with A.M. and P.M. sessions should receive specialist services equivalent to other teachers; they should not receive double specialist time to provide services to A.M. and P.M. sessions. The principal and kindergarten teacher and specialist should confer regarding how best to provide services for A.M. and P.M. kindergarten sessions.

Art, music, and physical education specialist schedules should include a 30-minute preparation period per day. Unallocated time before and after the student day should be used for special help, program-related activities, or school duties. Schedules for traveling art and music teachers at schools without an art room should allow for appropriate travel time between rooms. Under no circumstances are specialists to be scheduled to serve more than one school on any given day. This last policy was agreed upon because it was felt that school-day travel is non-productive and that there are ways to work around that issue.

Sample Schedules for Elementary Art Specialists

Figure 10.1 Four-period schedule — 70-minute periods.

8:00- 8:20	A.M.	Special help
8:20- 9:30	A.M.	Student contact
9:35-10:45	A.M.	Student contact
10:45-11:15	A.M.	Prep
11:15-12:00	NOON	Lunch (45 minutes)
12:00- 1:10	P.M.	Student contact
1:15- 2:25	P.M.	Student contact
2:25- 2:40	P.M.	Art program activities

The sample schedule depicted in Figure 10.1 provides 280 minutes of contact time, sufficient travel time, and 30 minutes of preparation daily. This schedule is the one that art specialists find most attractive. It may require a "rotation approach,"

110

which means that classes do not meet on the same day every week. The rotation concept will be described in subsequent paragraphs.

Figure 10.2. Five-period schedule — Variable time.

8:00- 8:15	A.M.	Special help/prep
8:15- 9:10	A.M.	55 minutes of student contact
9:20-10:15	A.M.	55 minutes of student contact
10:25-11:20	A.M.	55 minutes of student contact
11:20-12:05		45-minute lunch
12:10- 1:10	P.M.	60 minutes of student contact
1:20- 2:20	P.M.	60 minutes of student contact
2:20- 2:50	P.M.	Prep

The schedule shown in Figure 10.2 results in 285 minutes of contact time (two 1-hour classes and three 55-minute classes), sufficient travel time, and 30 minutes of preparation.

Figure 10.3. Six-period schedule — 45-minute periods.

8:00- 8:30	A.M.	Special help/prep
8:30- 9:15	A.M.	Student contact
9:20-10:05	A.M.	Student contact
10:15-11:20	A.M.	Student contact
11:00-11:45	A.M.	Lunch
11:45-12:05		Prep
12:05-12:50	P.M.	Student contact
12:55- 1:40	P.M.	Student contact
1:45- 2:30	P.M.	Student contact
2:30- 2:40	P.M.	Special help/program-related activities

The schedule illustrated in Figure 10.3 provides 270 minutes of contact time. Preparation time must be split between morning and lunch to accommodate six periods.

Staffing Formulas and Multiple School Assignments

Because schools differ in size, a formula must be developed to distribute specialists' time and talent in a somewhat equitable fashion. Additionally, a method has been developed to match schools of different size so that specialists will have full-time assignments for our specialists. In this section (a) a staffing formula for schools of different size, (b) multiple school assignments, and (c) rotating schedules versus weekly schedules.

Staffing Formula

A staffing formula was developed based on the number of classroom (including early childhood and exceptional education) teachers in school. This formula is shown in table 10.1.

Table 10.1 Staffing Formula

Number of classroom teachers	Specialist Allocation (in hours per day)
1-13	.3
14-15	.4
16-19	.5
20-21	.6
22-23	.7
24-or more	1.0

A school with nine teachers would be allocated 1.5 days of specialist service per week, or 3 days in a 10-day rotation (e.g., Mondays and alternating Fridays). A quick calculation reveals that a 6-period schedule would allow each teacher in this school the equivalent of 45 minutes of art per week. Because it was decided not to split days, the art specialist would spend 2 days at the school the first week and 1 day the following week, during which time all teachers would have two periods of art.

In some cases, larger elementary schools will require the provision of more than one full-time art specialist. In these situations, the formula is extended to accommodate all of the classes. Consultation between the art teachers and the principal will take advantage of teacher capabilities regarding assignment of grade levels and exceptional education responsibilities.

Multiple School Assignments

A district policy that does not support part-time staff has created a challenge in setting up service to all 107 schools. Accordingly, we were required to create full-time specialist assignments. This was accommodated by matching part-time assignments to create a series of full-time assignments. The following formula was used:

.2 + .8 = (1 day at school x, 4 days at school y)
.3 + .7 = (1.5 days at school x, 3.5 days at school y)
.4 + .6 = (2 days at school x, 3 days at school y)
.5 + .5 = (2.5 days at each school, e.g., MW and alternating Fridays or alternating weeks)

Because of the range of teachers in the formula, art specialists with two schools on the low end of the formula have been able to schedule 4-period days (70-minute classes), while those on the high end have had to schedule 6-period days (45-minute classes). Specialists have indicated a strong preference for the 4-period days in terms of preparation and movement. Invariably, situations arise after all matches have been made where no simple mathematical solution remains.

Rotating Schedules

One of the disadvantages of a weekly schedule is that there seems to be a predominant occurrence of "days off," programs, or other distractions on Thursdays and Fridays. Therefore, on a weekly schedule, classes scheduled for art on these days tend to miss art more frequently. The rotating schedule operates independently of the day of the week and simply skips "days off" or special events. Essentially, the number of classes to be served is plugged into the rotation (it could be a 4-day, 5-day, 6-day, etc., rotation). The art specialist projects the known "days off" and other interruptions and sets up the schedule, which is distributed to the classroom teachers. Unforeseen interruptions are accommodated, and the schedule can be revised without "skipping" any classes. Figure 10.4 provides a sample rotating schedule of 6 days with some typical interruptions.

This is a rotating schedule for 30 classes with 5 classes per day. For classroom teachers' convenience, the groups of classes have been named Red, Blue, Yellow, Green, Violet, and Orange. This can help in posting the current rotation in the office.

113

Figure 10.4 Staffing Formula

	Monday	Tuesday	Wednesday	Thursday	Friday
Week 1	Red	Blue	Yellow	Green	Testing
Week 2	Violet	Orange	Red	Blue	Yellow
Week 3	Green	Violet	Orange	Teachers	Convention
Week 4	Red	Blue	Yellow	Green	Violet
Week 5	Orange	Red	Blue	Yellow	Green

TEACHER AND PROGRAM EVALUATION

The educational necessity for continuing cycles of evaluation cannot be over-stated. "The unexamined life is not worth living" should be paraphrased to "The unexamined program (class, curriculum, practice) is not worth sustaining." Simply stated, assessment provides needed information for continual improvement.

From the perspective of the supervisor or administrator, issues of program evaluation are dealt with on the school level and the district level. The same is true for teacher evaluation, curriculum evaluation, and, perennially, grading and student assessment.

The following list is used by the district art supervisors and local school principals to collect data and to provide feedback to the teacher. It was developed in cooperation with the teachers and was designed primarily as a tool to analyze teaching and the classroom environment. It was not designed as an evaluative tool. However, in practice, it has become a source of information that may subsequently be used by the principal in developing the annual evaluation statement. To enable quick collection of observations, each item is provided with a "check scale" as follows:

1. Exceeds Performance Standards
2. Meets Performance Standards
3. Could Be Improved
4. Must Be Improved
5. Not Observed

The major categories contained in this supervisory observation form are Subject Matter, Classroom Decorum, Instructional Skills, and Human Relations. The greatest attention is given to Instructional Skills since this area is the one in most frequent need of improvement. Items in this section are derived from research on teacher effectiveness, clinical supervision, and mastery teaching as well as our accumulated experience in observing art teachers in action. The categories and items included on the form are as follows.

I. SUBJECT MATTER
    A. In sequence with the Milwaukee Public School art curriculum
    B. Daily and long-range planning is evident and clearly organized
    C. Daily lesson plans are appropriate to time and grade level
    D. Developed and presented in various and interesting formats
    E. Accurate and up to date according to subject-matter standards
    F. Correctly sequenced and presented during class period
    G. Appropriate visual resources are used to enhance instruction
    H. Confidently and knowledgeably presented
    I. Prepares art materials before class
    J. Organizes art materials for efficient distribution and retrieval

II. MAINTAINING CLASSROOM DECORUM
    A. Consistently communicates the expectation that school is a place to learn
    B. Creates an atmosphere that is at once purposeful and joyful
    C. Holds performance standards that are both reasonable and enforced
    D. Neither overasserts nor underasserts authority
    E. Uses both verbal and nonverbal means of communication with students
    F. Causes students' time to be spent on learning tasks and activities
    G. Fully uses all instructional times
    H. Treats the causes and manisfestations of disruption
    I. Maintains personal self-control

III. INSTRUCTIONAL SKILLS
    A. INTRODUCING A LESSON
        1. Obtains student attention and focuses on work to come
        2. Makes both short- and long-range objectives clear to students
        3. Makes timely transition from one activity to another
    B. CLARITY OF EXPRESSION
        1. Matches vocabulary to the students' grade and maturation levels
        2. Sequences information from the easy to the more difficult
        3. Uses illustrations and examples to establish a frame of reference
        4. Repeats as appropriate
    C. QUESTIONING
        1. Relates directly to lesson objectives
        2. Establishes knowledge base by asking lower order questions
        3. Applies and expands learning by asking higher order questions
        4. Maintains balance between drill and open-ended questions
    D. VARYING THE MODE OF PRESENTATION
        1. Uses a variety of methods (e.g., verbal, visual, audio, physical-

manipulative)

      2. Arranges physical environment to enhance instructional goals

      3. Provides both guided and independent practice

      4. Uses both group and individual instruction

      5. Engages the students in active participation in learning

      6. Student work is well displayed and is changed regularly

  E. RESPONSES

      1. Reinforces desired or correct responses and behaviors

      2. Uses a variety of reinforcers (e.g., verbal, nonverbal, immediate)

      3. Expresses disapproval appropriately

  F. RECOGNIZING PUPIL FEEDBACK

      1. Recognizes both verbal and nonverbal cues

      2. Sees what all pupils are doing, yet reacts only to significant cues

      3. Responds to feedback by changing the pace or mode of instruction

      4. Individualizes as necessary, considering students' learning styles and abilities

  H. ENDING A LESSON

      1. Summarizes major points presented in the class

      2. Incorporates application to upcoming lesson

IV. HUMAN RELATIONS

  A. Relates informally as well as formally with students

  B. Attentively listens to students' questions and answers

  C. Avoids prejudicial language

  D. Seeks student feedback.

The supervisory observation form represents an attempt to use regular and systematic evaluation measures with the ultimate goal of improvement of instruction. Not all items are necessarily covered in a given observation. The usual procedure is to have a "preobservation conference" at which time agreement is reached regarding the focus of the observation. Feedback is provided at the "postobservation conference." In most cases the checklist is left with the teacher along with comments, commendations, suggestions for improvement, and plans for future observations. In cases where "intensive supervisory assistance" has been requested by the principal, the postobservation conference may be held with the principal present. In these cases plans for improvement and copies of feedback may be left with the principal for the teacher's file.

Future Considerations

In a recent viewing of a videotape on the nature of paradigms, an interesting point was made regarding the "hazards" of paradigms. While rules and regulations allow people to deal with chaos, adherence to those same rules and regulations can blind one to creative solutions to new problems. Paradigms filter incoming experience and, as a result, make some data (or potential great ideas) "invisible" to some observers.

The information shared in these brief pages represents a paradigm for a certain time and a certain set of circumstances surrounding a large city district art program. We are currently in the midst of continuing reorganization — or "restructuring" (which is in some ways different than reorganization — to meet new demands upon urban education. New rules and formulas will need to be devised — just as those described here were devised to meet needs. But a greater need is for creative people to come up with completely different solutions to the problems of education in our society. Unless dramatic change is designed from within the field of public education, change could be enforced from without. A quintessential skill of the supervisor is the ability to balance change and stability to create a healthy, continually growing organization.

117

11

Partners in Art Education: Supervising Art Education at the State Level

MARTIN RAYALA

Wisconsin Department of Public Instruction

ACCEPTING THE CHALLENGE

Challenges for art education in the states are of such scale and number that state art supervisors could not expect to take them on single-handedly. This is why they rely on networks of dedicated individuals and organizations to join them as partners in arts education. These partnerships make quality art education happen in the states and make state art supervisors proud to be part of the team.

State art consultants are assigned a variety of titles, such as consultant, supervisor, director, or specialist, and their education agencies are labeled state education agencies, state departments of education, or departments of public instruction. Whatever the nomenclature, there is no doubt that state art supervisors are part of large and complex organizations that are ultimately responsible to taxpayers, legislators, the general public, parents, and the young people of the state.

Who Signs the Check?

A state art supervisor is a career professional who has devoted his or her life to improving art education and does the best possible job to make a difference in the field. That personal commitment is often the reason the person got the job in the first place. As part of the state department of education, the consultant is expected to consider the overall educational needs of the state and how the arts can best contribute to the big picture. The art consultant needs to strike a balance between the role of advocate for arts education and the position held within a state education agency.

Most state art consultants are the only ones in the state education agency assigned to advance the cause of art education. They are only a small part of a multilayered bureaucracy of hundreds of people looking after everything from school lunch programs to preparation of future teachers. People who have occasion to visit state consultants at work are often surprised to find that, in some states, the entire state education "department" consists of the state consultant in a small office or cubicle with a program assistant shared with two or more other consultants. It is not uncommon to find school district art departments with larger staffs, better facilities, and more resources than a typical state art education consultant. Because of limited staff and resources, state consultants have to be especially resourceful to accomplish their goals.

Realities of State Service: Wearing Many Hats

State art supervisors, not unlike other professionals, find themselves wearing a variety of hats in the course of their day-to-day work. Many have a variety of jobs because they supervise more than one arts area or have additional assignments outside of the arts. Some state consultants have responsibilities that range from supervising art, music, dance, theatre, and assessment to handling general education concerns.

120

The primary function of a state art consultant is to provide supervision, leadership, coordination, and consultation to art education programs in K-12 public schools, teacher preparation institutions, and art organizations. This is accomplished through the development and administration of state education agency programs and policies related to schools and through cooperation with national, state, regional, and local agencies and associations.

A Large Ship That Turns Slowly in the Water

One of the realities for state art consultants is that a state education agency is *a large ship that turns slowly in the water*. Programs and projects require long-range planning and can have long-term implications for education in the state. Standard procedures for activities of government agencies provide time and opportunities for input by the public and their elected representatives. The public's need and right to know that their money is being well spent creates layers of administration that, in part, contribute to some of the time and expense of administering government programs. Something that seems to be relatively simple to accomplish may be more complex and time consuming because of the structure of the government agency.

Legislation: The Power of Law

The influence of state art supervisors is determined, in part, by the degree to which they are or are perceived to be enforcers of laws or regulations. For most state art supervisors, their role as enforcers is more a matter of perception than of reality. There are not many rules or laws that regulate the teaching of art at the state level, since local control is still the rule in most states. Most state standards deal with all the curricular areas and rarely are specific to the arts alone. State departments of education typically set standards for teacher certification, building codes for schools, and health and safety requirements. Some states have mandates for textbook adoption, curriculum standards, and high school graduation requirements. Many art supervisors adopt a consulting role and prefer to effect change through education and advice rather than mandate.

Tools of the Trade: The Limits of Influence

State consultants have a variety of tools at their disposal to do their jobs. Some of the most common ways for art consultants to influence change in their states include writing curriculum, working with committees or task forces, organizing workshops, participating in conferences, writing articles, talking to individuals and groups of teachers, and monitoring state guidelines.

CURRICULUM DEVELOPMENT

Curriculum-Guided Change

Curriculum development is one of the primary responsibilities of most state art consultants. This became especially true during the decade of controversy over the Discipline Based Art Education (DBAE) model for curriculum introduced by the Getty Center. Art teachers began paying more attention to art history, criticism, and aesthetics in local curriculum and instruction. For many art teachers with already limited resources and student contact time, this seemed like "trying to squeeze 10 pounds of potatoes into a 5 pound sack."

Curriculum development at the state level helps provide the theoretical underpinnings for curriculum development at the local district level.

A state curriculum generally provides a framework upon which local districts develop a curriculum designed to meet the particular needs and expectations of the local school or district. Although there seems to be a growing trend toward specifying objectives or outcomes at the state level, most curriculum content is locally determined. The basic expectations are that curriculum be written and sequential, with specific goals and objectives, course content, scope and sequence, resources, and procedures for evaluation delineated.

Expectations for the content of art education have evolved over the years from a curriculum primarily centered around the elements and principles of design to more specific content in terms of objectives, vocabulary, concepts, and applications in fine art, folk art, crafts, architecture, photography, film, video, computers, graphic design, product design, art history, art criticism, and aesthetics articulated from kindergarten through 12th grade. There are fewer opportunities for teachers to design instruction around their personal strengths, while more emphasis is placed on providing a broad, balanced sequence of instruction for multiple interests and needs.

Task Forces: Representative Democracy

Curriculum writing and most activities of state education agencies are conducted with input from task forces composed of volunteers from among professionals in the

122

field. These include art teachers, administrators, school board members, university faculty, and representatives from appropriate education organizations. State departments of education rarely enact any mandates that have been developed without input from educators, public hearings across the state, and reviewed by legislators or other government agencies. What are perceived as mandates from the state department are actually responses to requests and expectations of individuals and groups within the state. The "state" is a convenient conceptual label for the collective will of the people.

CHANNELS OF COMMUNICATION

Communicating with constituents in the field is probably the most challenging task for state art consultants. The size of a constituent population affects a consultant's ability to communicate with all of them. The larger the state, the more difficult this becomes. Some states are so spread out geographically that it is difficult to travel efficiently from one part of the state to another. Budget considerations often prohibit a consultant from mailing to large numbers of constituents on a regular basis. As the use of electronic bulletin boards and electronic mail systems becomes more prevalent, it will be easier for large numbers of people to share information and ideas inexpensively and efficiently. Several state art consultants have such systems in place, but it will be some time before the number of teachers in the field who have the ability or inclination to use them is large enough to make electronic communication practical.

Workshops: Spreading the Word

A perennial challenge for state art consultants is the magnitude of their responsibilities in terms of numbers and geography. A state like Texas is so large the art consultant sometimes has to fly to workshops within the state. Even in states such as Michigan, Wisconsin, and Minnesota, if the art consultant set out to visit one school district each week it would take 5 to 10 years for this one individual to reach them all.

Bringing art teachers together from a number of districts in one place is a more effective way to spread the word! Most states have some form of regional network used to increase the scope and range of workshops or conferences. The challenge is finding time when teachers can be released from duties to attend workshops. State art supervisors typically participate in many weekend activities when teachers are free of teaching responsibilities. When an active state consultant is paired with an active state art education association, the number of conferences, workshops, and events can reach a saturation point. Most state consultants sponsor or participate in two or three such activities every month during the school year as well as events during the summer. It becomes necessary therefore, for state art supervisors and teachers to be selective.

Conferences: Rallying the Troops

Conferences can be a highly effective way for art educators to keep up with changes in the field and to renew their passion for teaching. Conferences are typically sponsored by organizations such as state art education associations, the state Alliance for Arts Education, regional organizations, and the department of education. The logistics of the school year cause most conferences to be grouped together in October-November and March-April. September and May are taken up with the flurry of activity beginning and ending a school year, while December and January are often preempted by holidays and school breaks.

State consultants often find much of their year devoted to planning and attending conferences. These include state and national art education conferences, state and national Alliance for Arts Education conferences, and a variety of other conferences such as those sponsored by the Getty Center or by state arts agencies. In addition to these clearly pertinent conferences there are a variety of related events, meetings, or conferences such as those of state historic preservation organizations, architects, designers, theatre designers, filmmakers, photographers, museums, art historians, philosophers, computer artists, and urban planners. Each of these provides opportunities to enhance art education in the schools, and these groups are often eager to initiate projects for K-12 school art programs.

In addition to the art-related meetings and events there are a variety of education-oriented activities state art consultants are expected to (or feel they should) attend to make certain the arts are represented. These can include professional organizations specifically for school administrators, principals, school board members, parent-teacher organizations, directors of instruction, gifted and talented, early childhood, social studies, humanities, children at risk, education for employment, environment, and special needs. Without representation by someone in the arts, these groups may forget or downplay the role of the arts as a basic component of all aspects of education.

124

Phone Calls and Letters: The Quick Fix

Responding to individual phone calls and letters is an important aspect of state art supervisors' activities. Often calls and letters come directly to the state art supervisor; sometimes calls and correspondence are referred to the art supervisor by someone else because of the nature of the question; and occasionally written responses must be prepared for someone else's signature, such as the state superintendent or the governor.

In any case, responding to calls and letters sometimes is not as simple and straightforward as it would seem. Because of all the meetings and conferences mentioned above, the consultant may not be available when the initial call is made. This sets off a sequence of events often referred to as "telephone tag" in which the two parties try to return each other's call. Letters or calls can sometimes require checking information with other individuals and can run into some amount of research before an adequate answer can be provided.

Handouts: Peddling Paper

State consultants often leave a trail of paper wherever they go. Handouts they have either created or are passing on from other sources are useful resources to help teachers remember ideas and to pass information on to colleagues. Often, the number of copies is in the thousands for any given item, which can add up in terms of copying, storing, and transporting. (Consultants often feel they are drowning in paper!)

Art Teachers: Limits to Communcation

Communicating directly with art teachers in the state on a regular basis is often not an option available to state art supervisors. State art supervisors respond to individual requests from art teachers and try to meet with groups of teachers from several schools simultaneously whenever possible. Consultants often rely on the communication network of the professional art education association in the state. Theoretically, most of the art teachers who are interested in information that might come from the state level are also the types of art teachers who would take the time and effort to join their professional organization. This is not always the case, however, and does not release the state consultant from his or her responsibility to serve all art teachers in the state.

Communicating with teachers through their school district is often the most feasible avenue available to art supervisors. This reduces the number of pieces mailed, and most states have established systems for regular communication with school districts. In Wisconsin, for example, it is more feasible to communicate with the 430 school districts than directly with the 1,500 art teachers. This method breaks down, of course, if the information is not passed on to the art teachers in a timely fashion.

ALLIES FOR ACTION

Professional Organizations

A strong professional organization is one of the most useful allies for a state consultant in communicating with art teachers in the state. Most consultants work with a variety of professional organizations. Consultants who supervise more than one arts area may find it difficult to attend all the conferences, workshops, events, and board meetings of all the organizations.

Consultants can find much of their time devoted to meetings or activities of professional organizations. While this is condoned and expected as a legitimate part of a consultant's job by most state education agencies, there is a thin line that must be walked to avoid misuse of taxpayers' money in the service of nonprofit organizations. It is generally not considered proper, for example, for literature of a professional organization to be mailed by the state education agency unless it is for a clearly defined state function.

The State Art Education Association

The state art education association is clearly the group most directly aligned with the mission of a state art consultant. The professional art education association provides leadership, communication networks, and valuable resources without which few state art consultants could be effective. Most of these groups are not-for-profit organizations completely run by volunteers with limited financial resources. Under these conditions, it is amazing the amount and quality of work art education organizations do.

One factor state consultants have to consider when working with state art education associations is that typically only one-fifth to one-third of the art teachers in a state are members of their professional organization. State consultants can encounter some ethical and legal conflicts supporting an activity or event if it is available only to members of the state art education association.

The State Alliance for Arts Education

The Alliance for Arts Education is another ally for many state consultants. Depending on the strength and leadership of the state alliance, a state consultant can find a good deal of time devoted to projects and meetings involving more than one arts area. This provides useful links to other arts organizations in the state as well as other education organizations such as those for school administrators, principals, school boards, and parents. The scope of these "alliances" is more characteristic of the state Alliance for Arts Education than most other groups with which a state consultant might work. This provides a broader view of arts education than is often obtained within a single arts organization.

The Citizen Advocates Organization

Most states also have some form of citizen advocacy groups for the arts. These groups are often registered as 501-C4 organizations, which legally allows them to include lobbying as a major part of their activities. Many of these groups retain a professional lobbyist. In general, the mission of these organizations is more closely allied to the state arts agency than to the state education agency. They focus largely on legislation affecting the state arts agency budgets and the conditions for artists and arts organizations rather than on issues relating to arts education. In fact, most consultants, as state employees, are restricted by law in the degree to which they can legally be involved with an organization that lobbies the state legislature.

With the recent attention the National Endowment for the Arts has been giving to arts education, however, more lobbying groups are beginning to ask how they can be of help in advancing the causes of arts education. Within the limits of the law, it is important for state art consultants to assist arts education organizations to make appropriate use of these lobbying groups. This might include something as simple as having a lobbyist explain the legislative process to arts educators or as complicated as having the citizen group work with the state art education association to help guide a bill from draft form to legislative approval.

Reaching Out: Friendly Ears

In addition to the individuals and organizations most obviously aligned with the mission of the state art consultant's position, there are many alliances that can be essential to the general task of making the arts basic to education for all students K-12. Not long ago the arts were set apart from general education and the art specialists perhaps even took some pride in their "special" status as individualists on the margins of the educational enterprise. In the 1980's this outsider status began to be reexamined as the arts started to be seen as one of the five basic academic subjects. Most prominent writers in education since the early 1980s identify five areas of basic academic education in the schools — language arts, science, mathematics, social studies, and the arts. As the arts started to be recognized as contributing to the overall mission of basic education for all students art teachers started making more connections with other aspects of schooling than in the past.

Language Arts, Mathematics, and Science: The Other Side of the Brain

Language arts education is traditionally the foundation for all education and is provided more time and resources in the educational system than all other areas. Students have over 12 years of required, regular instruction in the language arts during their K-12 schooling as compared to roughly 6 years of instruction in visual art during that time. As a result, most Americans are relatively proficient with verbal communication but function at about the sixth-grade level in visual communication throughout their lives.

Mathematics and science education became a national obsession when the Russians launched Sputnik. Traumatized by the shock of coming in second in the space race, Americans demanded that the educational system begin producing more top-level scientists, and the schools responded by a corresponding emphasis on science and math in the curriculum. The arts were not seen as a primary mission of education during this time, which was viewed as a national emergency. Years of this imbalanced educational diet have left many of our students without the life-giving nutrients found in the arts. We entered the 1990s with children at risk and a nation at risk.

Visual literacy and graphic communication are essential to intellectual development and hold, in part, keys to solving many problems in fields such as mathematics, physics, urban planning, and the environment. In 1953, for example, when James Watson and Francis Crick were in a race with scientists like Linus Pauling to discover the structure of DNA, all of the component parts were known. What scientists did not know was how it all fit together. When Watson and Crick envisioned a structure like a spiral staircase, which they called a double-helical structure, they uncovered the basic genetic structure, for all life forms. The image was the answer. What they were able to accomplish that no other scientist had been able to was to see what DNA could look like. Many such problems that currently resist solution by our best thinkers will require strong visual as well as verbal, scientific, and numeric thinking skills to be fully resolved.

For human intelligence to develop fully, visual thinking and graphic communication will have to be given appropriate status alongside verbal, scientific, and mathematical modes of thought. This will require teachers and students to acknowledge all modes of thought and respect multiple modes of inquiry. This calls for stronger alliances among the language arts, mathematics, science, and the visual arts.

Social Studies

As art educators began to increase their efforts to include sequential instruction in art history in the curriculum, they began to find more connections to the fabric of general education. Knowledge of history enriches one's understanding of the development of the arts in society, and knowledge of the arts enriches one's understanding of history. State consultants may find themselves increasingly involved with the state association for social studies education and may discover together ways to increase students' understanding of the arts as well as history and social studies.

A glance at a K-12 social studies curriculum reveals many obvious opportunities for correlating with art education. In Wisconsin, for example, art teachers are encouraged to align their art history instruction with the social studies curriculum in their schools. In fourth grade, when the history of the state is the focus of the social studies curriculum, art teachers are encouraged to teach about the art and artists of Wisconsin. This includes internationally recognized artists from Wisconsin such as Frank Lloyd Wright and Georgia O'Keeffe, as well as the Native American, folk and ethnic art forms, and the design arts of the state. In fifth grade the emphasis is on America, in sixth grade the world, and so on. This is a convenient pattern for scope and sequence that a district can chose to adopt for both art history and social studies.

Library and Media

Two trends in current art education lead toward increased interaction with school librarians and media directors. The study of art history, art criticism, and aesthetics leads students and teachers to the written word, which resides in libraries. Just as our largely verbally oriented school system needs to recognize the power of visual thinking and graphic communication in the development of the intellect, it is also necessary for art teachers to recognize that much knowledge and understanding about the visual arts are transmitted verbally and through the written word. Libraries provide print and media resources for students and teachers in arts education.

Increasing recognition of the role of the media arts in visual art education is another force leading art teachers to interact with librarians and media directors. The study of film and video as visual art forms, rather than as literature translated to images, leads art teachers to the technology of media. Librarians and media directors have already begun collecting the films, videos, slides, instructional materials, and hardware to help us get started on the media track.

Educational Communications

Film and video are not only increasingly important as art forms in schools, but the whole area of educational communications technology is important to education in general. Instructional television and distance learning strengthen the potential of visual learning and visual communication, which are the basis for part of what we try to accomplish in art education. All of this is not about "art" but about the power of visual images to communicate ideas and emotions in ways that are different from verbal communication.

Career Education: Vocation or Avocation?

Historically there were philosophic differences between the educational objectives of many vocational education programs and the arts. Not only did the two areas of the curriculum view themselves as having very different missions, but they were also in competition for students as elective subjects in secondary schools. As a result, some schools developed separate courses in art and vocational education for subjects such as photography, architecture, graphic design, and product design with very little cooperation or coordination between the departments. As visual arts curricula are expanded to include architecture and design arts such as product design and graphic communication, there is more room for both the vocational and the artistic components of these fields. Such coordination can only enhance the potential quality of our lives and the future development of our designed environments.

USING STATE RESOURCES

The State Arts Council

The state arts council can be an important ally of the state art consultant because it can help gain that visibility and public attention for important art education issues in ways that the state consultant cannot achieve as an individual. The state arts council is probably the most visible arts agency in each state. One source of its power is its singleness of purpose. The arts are the sole mission of the state arts council, while the state department of education encompasses all of the curricular areas and the total condition of K-12 schooling.

Another feature of state arts councils is that they are a granting agency. They give money to individual artists and arts organizations, and money talks. Each time the state arts council announces the completion of a grant review cycle, it makes the newspaper because people are anxious to see who got the money. Most state art consultants do not have programs that grant money to individuals or organizations, so they don't garner the same press coverage and public attention as the state arts council.

Another important plus for the state arts council is that it works closely with artists in the state on a regular basis. This perspective is important for art consultants, who may become overly focused on "school art" and lose sight of art in the "total picture". The state arts council can be a good barometer for current ideas and issues in the world of art in each state.

Artists in the Schools Programs

Not all programs of the state arts council have a direct relationship to the goals of state art consultants. The most obvious connection is with the Artists-in-Education program director. The Artists-in-Education (AIE) program places artists in the schools for a week to a full year to work with core groups of students and teachers. State arts agencies have done a good job of improving these programs to overcome some of the problems found in early years. They are aware that many art teachers are practicing artists themselves and can be offended by someone coming into their classes as the "real" artist. Program directors have also redesigned their programs to try to have the AIE residencies mesh more closely with the existing curriculum in the schools. State art consultants can be very helpful in this effort by working with the state AIE coordinator to design residencies so there is adequate preparation of the students before the artist's visit, and appropriate follow-up after the residency. Ideally, the artist's residency will contribute to the objectives of the ongoing curriculum plan of the district.

Some of the limitations of the Artists-in-Education program stem from the types of artists often available for residencies. Many artists in the programs are individuals with flexible schedules who use residencies to augment their income. This is one of the benefits of residencies for artists. Some artists, however, such as architects and designers, have less flexible schedules and less financial incentive to enter the programs. Since these types of artists are less likely to be represented in residency programs, students don't receive as broad a picture of the world of art as many teachers would like. State consultants can help by working to encourage architects and designers to join the programs as a public service and by encouraging art teachers to supplement the residencies with field trips or visits to the schools by architects and designers.

Folk Arts, Community Arts, and Percent for Arts Programs

State arts councils also have programs for folk arts and community arts and Percent for Arts programs that provide opportunities for partnerships with state art consultants. The coordinators of these programs usually do not include a background in education as part of their job descriptions, so the state consultant may have to approach them and suggest opportunities for partnerships with the schools. They have resources that can be directly applicable to state curriculum goals and objectives.

Percent for Arts projects, for example, provide excellent opportunities for units on art criticism because public artwork almost always sparks lively debate in the community about the nature and value of art. In Wisconsin the State Art Supervisor worked with the state arts council's Percent for Arts Coordinator to develop an art criticism unit for high school students. The students worked in teams as panels to select a work of art they felt would be appropriate for a particular site. Materials describing the site and slides of actual artists' work submitted for a real percent for art project in the state were provided from the arts council's files. The students practiced skills of art criticism while gaining insights into how art is selected for public places.

The State Legislature: Becoming Political Animals

Both the state education agency and the state arts council are arms of the state government, and their budgets, standards, and activities must conform to legislative mandates and withstand legislative scrutiny. State mandates such as high school graduation requirements in the arts typically require legislative approval. Since most state art consultants have come up through the ranks of artists and art teachers, the need to become "political animals" may run counter to their interests and inclinations. Nonetheless, it is becoming increasingly important that all art educators become more politically astute and learn to use the governing processes that are involved in group decision making in free democracies. This includes knowing how the systems work and knowing the people who make them work. One of the first steps is to overcome the artists' traditional cynicism and accept the government officials as real people who are neither corrupt nor self-serving. One of the keys to long-term survival in the political arena is to have a sympathetic understanding of people and the views they hold, even when strongly opposed to their point of view. It is alright to agree to disagree.

132

Museums: Educational Treasure Houses

Museums have come a long way since the days when their primary mission was to protect and preserve artifacts. Today many museums have curators of education who develop programs for children and adults to help them understand and enjoy the treasures contained in the museum. Informational graphics, attractive displays, differential lighting, supportive print materials, guided tours, audio tours, interactive exhibits, and special projects with schools are just a few of the developments in museums in recent decades.

"Mini-Museum" is a project of the Madison Art Center in Wisconsin in which classes get a behind-the-scenes tour of the museum and interview the people who do all the jobs — exhibit design, installation, conservation, attribution, publicity, and so forth. The students use this information to design their own exhibition. In the small community of DeForest, for example, elementary students decided to do an exhibit of original artwork from the homes of people in the community. They found over 100 works of art from 50 different countries, then designed the exhibit, installed it, prepared identification labels, printed an exhibition catalog, and conducted guided tours. Busloads of students came from neighboring communities to see the exhibit. The townspeople came to the school and were amazed at how much "culture" there was in their small town. The students and community members developed a sense of pride in their school and community as a result of this project, and the students practiced their art criticism skills, learned about the discipline of art history, and had good fun at the same time.

Universities and Colleges

University and college art education faculty can be indispensable allies for a state art consultant. They have access to current information and developments in the field of art education and regularly work with future and current art teachers. State consultants can find themselves in the position of reviewing and approving programs developed by college and university art educators who have often literally "written the books" on art education. Establishing a respectful collegial relationship with the students and faculty of state colleges and universities is especially important since they are guiding the development of future art teachers in the schools.

Universities and colleges can have a profound effect on the teaching of art in K-12 schools if their entrance requirements include a credit or more of the fine arts. If fine arts credit is not required to enter colleges and universities in the state, then students may find it difficult to find time to take high school art courses. This is especially true with the many requirements in areas such as foreign language, computers, advanced math, and science.

Teacher Preparation and Curriculum Change: Which Comes First, The Chicken or the Egg?

There is an interesting "chicken and egg" problem with curricular change in that it is difficult to change curriculum expectations if teachers have not been prepared for the changes. And, it is difficult to expect colleges and universities to prepare teachers for a curriculum that doesn't yet exist in the schools. Can teachers be expected to teach aesthetics or art criticism if they have never had courses in these subjects? Can colleges and universities be expected to require courses in aesthetics and art criticism if schools are not yet teaching these subjects?

Where is the best place to begin with curricular change? Do you prepare future teachers first and then make changes in the curriculum in schools, or do you change curricular expectations in the schools to spur change in teacher preparation programs? And who prepares the college and university instructors for these curricular changes?

One of the challenges for teacher preparation programs is that expectations for future teachers are beginning to include topics such as art history, art criticism, aesthetics, design arts, media arts, architecture, and computer graphics. If the art department has not been expanding to include these topics within their offerings, students will go outside of the department for these courses. At some institutions it is difficult for students to find appropriate courses that will help them become better teachers in art criticism, aesthetics, architecture, or some of the design arts.

FACING THE FUTURE

Let's Get Real: The Many Faces of Art Education

State education agencies continually develop educational programs of great expectations for students, such as those with exceptional educational needs, students at risk, gifted and talented students, and early childhood education students. Schools *are expected* to provide basic education, college preparation, education for employment, health education, sex education, environmental education, and computer training as well.

Schools are trying to find time for all of this by adding more periods to the school day, starting earlier in the fall, continuing later in the spring, lengthening the school day, increasing summer classes, hiring more staff, providing more social services, and building more schools. Many college and university teacher preparation programs have become 5-year programs despite what the catalog says. Art teachers are working longer days with fewer preparation periods, while trying to write and implement a new curriculum at the same time.

How can we hope to keep up with the avalanche of new expectations for students, teachers, parents, and the schools? It would be comforting if we could predict that this was all going to slow down, and things were going to level off and become more manageable. There are not many indications that this is going to happen. It is estimated that by the time a student starting school today reaches 50 years of age, 97% of the knowledge of the world will have developed during that student's lifetime! Put another way, today we only know 3% of what will be learned in the next 50 years! There was a time when teachers only needed a few years of college to become a teacher, and most people could do quite well with only a high school education. We will never see those days again!

It is exciting to realize that most people will be engaged in learning and growing all their lives. It is challenging to think that we all will be learning things no one ever knew before, and do not even imagine what they might be!

State art consultants are not causing all of these changes, nor are all necessarily eager to see them come. They are struggling to keep pace, just like everyone else. But as key partners in education, state arts consultants are working side by side with teachers, students, administrators, parents, higher education, and the communities to help provide the best educational programs possible for the schools of the 21st century.

Suggested Resources

Alliance for Arts Education, Kennedy Center for the Performing Arts, and American Association of School Administrators. (1987). *Performing together: The arts and education.* Washington, DC: American Association of School Administrators.

The College Board. (1983). *Academic preparation for college.* New York: Author.

Getty Center for Education in the Arts. (1985). *Beyond creating: The place for art in America's schools.* Los Angeles: Author.

Hatfield, T. A. (1983). *An art teacher in every school.* Columbia, SC: Whitehall Publishers.

McFee, J. K., & Degge, R. (1980). *Art, culture, and environment.* Dubuque, IA; Kendall-Hunt.

Katz, J. (Ed.). (1988). *Arts and education handbook: A guide to productive collaborations.* Washington, DC: National Assembly of State Arts Agencies.

National Endowment for the Arts. (1988). *Toward civilization: A report on arts education.* Washington, DC: Author.

Watson, J. D. (1968). *Double helix: Being a personal account of the discovery of the structure of DNA.* New York: Macmillan.

Wisconsin, Arts Board.I (1988). *Step by step: The Wisconsin plan for arts in education.* Madison: Author.

Wisconsin Department of Public Instruction. (1986a). *A guide to curriculum planning in art education.* Madison: Author.

Wisconsin Department of Public Instruction. (1986b). *A guide to curriculum planning in social studies.* Madison: Author.

12

Art Education Curriculum: A View from the Classroom

LARRY N. PEENO

Normandy, Missouri, School District

Introduction: The Prehistoric Curriculum

In the past, students spent extensive amounts of time doing "art work" outside of the art room — building and painting sets for school plays; designing programs; making class banners; drawing political cartoons for upcoming tax levies; making posters for PTA meetings, pep rallies, and to promote ticket sales; painting downtown merchants' windows for Halloween; making up the draw sheets for athletic tournaments; making table decorations for sports banquets; and doing graphics for the yearbook. They also participated in lettering awards of appreciation, making name tags for special affairs, and decorating the gym for the senior prom, etc., etc. — all at the whim of whoever wanted the job done. Unfortunately for some children, this type of program is still being used.

Also, a variety of written and unwritten curricula are being used. For example, there are guides presented as curricula, when, in fact, they are just collections of lesson plans placed in a three-ring binder and indexed by grade levels, studio areas, months, holidays, or whatever. Some of these guides are based on ideas, some on projects, and a few even on the actual art materials. A few art teachers defend the unwritten curriculum "because a written curriculum restricts academic freedom and doesn't allow enough creativity in the classroom."

The only commonality in these approaches is that there are no written, well-defined goals or objectives — no genuine accountability. Although significant gains have been made in this area, it appears that many art programs have made less than a positive impact on students, administrators, and the community. A major factor in this lack of impact is fragmented views of the art curriculum.

The next decade will provide major challenges for art teachers in the area of curriculum development and teaching. Teachers' attitudes about art will be extended beyond the production of art, art history, aesthetics, and criticism, to include the study of not only fine arts but applied arts, ethnic arts, folk arts, computer graphics, and Western and non-Western arts. Teachers will have to develop lesson plans with cognitive objectives that support critical thinking at all levels of the curriculum. This, in turn, will necessitate substantial documentation for higher order teaching and learning hierarchies along with sufficient knowledge of the learning styles of the students. It is not hard to see the confusion and anxiety that this influx of change will bring to the art curriculum.

It has been well documented in the literature that art is the natural unfolding of the child (Dewey, 1954), symbol making is basic to the human mind (Kellogg, 1959), and there is an innate desire to improve and expand these symbols (Langer, 1963). On the other hand, education in the context of "schooling" is not a result of maturation, but an outgrowth of culture (Feldman, 1980), and therefore art educators should not rely heavily on the natural or innate abilities of the learner, as some seem to do. This by no means reduces the validity of such abilities. In fact, just the opposite is true. Most children enter school with skills that more closely resemble art, music, and physical education than reading, writing, and arithmetic. This makes a very strong argument in defense of "art as basic," simply because it is innate. Therefore, it makes sense to exploit the already apparent cognitive methods of the child (Sommerville & Hartley, 1986); however, it is unacceptable to rely only on these cognitive abilities.

It is not enough that most scholars agree that art should be a part of every child's development. All art teachers will have to revise their thinking and insist that art be part of the child's schooling. Art will have to be viewed as a subject with content that can be taught, learned, and evaluated (as other subjects are treated in school). Art will have to be held accountable.

It is evident that an explosion in the art curriculum is upon us, and art educators must be prepared to accept this challenge and respond accordingly. As this article develops, I will illustrate how the computer can assist school districts and teachers in meeting this challenge.

Current Curricular Concerns

Although most art education programs have been centered heavily on the product, there is a growing concern to *redefine what will be taught* in the art class. Studio classes are expected to be more encompassing and to include a balance between culture and technology.

All visual arts (fine, applied, folk, ethnic, computer graphics) offer multiple solutions to a problem, a variety of media, diverse knowledge, and rich cultural insights, and they can stimulate personal interpretation. Individually, these areas allow positive contributions to a more pluralistic approach to studio art. Collectively, they add to the already overworked art curriculum. One method for the supervisor to deal with this surge of responsibility is to simplify the conditions under which the curriculum is written or revised and use a format with the flexibility to accomplish this. Although there is a gap between theory and practice, such a curriculum can be devised. It will, however, require the expertise of well-trained art educators.

Another cause for concern for art teachers has been the introduction of *cognitive thinking skills* into the curriculum and how the teachers will account for student progress in this area.

My colleagues and I have observed that in the past several years many students do not formulate their thoughts as methodically and creatively as students in previous years. This came to my attention as I taught art history. Many students could "read" well enough but could not tell me what they had read when asked to do so. When I gave a vocabulary quiz (written or oral), many students could respond correctly, but most failed to recognize the word and its meaning when it was used in conversation and/or classroom demonstration. In other words, students could pass the test, but couldn't apply this information to other situations that would arise.

It has been my observation that when students are given a length of time in which to think about an answer, more and more of them reply, "If you tell me the answer I'll know it." In the case of studio work, students want to be "shown how." That may be all right, but then they are satisfied with replicating what they observed, and no more. If several examples are shown, students will ask, "Which one do *you* want me to do?" Unfortunately, these are not just observations, but symptoms of a much larger problem.

Reports such as *The Nation at Risk* (1983) have pointed out that educational systems have, at least, reduced the ability of students to employ higher thinking skills. *The National Assessment of Educational Progress* (1981), when assessing students, found that even the better responses showed little if any evidence of well-developed problem-solving or critical thinking skills. A more recent report, *Crossroads in American Education* (1989), published by the Educational Testing Service, supported the same conclusion — that teachers should place less emphasis on students' ability to memorize facts and should adopt teaching methods that promote critical thinking. Teachers, administrators, students, and parents must share the responsibility for this situation. The responsibility is not ours alone.

Some colleagues have expressed the view that the message of the schools seems to be that teachers should teach the "right" answers. This appears to be justified by some districts in hopes of raising test scores. Although I know of no district that has admitted that they teach to the test, I do know of teachers in several districts that have said (with a smile) that they teach students how to take a test, and I am aware of at least one school district that tried to tie teacher evaluations to student test scores.

In April 1988, then Secretary of Education William J. Bennett submitted his findings in a report assessing America's educational progress since 1983. The report *American Education: Making It Work* found that every state reported itself above the national average in test scores. Although Bennett questioned the validity and scoring of these tests, it would seem that how the students arrived at those answers should have also been addressed. Nevertheless, it appears that what is important to the state will be tested and what will be tested will be taught (Wise, 1988). It is no wonder that some teachers conform to this process.

By the time students arrive at high school, they too have adapted to this process. Some will tolerate only what they have to learn — by the shortest means possible. Far too many students are satisfied with the minimum, and will do no more than what it takes to pass. Students rarely question a statement. I cannot remember the last time a student asked "why" or prefaced a statement with "What if ... ?" The irony is that some of these students will become teachers and will probably continue to refrain from asking such questions.

In bypassing the ability to think in favor of expediting skills education, some schools have systematically reduced teaching of higher cognitive functions to that of teaching facts. As a result, learning becomes fragmented, thinking reduced, and creativity retarded. It is quite obvious that the results of this kind of education will be felt (with severe consequences) in the near future and for a long time to come.

The innate thinking process (i.e., creativity) and the curriculum should be thought of as interdependent because student cognitive behavior can be modified by effective teaching methods (Feuerstein, Rand, Hoffman, & Miller, 1980), and, contrary to some research, thinking should not be thought of as a separate subject to teach, at least not with younger and low-achieving students (Weinstein & Mayer,

1986).

Research in *learning styles* has also had a very real effect on art teachers, who have to understand not only their own *teaching strategies,* but the students' learning styles as well. This, of course, must be added to what teachers already are assumed to know about student maturation levels, course objectives, core competencies, art skills and techniques, art vocabulary, individual lesson plans, and how all of this must relate to the total K-12 curriculum — a monumental task! One researcher indicates that when learning styles are matched with teaching strategies, there is an increase in academic achievement, improved attitudes toward school, and reduced discipline problems (Dunn, 1982). However, Weinstein and Mayer (1986) warn that learning strategies appropriate for one type of learning situation may not be appropriate for another, and Lochhead and Clement (1979) have suggested that there is a history of disappointment concerning the teaching of these skills.

Helping students to become independent learners and thinkers who assume responsibility for their learning and actions, whether in school or on the job, is essential. Students who know that their efforts will be successful will use previously learned strategies in other situations (Kurtz & Borkowski, 1984), and learning outcomes will be determined by the teacher and his or her ability to teach complex, comprehensive skills.

Another area of concern is *discipline-based art education* (DBAE). For better or worse, DBAE is the most comprehensive attempt at presenting art education as an academic discipline that has been seen in recent years. Those who have chosen the DBAE concept have had to modify their approach to teaching art, perhaps placing less emphasis on the art product. It would be safe to assume that in any given high school, most of the students taking art are not art majors, and many may never participate in making art again. Given these circumstances, perhaps the art product should not be the single criterion on which to assess student progress.

Through DBAE, students have had to be encouraged to talk, read, look, and write about art in a manner as never before. Since most adults engage in art through one or several of these same concepts, this allows for a broader base of creative expression and self-confidence than ever before. By using DBAE concepts art educators might be able to change attitudes about art in the majority of the population.

From time to time, I have heard principals, school board members, teachers, and citizens speaking of low scores in this or that subject and what to do about the problem. Instead of questioning the methods used in teaching those same subjects, they invariably come to the irresponsible conclusion that by doing away with or reducing the number of art classes, teachers could spend more time with children in subjects where scores are low. I must keep reminding myself of two things. First, this person to whom I am listening is a product of our educational system, and *we* have failed to positively enhance this person's attitude toward art. Second, I should

141

be thankful that I have the opportunity to change this attitude. However, I must confess that changing this seemingly universal attitude is almost impossible when dealing with adults. It is evident, however, that the time and place to begin to deal with one's attitude toward art is in the elementary and secondary schools. It is also evident that the DBAE concept can be a major factor in this effort.

DBAE can be integrated into most lesson plans. Caution must be taken to introduce one or more of the DBAE disciplines when it is most appropriate for the learner, rather than to simply integrate the curriculum with all four disciplines at once. It is important that each student gain an overall understanding of art rather than merely be exposed to the concepts of discipline-based art education.

It is implied in some art programs that all areas (art production, art criticism, art history, and aesthetics) are taught; however, upon close inspection, this doesn't always prove to be the case (McLaughlin & Thomas, 1984). The art product is observable and ongoing, but art history and criticism seem to be treated with lip service or indifference, while aesthetics is, for the most part, ignored.

DBAE is a sound approach that has been instrumental in placing the visual arts in a more academic setting that administrators appear to understand. However, some teachers have failed to make this connection. One possible explanation for this may be that when one works with creativity, one often works in some form of isolation. When dealing with one's own artistic talents, most artists choose to work alone. Art teachers are no exception, although teaching art often produces a different kind of isolation. One result is that art as a subject in the school program has not always been held accountable in the same manner as other subjects. This had led to the situation we face today: Schools are faced with accountability in art, and art educators are searching for ways to bring this about. We cannot continue to isolate our field and expect equal representation in the school curriculum and the school budget.

Developing a Curriculum

Before discussing the use of the computer in curriculum writing, I will mention several factors pertinent to the development of any curriculum. First and foremost is the teacher. Without the expertise of the teacher, we could see learner outcomes reduced to memorizing facts and learning skills. The teacher is the single most important element in effecting learning, and therefore must be the keystone to writing and implementing the curriculum. From preplanning through implementation, teachers must be allowed to maintain a level of autonomy in what and how they teach (Schwab, 1983). In addition, when teachers participate in curriculum development or in any decision making, they grow professionally, have greater job satisfaction, work harder, and integrate the assignment more readily (Alutto & Belasco, 1972). Whether it's a discipline or an attendance policy committee, teachers exhibit more self-esteem and higher morale when given the chance to be a part of the decision-making body. If the teacher is kept in the classroom, he or she cannot learn and respond to new ideas (Morrison, Osborne, & McDonald, 1977).

A second factor is the philosophy — one that is developed and understood not only by art teachers but administrators, the school board, and the community. The philosophy must be broad enough to allow academic freedom for the teachers as well as tap the creativity of the students. The philosophy must be unique and must establish and maintain art as an independent and essential subject matter area with content that can be taught, learned, and evaluated.

A third factor is selecting concepts upon which to build the curriculum and knowing the population. To aid in this process, the art teacher must become aware of student learning styles. This will reduce discrepancies between teaching strategies that may have been formulated during another time and were probably based on different assumptions and taught to a different population. On the basis of my own observations, it seems that many learning styles and teaching strategies are compatible, with little or no significant difference in learning outcomes.

It is important then, that the curriculum be constructed so that the selected concepts can be learned without being isolated. Most importantly, the concepts should be sequenced to promote effective aesthetic and cognitive growth in the classroom while infusing the element of critical thinking. The incorporation of these factors into the curriculum will encourage students to master a body of knowledge appropriate to their grade level and ability. Teachers and members of the community must be part of curriculum development. Without this essential input, the administration cannot expect the curriculum (K-12), to be fully implemented, much less to be expanded when the time comes (Trumbull, 1987).

The Curriculum and the Computer

Making changes in the curriculum has always been a problem, often because of the amount of work entailed. Using the computer can eliminate most of this frustration by allowing the writer to make revisions on an ongoing basis without disrupting the whole department or district. Changes can be made by page or section and inserted in a three-ring notebook as needed. This enables one to replace only what is needed and, in turn, save time, materials, and money. When organizing the curriculum, the computer is a valuable tool; when the curriculum is written and stored on a disk, the computer becomes an invaluable resource.

All schools operate on the energy created between and among teachers, students,

143

and administrators. There are many variables that contribute to this energy, one of which is being at ease with the curriculum — not just accepting it, but being able and willing to implement it fully or update it without the usual anxiety that seems to develop.

Before one begins to write or rewrite the curriculum, all existing guides and related material should be collected and reviewed, and the computer format should be determined. Next, it is very important to consider the needs of the district and how it might use the sort codes. Workshops should be advised for those who are not familiar with the system being used, and these workshops should be mandatory for those who have not previously worked with computers.

Although there are many good programs on the market, the one presented here has stood up to the many revisions and demands made by our state department of elementary and secondary education and our school district. The department format was generated using the Apple IIGS computer with 1.5 megabytes of memory, a color monitor (a black and white will work), two (3.5) 800K disk drives (one will work), and an Imagewriter II printer. The program used was AppleWorks 2.0 (Data Base), enhanced by an applied engineering program (Appleworks 2 Expander) that increased the data base from 6,350 records to 22,600 records, the word processor from 7,250 lines to 22,600 lines, and the clipboard for the data base and word processor from 250 lines to 2,042 lines. An extensive amount of memory and the ability to move and store numerous records are absolutely essential.

The next step is to decide what information needs to be stored. This should be planned carefully because most programs deal with limited space. Although this particular program is limited to 15 lines of information per record and our curriculum has been revised and additions made, there were no problems with this limitation.

Figure 12.1 is an example of one record of a curriculum objective for the course *Beginning Art*. This case deals with drawing, where the teaching objective is the elements and principles of design, with emphasis on the key skill pertaining to the use of the art vocabulary. The student objective is stated in behavioral terms and the evaluation method is listed. The SORT CODE and other sorting functions of the computer allow the user the convenience of "seeing" the curriculum as never before. The SORT CODE may contain any items a department and district deem necessary, such as the following: [BEGINNING ART 407] is the course name and numerical code used by the district to identify individual courses. [CC.E] identifies the core competency E, which reads: "Describe, interpret, and judge works of art, and use appropriate vocabulary to explain their (i.e., students) evaluations." [THFACT] is a code for a teaching hierarchy (TH), and in this case it's the FACT level. [LHMEN] is a code for the learning hierarchy (LH), and in this case it's the MEMORIZING level. (A system is being field tested at this time dealing with a 3 x 4 x 13 matrix in which there are 3 levels of the learning hierarchy and 4 levels of the teaching

144

Figure 12.1 Curriculum objective.

hierarchy, each with 13 cells (-12). In theory, teaching objectives as well as learning objectives can be identified by degree of difficulty, ranging from the concrete to the abstract. The lowest level of the teaching hierarchy is teaching facts, and the lowest level of the learning hierarchy is memorizing those facts.) [XI] means that this course is open to all grade levels, as opposed to a numerical code of 09, 10, 11, or 12 (grades). [FA] is a two-letter code for fine arts that is used to call up the art curriculum from the master file. The [S2] code means that this class is a two-semester course ([S1] would indicate one-semester course).

The ACTIVITY bar, another code bar, can be used to sort items such as BEGINNING DRAWING, which is the general activity to be taught within the Beginning Art Course. [0101.KS.3.B] is a series of codes, the first two digits (01) being the code for beginning and the second two (01) the code for drawing. This code would be used primarily at the district level. KS stands for key skill, and the

145

number 3 is the code for high school (number 2 for middle/junior high schools and number 1 for elementary schools). The letter B is the code for beginning level (A is the code for advanced level). [E01] is the code for core competency E, which reads: "Describe, interpret, and judge works of art, and use appropriate art vocabulary to explain their (i.e., students) evaluations." The 01 is key skill number 1 and reads: "The learner will describe the appropriateness of media and techniques used in works of art." T.O. is the teaching objective and S.O. is the student objective. The EVALUATION line is coded as to how the student objective outcomes are evaluated. TEXT is space given for any text and/or reference notes that one may wish to use.

Figure 12.2 shows the format for a lesson plan. The SORT CODE is layed out basically the same as in the curriculum objective format. The [Beginning Art 407]

Figure 12.2 Format for a lesson plan.

File: ART. LESSON. PLNS   REVIEW/ADD/CHANGE   Escape: Main Menu

Selection: All records

Record 40 of 42

SORT CODE: [Beginning Art 407] [CC.B] [THCON] [LHUSE] [X] [FA] [S2] [DBAE]
ACTIVITY: Beginning Drawing [0101.KS.3.B] [B07]
DIRECTIONS-: 06. Use the principles and elements of design to make a critical
- : analysis of selected art work. The learner will analyze the influence of
- : context on color appearance.
- : -
A.O.- : To talk more intelligently about art.
- : -
- : -
- : -
MATERIALS - : Slides, books, visuals
MATERIALS - : -
MATERIALS - : -
- : -
EVALUATION - : A teacher observation, a pencil and paper test
----

Type entry or use @ commands   2/13/89 7:28 P sections contains the course name and numerical code. The [CC.B] code is the core competency B, which reads: "Recognize and successfully employ the elements and principles of design." [THCON] is the code for a teaching hierarchy (in this case the CONCEPT level), and [LHUSE] is a learning hierarchy code (in this case the USE level). (Both the teaching and learning hierarchies are of a higher order than in Figure 12.1) [X] means that this course is open to all grade levels (as opposed to 09, 10, 11, or 12). [FA] is a two-letter code for fine arts and [S2] is the code for a two-semester course. The only addition is the [DBAE] code, which is used in this format to indicate that the lesson is discipline-based art education.

The ACTIVITY bar is sectioned into Beginning Drawing, which is the activity to be taught within the Beginning Art Course. [0101.KS.3.B] is a lengthy code to be used when retrieving this lesson plan from the master file. The first two digits (01) are the code for beginning and the second two digits (01) are the code for drawing. KS stands for key skill; the number 3 is the code for high school; and the letter B is the code for beginning level. [B07] is the code for core competency B, which reads: "Recognize and successfully employ the elements and principles of design"; 07 is key skill number 7 and reads: "The learner will analyze the influence of context on color appearance."

The DIRECTIONS category consists of a sequence number (06), the core competency B, and the key skill number (07). The A.O., or ACTIVITY OBJECTIVE, is a more global objective for the lesson plan. (An objective of this nature may cover one or several lessons or an entire unit.) The MATERIALS section is self-explanatory, and the teacher lists the best ways to document the progress of the student in the section coded EVALUATION.

Figure 12.3 is the vocabulary format and contains items of simple explanation. The SORT CODE contains the FA code for fine arts and any other information as one deems necessary. The ACTIVITY section contains a list of all the activities where the word is used. The WORD section contains the vocabulary word and its definition, and the DEPARTMENT section is self-explanatory. The COURSE section contains a list of all the courses where the word is used. If the word is used in all courses, the section should be coded All.

Figure 12.4 is the slide collection format. The SORT CODE section contains such items as [ADVANCED ART 413], the course title and numerical code that are used to retrieve slide information from the master file. [HS 047] is a code for the high school (HS) version of *(History of Art* by H. W. Janson *History of Art for Young People* by H.W. Janson), and 047 is the page number where the slide and/or reference can be found. The ACTIVITY section contains the activities in which the slide and/or visual is used. The TITLE section is self-explanatory, as are the sections coded ARTIST and BIRTH/DEATH.

In the NATIONALITY/ORIGIN section, nationality is used when the artist is known; when the artist is not known, country of origin is used to identify the artifact.

Figure 12.3 Vocabulary format.

File: ART. VOCABULARY   REVIEW/ADD/CHANGE   Escape: Main Menu

Selection: All records

Record 1 of 474

```
------------------------------------------------------------------------------------
------------------------------------------------------------------------------------
SORT CODE: [ ]   [ ]   [ ]   [ ]   [ ]   [ ]   [FA]
ACTIVITY: [Jewelry] [Advanced Sculpture]   [ ]   [ ]   [ ]   [ ]   [ ]
WORD: ABRASIVE - -A substance used for grinding and polishing, such as emery,
WORD: pumice, rotten stone and rouge.
WORD: -
WORD: -
WORD: -
WORD: -
DEPARTMENT: Art
COURSE: Arts and Crafts, Advanced Art
------------------------------------------------------------------------------------
```

Type entry or use @ commands   2/13/89 7:29 P

The sections MEDIUM, STYLE/SCHOOL, YEAR OF ART WORK, SIZE, PERIOD, and LOCATION OF ART WORK are all self-explanatory. The REF-ERENCE/TEXT section is reserved for a reference and/or textbook and page number used to identify or describe the slide. The FILE LOCATION is an index used to catalog slides and/or visual. In this case, A identifies the cabinet, 1 the drawer, and 117 the slot where the slide is located.

This is a user-friendly program and, because the process is not complicated, anyone can learn it and improve their productivity in curriculum writing. Now, after the above groundwork and brief outline as to "how," an explanation is in order as to "why."

The true versatility of the computer is realized when one needs to look at aspects of the curriculum other than the sequence of courses and/or lessons. For instance, the district coordinator may want to look at all the grade levels where line or color is taught. Once that has been accomplished, he or she may want to look even further, at all the stated objectives for teaching line or color. Then he or she can look up lesson plans to see how the lesson is approached. Should there be a discrepancy along the way, a classroom observation of that particular lesson might be called for in order to make any adjustment. Whereas several observations may have been

148

12.4 Slide collection format.

File: ART. SLIDE. COLL   REVIEW/ADD/CHANGE   Escape: Main Menu

Selection: All records

Record 1 of 2032

```
-----------------------------------------------------------------------------------------
-----------------------------------------------------------------------------------------
SORT CODE: [ADVANCED ART 413] [HS 047] [ ]   [ ]   [ ]   [ ]   [ ]   [FA]
ACTIVITY: [ART HISTORY] [ ]   [ ]   [ ]   [ ]   [ ]   [ ]   [ ]
TITLE: Mistress and Maid
ARTIST: Achilles Painter
BIRTH/DEATH: 5th century B.C.
NATIONALITY/ORIGIN: Italian
MEDIUM: Pottery (Attic white-ground lekythos)
STYLE/SCHOOL: check
YEAR OF ART WORK: c. 0440 - -0430 B.C.
SIZE: 16" high
PERIOD: Ancient, Greek
LOCATION OF ART WORK: Staatliche Antikensammlungen, Munich, Germany
REFERENCE/TEXT: History of Art (2 ed.), Janson, H.W. p. 109
FILE LOCATION: A-1-117
-----------------------------------------------------------------------------------------
Type entry or use @ commands                                    2/13/89 7:32 P
```

needed to identify the original discrepancy, scanning the curriculum via the computer will certainly take less time than any one observation.

An art teacher who wants to give a substitute a class roll and lesson plans for a particular unit has only to key in the correct code. A word of caution: Using this system, it is very easy to overwhelm the substitute with too much information, even if he or she is certified in art.

The ability to call up core competencies or certain key skills along with teaching and learning hierarchies will prove to be indispensable in defending accountability. The ability to examine the K-12 gifted and talented program, while at the same time checking that the elements and principles are covered at the proper grade levels, will expedite revision when necessary. It will be easy to examine how many times and what activities use each word of the glossary. You will be able to review the curricular format for discipline-based art education, examine areas that may need strengthening, and lessen the impact on others. It is also possible to include teset questions so they may be checked against goals, objectives, competencies, and key skills, thus verifying that the curriculum content is being tested. The combinations are limited only by one's creativity.

Summary

Although the list of curriculum problems is not complete, it is worthy to note that those mentioned will create enough confusion in most programs. Writing across the curriculum, the hidden curriculum, ethics, and honesty will all be under consideration for inclusion into the curriculum at one time or another.

This decade will see a rush to write and revise curriculum in art education. If changes are not made over a sufficient period of time and with the proper leadership, concepts like discipline-based art education could deteriorate into a studio-based humanities program, taught in the language arts department by English majors. Attitudes about art will have to shift to less emphasis on the product and include more reading, writing, and talking about art and works of art.

Visual arts, however, will always occupy center stage in art education. Making visual arts more pluralistic is cause for concern, not so much in the elementary schools but certainly at the secondary levels. It has been my experience that secondary art teachers are much more product oriented and do less cross-discipline sharing than elementary art teachers. To help modify this will require a strong commitment from colleges and universities that teach art education and a change in attitudes about art education from studio art teachers in higher education.

There are many factors that interfere with the thinking processes of students, and a fragmented curriculum is preeminent. When this interference is removed, students will be allowed to think rather than be taught how to think. Students must be able to analyze, compare, and infer in order to move beyond mere problem solving to the more creative cognitive process of problem making.

There seems to be a trend toward teaching curriculum objectives as ends in themselves. When this structure is used, the result is "piecemeal thinking." If we believe that success in new learning depends on prior knowledge, then we are only compounding the problem by continuing this approach. Also, it is common knowledge that when structure is applied too long in an academic setting, the results are retardation of creativity and the inability to work independently on tasks that require higher cognitive functions.

Using the computer is not the complete answer to the complex problem of curriculum writing. It is, however, a major step in the process. It will enable one to create new documents, revise formats, or produce an overview of any aspect of the curriculum without elevating the emotions of the entire art staff. Ongoing modifications can be made with less consideration for the cost factor and more consideration for teacher input.

Conditions must open up to allow the art teacher maximum input into all levels of district policy, not only in the curriculum but in personnel matters, scheduling, facilities, art materials, and the budget. There is also a need for input from art teachers into the organization of the school. These changes will not occur unless art teachers make them happen. The prognosis is clear: If art educators are to make a positive impact on the future of their curriculum, they must provide the tangible evidence themselves, and no area can be left unchallenged.

References

Alutto, J. A., & Belasco, J. A. (1972). Patterns of teacher paticipation in school system decision making. *Educational Administration Quarterly, 9*, 27-41.

Bennett, W. J. (1988). *American education: Making it work.* Washington, DC: U.S. Government Printing Office.

Educational Testing Service. (1989). *Crossroads in American education.* Princeton, NJ: Author.

Dewey, J. (1954). *Experience and education.* New York: Macmillan.

Dunn, R. (1982). Teaching students through their individual learning styles: A research report. In *Student Learning Styles and Brain Behavior.* Reston, VA: National Association of Secondary School Principals.

Feldman, D. H. (1980). *Beyond universals in cognitive development.* Norwood, NJ: Ablex.

Feuerstein, R., Rand, Y., Hoffman, M. B., & Miller, R. (1980). *Instrumental enrichment.* Baltimore: University Park Press.

Kellogg, R. (1959). *What children scribble and why.* Palo Alto, CA: National Press Publications.

Kurtz, B. E., & Borkowski, J. G. (1984). Children's metacognition: Exploring relations among knowledge, process, and motivational variables. *Journal of Experimental Child Psychology, 37*, 335-354.

Langer, S. K. (1963). *Philosophy in a new key* (3rd ed.). Cambridge, MA: Harvard University Press.

Lissner, R. J., & Apple Computer, Inc. (1983-1986). *AppleWorks integrated software.* V2.0. [Computer program]. Cupertino, CA: Apple Computer, Inc.

Lochhead, J., & Clement, J. (1979). *Cognitive process instruction.* Philadelphia: Franklin Institute Press.

McLaughlin, M., & Thomas, M. A. (1984). *Art history, art criticism, and art production: An examination of art education in selected school districts* (Vols. 1-3). Santa Monica, CA: Rand Corporation.

Morrison, T. R., Osborne, K. W., & McDonald, N. G. (1977). Whose Canada? The assumptions of Canadian studies. *Canadian Journal of Education, 2*(1), 77.

National Assessment of Education Progress. (1981). *Reading, thinking and writing.* Denver: Author.

National Commission on Excellence in Education. (1983). *A nation at risk: The imperative for educational reform.* Washington, DC: U.S. Government Printing Office.

Schwab, J. J. (1983). The practical 4: Something for curriculum professors to do. *Curriculum Inquiry, 13*, 239-265.

Sommerville, S. C., & Hartley, J. L. (1986). Art. In R. F. Dillon & R. J. Sternberg (Eds.), *Cognition and instruction* (pp. 241-298). New York: Academic Press.

Trumbull, D. J. (1987). On changing perspective: An examination of teachers' dilemmas. *Journal of Curriculum and Supervision, 3*(1), 45-60.

151

Weinstein, C. E., & Mayer, R. E. (1986). The teaching of learning strategies. In M. C. Wittrock (Ed.), *Handbook of Research on Teaching*. New York: Macmillan.

Wilks, M. (1986-1987). *AppleWorks 2 expander. V1.1.3.* [Computer program] Carrollton, TX: Applied Engineering.

Wise, A. E. (1988). Legislated learning revisited. *Phi Delta Kappan, 69*, 328-332.

13

Arts Networking as Staff Development: The Cultural Community as Staff Development Resources

CAROLYN WHITE-TRAVANTI

Milwaukee Public Schools

Background

When an experienced art staff already has strong technical and classroom management skills, the art supervisor's approach to staff development must be reevaluated and redesigned. The challenge for the supervisor is to analyze and define needs and design in-service courses that fulfill these needs.

In the process of analyzing needs, some facts became apparent. In most cases, there is only one art teacher in a school, and this creates a kind of artistic isolation. Most of the art teachers did not know each other or know each other's art teaching processes. Art teachers were seldom seen at art openings and receptions at local galleries and museums. Few art teachers took students, even on an occasional basis, to local galleries, museums, and other art community resources.

An externally generated need occurred when the art teacher was asked to explain, define, and defend the field of art, especially recent "art news," to other members of the school staff. This situation demanded that art teachers become even more knowledgeable regarding the field of "art" than they had been prepared for by their university education. This positioned art teachers as spokespersons for the entire field of art with students and faculty alike, a role that they may not have ever desired and that made some of them extremely uncomfortable.

Believing that these unique needs could be met successfully by staff development programs, the art supervisor decided on the following goals:

• To bring art teachers together on a regular basis.
• To keep the group physically and intellectually involved by including stimulating and unusual experiences.
• To expand their knowledge base of the "broad field of art" by introducing them to previously unknown situations and opportunities.
• To introduce teachers to community artists and spaces that they could later incorporate in their classrooms.
• To build a sense of collegiality among the participants.
• To increase teacher networking across grade levels and schools.
• To create a sense of excitement for the diversity of art and artists.
• To develop their awareness of the role of art teachers in the local art community.
• To encourage teachers to include community art resources within the art curriculum by field trips or showing "I was there" slides to students.
• To increase students' awareness and knowledge of the local art community and resources by involving the art teachers.
• To refine teachers' career information within the art field.

With these goals clearly in mind, some designs for staff development activities were formulated.

Using Local Arts Institutions as Resources

When scheduled meetings for all art teachers are held consistently at a variety of local arts institutions, the result is the beginning of demystification of those institutions. As art teachers become familiar with an institution's permanent

154

collection, its physical floor plan, and whom and how to contact for tour content and scheduling, a positive and interested attitude emerges. These meetings can be held at art museums; natural history and local history museums; commercial art galleries; school art galleries in elementary, middle, and high schools; college and university art museums and galleries; architecturally important buildings; studio buildings that house groups of diverse artists; offices of professional arts organizations; and artist-run profit and nonprofit galleries. The supervisor can disseminate information regarding these institutions and can act as a contact person and a one-stop information center. By maintaining membership and ties to these arts institutions, the supervisor promotes and assists in their use.

This direction and support by the supervisor facilitates the teachers' incorporation of community resources into their students' learning activities. Encouraging teachers to incorporate the permanent aspects of a resource in their planned activities enables them to reuse that material in the future and allows them time to research segments in depth.

Using the Local Artist as a Resource

Most local artists are extremely willing to share insights into their artistic vision and demonstrate techniques to students and teachers. This excellent resource can be used to dispel misconceptions and stereotypical images associated with artists, can become a source of career education information, and can act as positive role models for students When a student (and one always does) asks an artist "Do you make lots of money?" the artist's response almost always includes the phrase "I really like my work." For some students, that statement opens up a whole new viewpoint toward future life options.

Connecting with local artists requires some pleasurable detective work. The art supervisor can make initial contacts by regularly attending exhibition openings and receptions. Asking an artist whether he or she would be interested in spending time with teachers and students, either as a volunteer or for a small honorarium, and exchanging contact telephone numbers to talk further about this idea can create wonderful staff development opportunties.

Involving a group of artists who are involved in a consortium can expand artistic and educational possibilities. In Milwaukee a group of artists representing a number of art disciplines in the visual and performing arts are housed in an older, centrally located high school. These Lincoln Center for the Arts studio spaces are operated by the Milwaukee Public Schools, with artists and groups paying for their rent by providing specified number of hours to teachers and students in the school system. The barter system offers performances, informances, workshops, residences, and demonstrations in the school and performances, demonstrations, studio visits, and internships at the Lincoln Center for the Arts. A school can schedule a group of students to visit two or three artists or groups in a block of time. This activity is promoted by mailed announcements to schools and through word of mouth, under the direction of the art supervisor.

One of the goals of bringing artists into the schools is to educate others about the job of being an artist. Referring to artists as self-employed small business people who use their time to produce a product or performance for which they expect to receive pay helps explain to students and school staffs the rationale for an honorarium. Artists should be offered an honorarium for their time and expertise, even if it is small. Artists who are employed by a business may have their time donated by their employer. The art supervisor can contact local businesses that employ artists and recruit speakers and demonstrations for schools, furthering career education information for both students and teachers.

The art supervisor can obtain membership lists of artists' organizations to facilitate contact with other artists. These groups usually have yearly exhibitions that provide the art supervisor with an opportunity to preview work and meet new artists.

Perhaps the hardest artists to find are folk artists, since they may not call themselves artists and do not join art groups. One solution is to observe the neighborhood, making a record of yards and houses that exhibit folk art characteristics. Using these visual records during a discussion of folk artists and traditional ethnic artists can provide leads from students to artistic neighbors, relatives, and friends. Inviting these artists to participate in school art fair activities or to appear as a classroom presenter and demonstrator successfully incorporates another level of the artistic community into the classroom.

The Art Collector

Art collectors who can be persuaded to discuss their personal collection provide invaluable insights into the process of collecting art and the chosen focus of their collection. Usually they will tell lively, informative stories of their personal relationships with the artists represented in their collection. The contrast between the successful, educated collector and the folk artist whom he or she respects generates lively discussion with art teachers on both social and aesthetic issues. Art collectors have different approaches and attitudes, with each collector basing the selection of art objects on a different set of values and tastes. A bank may want its exhibited collection to epitomize intelligence, seriousness, and solidity. On the other hand, an individual's collection may represent an ethnic interest or stylistic preference. As a result, knowledge about a variety of collectors and their motivations in collecting can significantly further insights and result in art teachers acquiring deepened knowledge about the various roles that art plays within our communities.

SOME STAFF DEVELOPMENT MODELS

The Weekend Culture Cruise: "Art Moves"

This model was designed to accomplish as many of the originally listed goals as possible and to incorporate local art resources. The model uses a weekend format to involve art teachers in 12 hours of intense activities. The beauty of this model is that it can be reoffered time after time by changing and introducing different local art resources. All travel between scheduled places is done in personal cars or on foot. A sample schedule follows:

Friday, 6:00 P.M.: Katie Gingrass's recently opened downtown gallery shows contemporary local artists. Katie will discuss the business of opening a gallery, her education and background in art, and process she uses to select gallery artists.

Friday, 7:30 P.M.: Michael Lord's gallery shows nationally known artists and some local artists. Michael will discuss the business of running a gallery from his perspective, his unusual gallery space, and his beginning interest in art. Michael will clue the group on the maneuvering involved in spearheading the acquisition, donation, and installation of a large Calder mobile at the Milwaukee airport.

Saturday, 8:00 A.M.: Bradley Sculpture Gardens, an internationally known collection of contemporary sculpture in a parklike setting, is one of only three similar gardens in the world. The scheduled tour with the docent would be an in-depth version. A student tour would be geared to the students' grade level. There are three large sculptures by Ernie Shaw included on the grounds. Since Ernie Shaw also was displayed at Lord's Gallery, teachers have an opportunity to mentally transfer a piece from the gallery to its proposed location.

Saturday, 10:30 A.M.: Back downtown to the artist's district — John Gruenwald's studio. John is a master lithographer who prints his own work, along with the works of national and local artists. John shares a warehouse floor with other local artists and also has created a living space there. He demonstrates the lithography process

157

and shows other artists' work that he has printed.

Saturday, 12:30 P.M.: Lunch as a group at a restaurant located in the neighborhood.

Saturday, 1:45 P.M.: Posner's Gallery, a newly opened, high-tech space in a renovated warehouse. This gallery carries predominantly national artists, specializes in limited edition contemporary prints, and retails nationally. Judy, who represents and carries hundreds of artists, discusses the gallery business from her perspective.

Saturday, 3:30 P.M.: Artists' studios (back into the cars). Chuck Toman, a local electronic sculptor, discusses his fascination with and attitude toward our current cultural obsession with electronic technology. Leon Travanti, a painter and designer, discusses his interest in fantasy and illusion as perceived in a variety of group celebrations, especially festivals, parades, and carnivals.

Three weeks later, 4:00 P.M.: The final meeting of these teachers is held to share their solutions to the homework assignment, which was to design, test, and bring examples of a lesson plan that incorporates and shares with their students a significant aspect of this in-service program.

The Art Museum Encounter

The art supervisor, working cooperatively with the Milwaukee Art Museum, designed in-service courses and programs that would assist art teachers in effectively using that local resource in their current curriculum. Two of these programs are aimed at the integration of the art and social studies curriculum at the fourth- and sixth-grade level.

All art and social studies teachers are provided with a packet of teacher materials for classroom use. This packet is designed to assist them in preparing students for a core-related, scheduled museum tour. It contains 20 black and white and some small color reproductions of artworks selected from the permanent collection that will illuminate and/or illustrate a social studies concept. Pertinent artistic, social, geographic, economic, and historic information is provided for and keyed to each of the reproductions. Suggested research and activities for students in both art and social studies are also keyed to each reproduction. A glossary, basic museum and tour information, and a loan form for slides of the artworks are also included in the packet. To further ensure the success of the activity, the art supervisor arranged to have the cost of the buses to bring all sixth-grade students to the museum funded by

158

the Milwaukee School Board, as part of a systemwide grade-level field trip program.

Teacher in-service courses are held at the museum each semester to assist teachers in familiarizing themselves with this resource. Currently, six 2-hour inservice meetings focusing on the fourth- and sixth-grade art and social studies program, have been scheduled.

Scheduled for the near future is *Insights Into Art History*, a two-semester museum in-service program that will teach art history from exhibited artworks rather than from slides This intense and fascinating 12-hour discussion/tour of the museum's collection will be developed chronologically and led by the director of museum education. Teachers will design lesson plans for each 2-hour discussion, incorporating art history into their curriculum.

Artists in Residence in the Schools

An artist's residency in a school can provide multiple benefits for students, school staff, and especially the art teacher. The art teacher can benefit from the unique opportunity to operate as half of a team with the artist. Interacting with another creative person and acquiring insights into attitudes, motivations, and visual resources, as well as different technical approaches, can act as a catalyst for new approaches to teaching. The artist also affects the school staff, helping to rectify preconceptions and misconceptions about the "life of an artist." Also, by bringing a fresh outlook to the situation, the artist helps the staff reexamine solutions and try new approaches. During the residency, school activities are usually occurring at a fast pace, the interest level is high, and students are highly motivated. As a result, a lot of ground is covered, and the enjoyment is evident. This situation directs the staff's attitude in future planning for activities and pacing.

Since, in an effective residency, the artist usually spends a few days at the school, a residency tends to require a financial outlay from the school. School residencies can be financed by matching funds from the school and an outside agency such as the state arts board, a parent teacher organization, a local business, a charitable foundation, or a school-sponsored fundraiser.

The required process of writing a grant or a proposal in order to obtain funds for the in-school artist residency takes time, but is crucial to the success of the residency. The planning and discussion that takes place among the faculty is invaluable as interest and enthusiasm extends from the small planning group to the full faculty. This writing of the grant or proposal requires that the school task force consider all aspects of the residence, how it integrates with and complements various disciplines, the best ways to schedule students and artist into the school day, the types of student activities that will introduce and lead up to the residency, and ways to involve parents and the local community. The art supervisor, acting as a source of inspiration, an advisor, and a resouce to the group, can help develop the proposal and suggest additional solutions and connections.

The "Hands-on" Encounter

The "hands-on," technically based in-service program that offers art teachers the time and opportunity to become artistically involved with a particular medium, especially under the leadership of a well-known local artist, is extremely successful.

One approach used in Milwaukee is to contract with a local artist who provides his or her expertise, tools, and studio space for the required 12 hours of in-service time. These in-service programs have included the techniques of limestone sculpting, stained glass work, Japanese woodcuts, silk-screen and photo-screen processes, collagraph and lithographic printing, and ceramics and metal working. Teachers involved in these programs gain renewed insights into the process of creation with the accompanying satisfaction of completion.

Smorgasbord "hands-on" in-service courses include a number of presenters, each demonstrating, modeling, and guiding the teachers in a particular technique or a series of activities for a specific grade level. Most of these presenters are excellent art teachers modeling for each other their very successful studio class activities. These programs are very popular with art teachers and are well attended.

Other smorgasbord offerings are one-time sessions demonstrating new materials and allowing art teachers opportunities to try out and experiment with those materials. New resources are available for examination at the same time.

IMPLEMENTING THE EXPERIENCE

Teacher Activities

All offered in-service activities require teachers to submit lesson plans that imbed into their curriculum aspects of that activity. The last meeting of the in-service program is devoted to group discussion and sharing, further enhancing networking among the teachers.

At our regularly scheduled group meetngs of art teachers, selected teachers are asked to describe their lesson, the student activity, and its place in the school curriculum. These teachers bring slides, videos, student work, and enough copies of the lesson plan for all present.

Evaluation

A staff development project is evaluated in a number of ways: First, the teachers' opinions are sought, stressing the importance of their response to the art supervisor. Second, they are asked for their advice on how to provide teachers with even better future in-service activities, whether a particular activity should be offered again, and so forth. Teachers' opinions are respected and acted upon in future plans. Third, teachers fill out a rating scale and make written comments. Fourth, the submitted lesson plans from each in-service activity are carefully read and evaluated. Did the teacher incorporate new attitudes, insights, connections, and/or techniques into his or her curriculum? Finally, as in art classes, a percentage of the evaluation must be based on the instructor or organizer's observation and the participant's performance. Some key questions guide the observations: How was the attendance? Were teachers on time? Were the participants attentive, interested, and enthusiastic? Did discussions arise? Was the discussion focused on in-service topics? Did teachers ask the presenters questions? Did teachers start to "network" with each other and the presenters? Did some of the submitted plans exceed expectations? What percentage of the plans were at the minimum expectation level? Did teachers try new ideas? Did teachers produce evidence of using plans with students and being successful?

Not all evaluation should be accomplished immediately — evaluation must be a continuing process based on observation. When the influence of a staff development activity continues to show up in the teacher's planned school and outside activities, it is a good indicator of the activity's success. Recent observation provided a number of clues to the success of past staff development activities.

The all-school Art Attack Day scheduled the following spring by a participant of the Art Moves in-service program was a positive evaluation, since it involved bringing local artists into the school to demonstrate and discuss their art with students and parents. Art Attack Day was extremely successful and now is scheduled regularly. Art Move spin-offs are occurring in other schools.

More art teachers are seen at museum and gallery openings. Some of them have become fearless museum goers and have developed the ability to convince principals to allow, and even fund and encourage, students at all grade levels to attend art museum field trips.

Teachers who are not teachers of art have also been involved in the in-service activities. The fourth-and sixth-grade teachers and the social studies teachers consistently register for these activities, and they and their art teacher cooperatively work out integrated lesson plans.

A high school geometry teacher used her photos from the Bradley Sculpture Garden to create an independent learning package for her students to use. A high school principal joined in an in-service activity and visited the studio of a sculptor who uses complex computers and programs to run a fountain (*Stephen Pevnick's*

Rainfall) that creates designs and spells words with drops of water.

The bringing together of the art community and educational community is starting to work. Each success points out additional approaches yet to be tried, but at least the wall has windows and doors.

14

The Role of the State Art Specialist: Executive Management Survival Skills

MAC ARTHUR GOODWIN
South Carolina State Department of Education

Background

The state art consultant must play an important role in promoting quality art education. He or she is called upon to provide technical assistance to districts in staff development, curriculum development, facilities planning, and program assessment. In order to accomplish these tasks, it is important that the state art consultant develop executive management survival skills. These skills are the focus of this chapter.

A survey of numerous documents on management in the executive arena reveals the following essential skills. Effective management requires (a) time management and effective decision making, (b) the ability to concentrate on performance, (c) an understanding of the developmental stages of programs, and (c) an understanding of political ramifications, leadership, and resourcefulness.

Time Management: Effective Decision Making

The basis of time management is the ability to control events. In order to manage time effectively, one must understand the nature of events going on around oneself. Daily occurrences make up the substance of time.

Differentiating between events that one can control and those that one cannot control, and the continuum between the two extremes, is crucial. Charles R. Hobbs (1987) refers to such events as anticipated events and delineates them along the following continuum (with suggested solutions).

• Events you think you cannot control, and you can't. Adaptability is most appropriate in these cases.
• Events you think you cannot control, but you can. Goal setting is most appropriate in these cases.
• Events you think you can control, but you can't. Gaining a realistic perspective is essential in these cases.
• Events you think you can control, but you don't. Exploring alternatives is necessary under these circumstances.
• Events you think you can control, and you can and do. This is the result of goal setting, consequential planning, and carrying out the necessary activities that lead to success.

Urgency is the principal enemy of effective time management. There are a lot more trivial urgencies in your day than vital urgencies. Knowing the difference is crucial. The key is the ability to prioritize anticipated events. Vitally urgent events are those that yield high to moderately high payoffs; trivially urgent events range from those that yield low payoffs to those that are a complete waste of time. In many cases, urgencies have little to do with priority; rather, they involve actions and responses.

Effective decision making is also an important skill. This involves developing the ability to identify the strategic and generic elements of a situation, thus avoiding solving the same problems twice.

Effective, proactive time management requires the ability to anticipate and prioritize. In addition, goal setting and delineating appropriate objectives and planning strategies are essential. Implementing activities and evaluating results effectively and efficiently are the hallmarks of good time management.

Concentration on Performance/Focusing

Concentration of power is the ability to focus on and accomplish your most vital priorities. Concentration means focusing on something; power is the ability to produce effect. Concentration of power, then, comes in two parts: the ability to focus and the ability to produce effect, or accomplish.

Concentrating on areas of outstanding performance will yield big payoffs. Rather than doing things right (efficiency), it is better to do the right thing (effectiveness). Focusing on strengths is an important skill, more important than focusing on weaknesses. Start out with what can be done; do not start out with limitations (DeGarmo, 1988).

Thus, a periodic statewide diagnostic survey of art education is crucial to effective management. Understanding the political and educational climate and needs and available resources is important to focus needed energies. Concentrating on performance and focusing are the necessities for orchestrating program reform.

Understanding Developmental Stages of Programs

Providing technical assistance to diverse school districts is problematic, to say the least. The needs of a district with art specialists might be quite different from the needs of a district without art specialists. Technical assistance provided in a district with administrators conversant in the arts might require one approach. A district where administrators are not conversant in the arts might require another approach. The state art consultant must be knowledgeable and confident, yet extremely flexible.

The state art consultant must understand and recognize the developmental stages of art programs. Programs are often at different developmental stages within a district. Thus, assessments and assistance are given within the existing framework and developmental levels of the program.

165

Understanding Political Ramifications: Communication, Leadership, and Resourcefulness

The state art consultant must understand the political ramifications provided by state and national perspectives and policies as well as those at the district level.

State and national policies are being made more frequently and are affecting more programs. Often, by the time local district personnel learn about recommended changes, policies have already been promulgated and regulations are in place. Thus, it is important that the state art consultant have some knowledge of the political process. Knowing the key player in the political arena is crucial to effecting changes that promote art education reform.

It is also important for the state art consultant to understand the political ramifications of his or her role at the district level. Policies vary from district to district — no two districts are exactly alike. Thus, there is no assurance that what will work in one district will necessarily work in another, and what works is not always good. Contemporary notions toward site-based management recognize principals as the instructional leaders of their respective buildings. Thus, the emphasis, support, and even philosophy of the art program might vary significantly from school to school. This is often the case in school systems that do not provide coordination at the district level.

In many cases two agendas exist within a single district. One is promulgated by the administration, and is usually more global, taking district- and schoolwide concerns into consideration. The other is promulgated at the classroom level and is usually predicated on student/teacher welfare. It is important to note that both perspectives are important, and as such must be dealt with effectively in order to provide quality art education programs.

The state art consultant's positions affords opportunities for the development of an important knowledge base. In this information age, the state art consultant must be a skilled information manager. He or she must be adept at communicating vital information and obtaining what he or she needs to know. Successful communication requires clear writing and speaking skills as well as an effective delivery system. Consideration must be given to publishing a regular update and articles in publications of other constituencies. An informed constituency is usually a supportive constituency.

The state art consultant must provide leadership and be knowledgeable about and actively involved in organizations and constituencies that have an impact on education policies.

The state art consultant must be resourceful. Knowing all of the answers is not as important as knowing where to find them. He or she must be able to network with other persons and resources in order to provide assistance and sustain program improvement. Thus, attending state and national education conventions in the arts is essential. It is also important to be conversant with current literature, research, and trends in the field.

Conclusion

The state art consultant is an executive manager. He or she manages staff development, curriculum development, facilities planning, and program development, all in the context of time management, performance, and national, state, and local politics. Here I have discussed the role of the state art consultant in this context. The responsibility of the state art consultant is not one of replicating efforts of higher education teacher training programs, efforts of curriculum development specialists, efforts of the arts commission in an attempt to protect the sanctum of the Department of Education; rather, his or her responsibility is to maximize the efforts of each of these entities. The state art consultant must be an effective manager to bridle unlimited energies and effect significant art education reform.

References

DeGarmo, S. (1988). The art of being an executive, *Success*. New York: Success, Inc.
Hobbs, C. (1988). *Time power*. New York: Harper & Row.
Bliss, E. C. (1976). *Getting things done*. New York: Charles Scribner's Sons.

15

Coordinating the Fine Arts

PAUL PATTERSON

U-46 School District, Elgin, Illinois

Introduction

There was a time in public school administration when it was rather common to find a director of art education, a director of instrumental music education, and a director of choral music education — each serving as district administrator for that program. These administrators were subject specialists who sometimes functioned much like lead teachers. In some respects, this dual role kept those in arts administration in an educational twilight zone — more than teachers but less than administrators. Times have changed! For many school districts, the days of individual discipline specialists serving as district administrators are gone. Many districts have folded all the responsibilities for arts adminstration into one position: the coordinator of fine arts.

Arts educators tend to find this change lamentable. Nevertheless, the era of the generalist arts administrator has dawned. This is a trend that will continue, given the economic and political climate of many school districts. In a nutshell, most districts find it more economical to hire one generalist administrator than several specialists. In some respects this legitimizes the position of arts administrator by providing a status equal to other curricular positions and perhaps lessening the potential of elimination of the arts administrator's position due to cutbacks, while still allowing the perception of a streamlined central office administration.

In my school district the position of coordinator of fine arts evolved from two positions — director of music education and director of art education. At the peak of financial troubles, the director of art education retired, and the position remained unfilled. The director of music education subsumed the responsibilities for art education by default. When the director of music education retired, the district posted one position. That position became coordinator of fine arts.

Obviously, this kind of change doesn't come about without creating new questions. From the perspective of one case study, I would like to examine three of those questions: (a) What does the position of coordinator of fine arts entail? (b) How does one provide leadership for all the arts with personal expertise in only one area? and (c) How is this leadership used to solve the problem of lack of an elementary art program?

Background

School District U-46 is Illinois' second largest school district, covering 90 square miles and including portions of three counties. Located within district boundaries are five communities and portions of three other communities. There are 31 elementary schools, 6 middle schools, and 3 high schools serving a student population of over 27,000 and employing 1,500 teachers and administrators. This district is ethnically diverse, with over 60 different languages spoken. It is also geographically diverse, encompassing rural, urban, and suburban environments. The district budget is approximately $90 million, 42% coming from state aid. Per pupil costs run slightly below the Illinois state average. Fifty-five percent of the students seek some post-high school education, and ACT scores run slightly above the national average. The district is a microcosm of America.

The Position of Coordinator of Fine Arts

The perception held by many that central office administrators wield massive amounts of power is mostly myth. Certainly, money is power, but money and the ability to allocate it to programs has become an increasingly rare commodity in most school districts. The power of central office positions comes more from the evolutionary and dynamic nature of these jobs and how these dynamics can be used or abused by those holding the positions. The parameters of any administrative position are defined by history and environment. Understanding how these two elements affect the role of a coordinator of fine arts helps one to be more effective in the position.

I believe the overall responsibilities of coordinator of fine arts fall into three basic categories: (a) staff, (b) budget, and (c) curriculum. I shall now look at these responsibilities and how they evolved in my case.

Staff

Most central office administrators have few direct line responsibilities (responsibilities for recruiting, interviewing, hiring, and supervising staff). One exception is the administrator in charge of itinerant staff. If the teacher is an itinerant (traveling to more than one building), then staff responsibility falls to a district-level administrator. If the teacher is building-based, then staff responsibility is also building-based.

In Illinois School District U-46, the music staff is considered itinerant. All except secondary choral teachers travel to more than one building. Therefore, I hold all these line responsibilities for the music staff, which I exercise with cooperation from building administrators. On the other hand, the art staff is considered building-based. Therefore, line responsibilities fall to building-level administrators. My role in art staff matters is purely advisory, at the request of the building-level administrator.

Nontenured teachers are evaluated five times a year for 2 years. Once tenured, teachers are evaluated every other year from one to three times. Each building administrator evaluates music staff once (since there are usually two buildings involved), and I evaluate each staff member three times. I make the final decisions about music staff, with support from the building administrator. All tenured music staff evaluations are my responsibility. All art staff are evaluated by building administrators. Tenured art staff may request that I serve as an evaluator. Currently, there are 46 music teachers and 20 art teachers.

Historically, the role of this office regarding line/staff responsibilities has been very proactive in music and inactive in art. Environmentally, the district functions within a very clearly defined and thorough set of employment practice guidelines that are developed through contract negotiation. We have the largest National Education Association (NEA) affiliated union in Illinois.

Additional staff responsibilities involve organizing and implementing in-service programs for all music and art staff at district in-service meetings two or three times

171

a year. These programs are developed with staff input, involve a wide range of current issues, and include the use of outside presenters from university or professional ranks.

Budget

Funding for supplies and support materials may be found in building-level and district-level budgets. Each is targeted for specific needs. I administer an annual budget of around $70,000. As coordinator of fine arts, I approve, process, record, and direct purchases.

My other budgetary responsibilities include developing and directing an advocacy for greater fine arts funding to my superiors and the school board, pursuing other funding sources through grants, developing age and obsolescence needs, and trying to maintain a consistent quality standard for supplies ordered (especially important in art materials). At times these duties are exercised through teacher committees; sometimes they involve going outside the district to learn what is available in the field.

In 4 years, I have been able to obtain slightly over $60,000 in outside funding from grants. These grants have helped complete a major curriculum writing effort in art, music, drama, and dance. All materials have received enthusiastic support. Additionally, the grants have permitted the district to bring in professionals in the arts to work with both students and staff. Fine arts funding at the district level has expanded somewhat, and funds are now distributed more equitably among all aspects of fine arts.

Historically, this office has been inactive in financial support of art. When the art program was subsumed under one administrator, the financial support at the district level for art was dissolved under the coordinator of fine arts; but very slowly. Environmentally, the district has gone through a series of recurring financial problems brought on by a combination of rapid growth and declining state aid. Given the level of state aid we rely upon, any cut has a dramatic impact.

Curriculum

For central office administrators, curriculum is the largest area of responsibility and potential influence. Primary tasks involve trying to maintain a uniform district program that provides equal opportunity to all students, developing and recommending curriculum policies and guidelines, serving as a liaison to community groups, being an advocate and facilitator of arts education, promoting the district as an arts leader, and influencing organizations on behalf of the arts at all levels.

These duties involve educating oneself to the issues confronting each of the arts disciplines, finding local experts who can work with the district in developing responses to these challenges, organizing teacher committees to develop new curricular responses, and being an active participant in influencing support organizations. These organizations include parent groups, local arts groups, and state organizations in the arts or in general education. Additionally, one must keep active membership in appropriate national organizations to stay informed of national issues in the arts and general education. Both state and national curricular initiatives are pushing the role of coordinator of fine arts to a new dimension.

Illinois state law has expanded curricular responsibilities through the Education Reform Act of 1985, states that the fine arts is one of the primary purposes of schooling. The act defines fine arts as art, music, drama, and dance and mandates that school districts develop a learner assessment plan in all of these arts areas for Grades K-12. The plan must include establishment of goals, assessment of those goals, plans for improvement, and reporting of all aspects of the plan to a variety of publics. This sweeping legislative reform has changed many aspects of the arts curriculum. New questions are being asked: What do we do with drama and dance in the curriculum? How do we go about setting goals for each of these areas? How do we assess the arts? This has caused educators in Illinois to reassess what they believe should be involved in children's arts education. Not surprisingly, these new mandates have stirred considerable debate. But debate aside, school districts have been confronted with the need to seek solutions as these mandates have been implemented.

The biggest challenge to the coordinator of fine arts, especially in light of these new state and national initiatives, is the question of how to provide leadership in all arts areas. No matter how diverse the background of a coordinator of fine arts, I doubt that anyone could develop real expertise in all the areas of the fine arts.

Strategies

Earlier I stated that I believed central office administrative positions are evolutionary and dynamic in nature and that this is affected by history and environment. Understanding how history and environment have developed enables one to respond to the challenges of this leadership effectively. These dynamics define how the game of educational leadership is played locally. I believe that leadership is then developed through four broad categories: (a) personal credibility, (b) visibility, (c) autocracy versus empowerment, and (d) understanding and playing the game.

Personal Credibility

The coordinator of fine arts must deal with a wide variety of groups — both peers and superiors — both inside and outside the local educational establishment. Being an effective leader with these diverse groups requires a high standard of personal credibility. People must have confidence that you have a sense of fair play, a set of personal and professional values, a sense of honesty, and passion in your approach to people and problems.

No person can be all-knowing in every area. Having high personal credibility means *admitting what you don't know, spending time and effort to educate yourself,* and *seeking support from others who are experts in these areas.* Instead of being an all-knowing "guru," you are a facilitator of ideas and people. It also means being willing to admit an error or a mistake. We are all mortal, so it's no sin to make a mistake. Sometimes, however, the ego of self-importance interferes. If you are credible, people will respect you, even if they disagree with you.

Visibility

As a leader of each of the arts, it is critical that you are visible. First of all, be visible in classrooms. This is not meant to be a misguided notion of "big brother is watching," but an active expression of your interest. It's easy to become isolated from staff. Desk duties must not interfere with the need to see, be seen, listen, and talk to teachers.

Advocacy is also a big part of the job of coordinator. To be an advocate, you must be visible — gathering knowledge and information and supporting the diverse groups you represent. The garnering of support is an ongoing reciprocal process. It means maintaining contact across a broad base. A colleague of mine defines his role as administrator as one of "being there." "There" is wherever things are happening that can affect your programs.

As part of this visibility, it is essential to develop a vision. This vision should be global, and should involve two aspects: (a) a vision of *what is happening in all the arts* in your district and (b) a vision of *what is possible in the arts* in your district. These visions must be shared with the staff. The coordinator of fine arts deals with a variety of disciplines as well as teachers scattered to the four corners of a school district. A common vision that welds this diverse group into one is critical to continued success.

Autocracy Versus Empowerment

The Carnegie Report *A Nation Prepared* has gotten press recently with its recommendations that teachers be empowered to have more autonomy. The debate over the recommendations has raged on both sides. I think the era of autocratic leadership is over. The strength of an organization is its people. Empowerment to me means recognizing the importance of participation by individuals. It means working together on problems, working with committees, and using managed group processes to solve problems.

The use of a committee, however, involves gaining a clear sense of the issue before you and researching it through reading and discussion with others who are

174

experts on the issue. Then is the time to formulate the committee to deal with the problem and to guide them as they seek solutions. Committees must be broad based to include all the faculty factions, as well as those who might be able to influence decision making. There's nothing like a committee arguing a hot topic that affects committee members professionally. When an agreement is reached, many members may have experienced a change. The power of the group consensus is greater than any individual or faction.

Understanding and Playing the Game

Arts educators tend to be purists. They view their profession in pure terms, they view problems in pure terms, and they try to seek purist solutions. The ideas of compromise and game playing are repugnant to many arts educators, who seem to believe that these practices somehow denigrate their professional worth. Educational decision making is a game, one that, in my opinion, most arts educators have not been very good at playing. Purism keeps us as outsiders, inflexible and unwilling to face new challenges. Too often decisions have been made without us.

To be a participant in the game of educational decision making, you must have a clear sense of who you are, what you are, and what you want to be. That's the vision I spoke of earlier. Then you learn how the game is played in your district. How are decisions made? What are the procedures, processes, and purposes? Some of these are written rules, some are unwritten. Who are the "influencers?" They can be found in many places, on every side of the issue. Who are they and what do they want? Who is making the rules for the game? The more information you have about how the game is played, who is playing it, and what their interests are, the better chance you have to be a successful participant. Recognize, however, that it is a game. You will win and lose. You can't win without compromise, so it's important to know what you are willing to compromise without sacrificing the vision, and know that you cannot win all the time or do battle on every issue.

You cannot confront every issue in an uncompromising fashion and retain credibility. You don't want people to cringe and run for cover every time you enter the room for fear of your latest crusade or rampage. Wars are fought all the time in the central office. If an organization is good, it is diverse and filled with strong people. Learn how to help others fight their wars. Learn how to make your point with "influencers" without alienating them. Learn when you must fight a war, then do it without fear. In the end, your success relates to how you are perceived as a leader.

As the coordinator of fine arts develops game playing skills to a high level, he or she must be a powerful advocate for each of the arts. One of my art teachers paid me my greatest compliment (after the presentation of our elementary art proposal to the school board), when she said that I was a more powerful advocate for art education than an art educator could be. I was serving all the arts, not representing any one specialized interest.

175

Reinstituting the Elementary Art Program: A Case Study

The school district eliminated the elementary art program in1978 at the height of ongoing financial problems. At that time, elementary physical education and elementary music were dropped as well. The school board decided to solicit elementary classroom teachers regarding priorities for reestablishing these programs. The programs were prioritized as follows: music, physical education, *and then art*. This priority was followed. When I came to the position of coordinator, no proposal for elementary art had been formulated.

Obviously, I was not personally going to initiate a technical discussion of art education that would lead to an elementary art proposal. First of all, I had to find money; it was going to cost something to get a consultant and develop a teacher committee. I also had to become aware of what was going on in art education. What were the current issues and ideas? Although it took a couple of years, we did receive a grant. It meant going out in the state; talking to people; finding out what was going on in art education, who had money, and how I could get some of it; and so forth. During that time I was able to do some reading about issues in art education. I also did some research on who was out there in art education, who knew how to lead groups, and who could serve as a consultant for us.

Part of the process involved learning how the old elementary program worked, what its advantages and disadvantages were, and how it was received. Also, it was important to be aware of what was possible for our district, at least in broad terms. As music and physical education came back into the elementary schools, how was it done? Who led the process of proposing it? How was it received? Much information was needed before we entered the first stage of meetings. Then the committee had to be developed.

Every art teacher in the district wanted to be on the committee. That wasn't possible. The committee had to have broad representation. What did that mean? I decided to keep the committee at a manageable level of nine active members. There were four art teachers (all of whom at one time taught in the "old" elementary program), two elementary classroom teachers, and one parent. The parent ran a parent volunteer art program in her school that was successful and had spread through the district. Three elementary principals were asked to serve as ad hoc advisors. I was very frank with them. They could come to meetings if they wished, but what we really needed was to have them edit our proposal once it was written and write letters of support that would become part of the total package. This information was shared with the consultant. By the time our consultant began to meet with the committee, she knew everything there was to know about the task before us, who was involved, what attitudes were represented, what we hoped the outcome would be, and what forces we had to combat.

The meetings with staff were great! Raging debates, arguments big and small, led

176

to consensus on a proposal that was unique in some respects and embraced the best of what we could offer in art education. I chose to take a more passive role in these meetings for one reason: It was very important that I not be perceived by the committee as trying to influence outcomes directly: I was, however, actively pushing my concerns through the consultant. She and I spent time after each meeting going through every step of what had happened and what was going to happen next. I tried to provide an environment that was conducive to work, keeping the coffee pots filled, getting donuts, getting things typed as needed, providing proper materials and utensils, and providing lunch in the meeting room. In a very limited time, we needed to get a lot done, and we did it.

Once completed, the final product was taken through the proposal process. In our district this is a fairly standard procedure. Fortunately, we were able to expand the traditional process, thus creating more broad-based support for art education in the elementary schools and for our proposal. We asked the district Citizens Advisory Council to study our proposal and sought their support for it. This body functions at the discretion of the school board, and it usually does not study proposals such as ours. At the same time we asked the Instructional Council, consisting of teachers, administrators, and parents (who make recommendations on curricular issues to the superintendent), to become familiar with and to support the proposal.

The evening our proposal was presented, the school board heard a report from the Citizens Advisory Council, received letters of support from elementary principals, and heard a presentation of the broad-based writing committee, all strongly endorsing adoption of the proposal. When we had completed our presentation, the school board applauded us. This was the first time that had ever happened in this district! It was especially impressive coming on behalf of an elementary art proposal that began with serious controversies, and little support — but ended with a broad spectrum of support from art specialists, classroom teachers, principals, and parents. The board adopted the proposal.

Footnote

A Concluding Word

I never really wanted to be an administrator. After 17 years as an orchestra teacher, I became coordinator of fine arts. This was not a traditional career move for me or a realization of a life ambition, but more a quirk of circumstances. Just after my appointment was announced, I saw one of my former orchestra students. He approached me and asked, using a phrase I had immortalized in my classroom, "So, how does it feel to be 'one of those idiots downtown'?" It has caused me to pause and reflect many times about whether what I was doing was making a difference or merely adding to the idiocy. I do believe that I can make a positive difference for arts education from the position of coordinator of fine arts. When I stop believing that, I will quit. I certainly do not want to become "one of those idiots downtown."

16

Evaluation of Art Learning

SANDRA FINLAYSON

University of Oregon

Introduction

The visual arts teacher, specialist, and administrator is in a position to provide insight and leadership concerning the manner in which the learning of art students is evaluated. The suggested insight is based on a blend of experience, purpose, and information. There are several different aspects of evaluation of student learning to be considered.

This chapter will address two major topic areas prior to a concluding commentary with recommendations. The first section will focus on the evaluation context, with subsections on the numerical representation of student learning, evaluative approaches traditional to the art learning setting, and standards from the test and measurements field. The second major section will address trends, research, and issues germane to evaluation of the art student's learning. Subsections will include trends affecting evaluation in general education and research development within the field of art education regarding evaluation and/or assessment of student learning. Emerging issues shape recommendations when considerations of the meaning of art learning are juxtapositioned against evaluative practice.

The Evaluation Context

In what social/professional context do art educators and learners find themselves? In recent years we have been teaching and living through the back-to-basics movement with its accompanying emphasis on accountability. Demands for program accountability have filtered toward teacher accountability and, simultaneously, have held implications for student accountability.

Questions have multiplied. Can we legitimatize our position and our worth? What do art students learn? How can others be made aware of this learning? Is our present curriculum amenable to publicly represented evaluation?

The exploration of definable disciplines or domains of art learning has provided rallying posts. The possible deemphasis of student creative expression in the studio has left many concerned. The battle cry of "what can be tested will be taught" has elicited skirmishes and research forays from many positions.

In order to work critically, responsively, and creatively with accountability/ evaluation issues, we must know the traditional elements and principles of evaluative design. Three of these traditions have been selected for describing the evaluation context: (a) numerical representation of student learning, (b) evaluative approaches traditional to the art learning setting, and (c) meanings of test purpose, validity, and reliability.

Numerical Representation of Student Learning

Numerical representation of student learning has been present as an evolving tradition within general education throughout the 20th century. The statistician's enchantment with normal distributions and the public need for information about people in particular settings have served as springboards for the production of evaluative instruments that measure individual or group differences. These differences may be in readiness, something learned, a capability, a personality trait, a perceived "disability," a preference, or any other characteristic one is able to record, measure, and disclose. Overwhelmingly, the disclosures or outcomes are represented by a numerical score. That score may then be viewed relative to the scores

180

of other individuals, relative to particular standards, relative to the norm, relative to other capabilities within the examinee, or relative to other selected points of reference. Correlations between scores proliferate.

However, the score only stands for the characteristic or capability being represented. The score *is not* the characteristic, and the characteristic *is not* the score. Rather, the score is a numerical representation of a relationship of certain sampled responses of an examinee or group to other examinees or groups or to the self. The score is a relative construct and a mathematical construct.

Imagine numerical representation of student learning as an aspect of the mathematical metaphor, as opposed to a linguistic or visually symbolic metaphor. Any metaphorical structure simultaneously reveals and discloses ways of thinking, thus obscuring and eclipsing understanding and communication (Bowers, 1988; Lakoff & Johnson, 1980). In our enthusiasm to reach understanding through metaphor, we sometimes ignore the limitations of the metaphor in use. In the instance of numerical representation of art student learning, what the numbers don't tell us may well be more eloquently "spoken" by the visual.

And what the numbers do tell us and how they are "worked" is to be treated with respect. There are incredible, fantastic, extrapolative formulae that deal with interrelationships of data gained through measurement (Linn, 1989). Consider this as the mathematician's artwork. Certainly, numerical methods are many people's life work and are creatively pursued. Yet, still, the score is *not* the characteristic, and the characteristic is *not* the score.

Our habituation to the numerical representation of student learning based on the assumption of "normal" distribution has become so pervasive that we may be missing some very important points. Who is "normal"? Those whose numerical scores indicate some belonging to the group congregating about the mean are just as unique and given to being themselves as those "outliers" whose numerical representations rest at the extremities of the continuum. I've yet to meet anyone who is just like me! Or you! Or to have any two students who were so much the same as to merit representation by the same mark.

Also, we work in a field in which, for many teachers., idea, expression, and skill development within individual students (with respect to the capabilities with which they enter the classroom) has been a lifetime instructional ideal. Naturally, many of us feel uncomfortable with "marking," because we have felt the limitation it can have on student affect, motivation, and self-confidence (Gerhart, 1986, Hull, 1984).

Evaluative Approaches Traditional to the Art Learning Setting

Various resources are available that may broaden our understanding of evaluating student learning in the art education field. This subsection will include evaluation of the learner as apprentice (Gardner & Grunbaum, 1986), art education texts that have chapters on evaluation as resources (Day, 1985), Wilson's research on art test items relative to a taxonomy of art education behaviors (1971), and selected reports that documents groups of art tests (Clark, Zimmerman, & Zuermuehlen, 1987; Educational Testing Service, 1987; Finlayson, 1988; Gardner & Grunbaum, 1986; Johnson & Hess, 1971).

Evaluation of the learner as apprentice. Fundamental to the history of evaluation of the art student's learning is the apprenticeship. During the apprenticeship, evaluation was an ongoing process of communication between the less (or differently) experienced and the more experienced person. This communication may or may not have been verbally explicit. "Assessment ... was for the most part implicit: when the student advanced to a higher level of competence, fresh assignments would be posed and one's status subtly upgraded" (Gardner & Grunbaum, 1986, p. 6)

In my estimation, the apprenticeship, or a learning relationship between the less experienced and the more experienced and the communication within that relationship, is another way of talking about the evaluative character of ongoing critical exchange and guidance within the learning setting. The assessment may or may not be in words. It may be looking thoughtfully at that which the less experienced person is working on. It may be helping to shape the learner's hands in order to work with a particular tool. It may be purchasing materials in which there has been an expressed interest. It may be respectfully leaving the person alone to do his or her work. It may be the verbal exchange of the critique in which the less experienced person's purposes and process are explored. It may be clapping one's hands with excitement and joy as the less (or differently) experienced person reveals the visually delightful.

Selected art education texts with chapters on evaluation. It was determined that texts representative of handbooks for art educators that included chapters on evaluation (Day, 1985) would be reviewed. *Creative and Mental Growth* (Lowenfeld, 1957; Lowenfeld & Brittain, 1987) was included as representative of the position opposing grading of student artwork. *Approaches to Art in Education* (Chapman, 1978), *Children and Their Art* (Gaitskell, Hurwitz, & Day, 1982), and *Educating Artistic Vision* (Eisner, 1972) provided examples of approaches supporting multiple means of evaluating student learning.

The Lowenfeld (1957) and Lowenfeld/Brittain (1987) perspective is that of protection of the child/student's burgeoning expressive nature through the stance that "grading in art has no function" (1987, p. 175) and that the imposition of the teacher's values in an evaluative situation is meaningless to the child. In the most recent edition of *Creative and Mental Growth* (1987), Brittain cited several studies that support the idea that impending evaluation may negatively affect creative production, levels of student interest, or preference for complicated problems rather than those more easily mastered. (p. 175-176).

The concept of evaluation reaches beyond grading. With growth as a concurrent concern, whether or not evaluation is occurring may need to be ascertained. Chapman's work (1978) provides a plethora of ways for obtaining records of student work and learning that are subject to evaluation. These include portfolios of two-dimensional work, photographs of three-dimensional work, student diaries serving as records of responses to personal development, tape recordings of interviews and discussions, videotapes demonstrative of student involvement, and in-class sign-up sheets to chronicle responsible behaviors and activities. The interview and unobtrusive observation are cited as tools to more clearly disclose how the student thinks, feels, and sees. Anecdotal records and checklists regarding attitudes and knowledge are seen as possible forerunners to periodic summary reports of student growth made jointly by student and teacher. Tests are presented as a manner of checking factual knowledge and the student's ability to recognize, interpret, and apply concepts in a hypothetical situation.

Gaitskell, Hurwitz, and Day (Gaitskell, Hurwitz, & Day, 1982) present evaluative strategies from a substantively different perspective. The influence of the behavorial objective and Bloom's *Taxonomy* (1956) is strongly in evidence as the author links the predetermined, desired educational outcome with "formal" evaluations, including teacher written tests and standardized art tests. A few example questions are cited. However, these questions appear to seek responses representative of learning of the "knowledge level" (p. 496), with no example items directed at the comprehension, application, analysis, synthesis, or evaluation levels (Bloom, 1956). The potential triviality of test items that are easy to compose is noted.

The authors give recognition to the challenge and complexity of evaluating developing expressiveness and artistic creativity within the student. Approaches such as checklists, anecdotes, portfolios, personal files, and narrative progress reports are subsumed under the heading of "informal" methods of evaluation.

Eisner's work, *Educating Artistic Vision* (1972), presents information about evaluating student learning that, by the style of its authorship, underscores the notion of the importance of the development of critical thinking skills by promoting their use by the reader. Evaluation, testing, and grading are defined, and evaluation is seen as a process of securing information in order to improve the educational process. Testing is regarded as a method of sampling student abilities and grading as the assignment of a symbol indicative of the student's achievement relative to specified criteria. Eisner argues for the addition of brief evaluative statements with the parent/teacher conference to the grading process.

Eisner explores the relationship between the general view that an educator holds about evaluation and the view one holds about the educational process. Expressive objectives with unspecified outcomes in which valuable qualities within the work are discovered and displayed *after* the process necessitate a differing evaluative approach, classroom milieu, and level of risk taking than specified behavioral objectives. Eisner's approach runs parallel to Hull's (1984) in support of the development of the critical abilities of the student/learner with the end in mind of self-critique and evaluation of progress.

Eisner's way of identifying characteristics of landmarks in creative activity, vis-à-vis boundary pushing, inventing, boundary breaking, and aesthetic organizing, provides the reader with a basis for increased acuity in day-to-day recognition of creative activity. A variety of ways of collecting and recording information pertinent to the evaluative process are noted.

All of the aforementioned authors include summaries of stated goals of art education, philosophies, and/or rationales prior to their comments, essays, or chapters on the topic of evaluation of student learning. Each links, to varying degrees, the "means" (strategies, objectives, process) with the "ends" (disclosure, evidence of learning, grades) (Eisner, 1972). Each recognizes and provides examples of varying ways to gather information on student learning suitable for evaluative purposes; Chapman provides the greatest diversity in techniques suitable for the classroom teacher. Eisner provides the most verbal support for the unspecified outcome, with flexibility and artful teaching as keys to evaluation of this outcome. All of the writings support the notion that evaluation of student learning in the visual arts is grounded in a multiplicity of approaches.

Wilson's research on art test items relative to a taxonomy of art education behaviors. An investigation of Brent Wilson's work, which includes a variety of questioning techniques and test item construction appropriate for identifying learning relative to the visual arts (Wilson, 1971), provides additional evidence regarding the aspect of multiplicity in evaluative approaches.

Wilson's scholarly work (1971) provides a substantive statement on the complexity of harmonizing art education objectives with behavioralists' theories of evaluation. This work represents not only extensive research and a sensitive atunement to the realities of art education, but also the overlapping effect of Wilson's doctoral studies (Johnson & Hess, 1971) and his administrative role in the development of the art testing instrument of the National Assessment of Educational Progress (NAEP). Numerous scholars, art educators, and assessment specialists worked together to consider prospective items for the NAEP in art. (Note however, that the diversity of item types in Wilson's [1971] work did not carry over into practice in the NAEP in art. A much more narrow range of item types is found in the NAEP Released Exercise Set.)

A hybrid taxonomy, not unlike Bloom's (1956), appears in Wilson's listing of art education behaviors (1971). These "behaviors" include perception, knowledge, comprehension, analysis, evaluation, appreciation, and production. Test item examples with expanded descriptions of purpose for each of these classifications follow essays developing their meaning. Certain items given as examples of questioning approaches were developed by Wilson; however, most were pulled from existing tests, both published and unpublished, ranging in date from 1940 to 1971, with strong concentration in the late 1960s. Wilson also includes support for the "fluid teaching structure" (1971, p. 556) frequently occurring in the art classroom, for which behavioral objectives are not appropriate.

Selected reports that document or list art tests. In addition to Wilson's bibliography (1971), there are several resources that refer to art tests. Keep in mind that the purposes of art tests vary, as do the purposes of authors who group or list tests. An explanation about the meaning of test purpose will follow in the section on standards from the test and measurement field.

Tests in the Arts was published by CEMREL in 1971 (Johnson and Hess). The purpose of the document was to "locate, review, and develop a comprehensive index and set of abstracts of all known measuring instruments and tests applicable to the arts" as well as "to provide a brief but comprehensive overview of the various psychometric methodologies utilized in the development of the instruments" (p. 1). I do not think the second goal was met. Art, dance, drama, film, literature, music, and creativity are domains in which the tests were indexed. A "response taxonomy" in art is drawn from the review of 32 submitted tests that characterize the (a) item type or method of response and (b) the response construct (what, in actuality, the reviewers thought was being measured). Critical commentary is included, and suggestions for test developers are made. Most criticisms center around the lack of data about the validity and reliability and/or absence of technical manuals, test construction rationales, and awareness of standards from the test and measurement field.

The Educational Testing Service publication *Annotated Bibliography of Tests: Art* (1987) "contains tests for elementary school through adult level, including measures of pictorial creativity, achievement in design, interest and attitudes, knowledge, art education, art history, and aesthetics" (p. 1). Upon review of the test

185

abstracts in this listing, I would say that the purposes of the tests are either broader *or* more specific than those implied by the general, introductory statement. The tests were created by universities, independent research institutions, or individuals and are available from institutions, individuals, ERIC, ETS's test collection, or test marketing companies. Most publication dates fall after 1970, with a few older "classics" whose publication rights appear to have been purchased by a marketing company. Many of the tests have specific market appeal linked to the stated test purpose. No notation is given with regard to validity methodology or reliability estimates of specific tests.

Clark, Zimmerman, and Zurmeuhlen (1987) offer a more historical overview of art testing in the appended chronology of *Understanding Art Testing,* which includes art tests dating from the early 1900s. They list 45 tests, inventories, or scales designed to reveal a variety of characteristics related to artistry. Only a handful are also included in the ETS bibliography; several are included in the CEMREL document. Only dates, authors, and test titles are given. The exception is the considered treatment of the work of Norman C. Meier within the text. Meier, a psychologist, developed the "interlinkage theory of special ability" in which he sought to describe the characteristics, capabilities, processes and circumstances that lead to the development of artful competence (pp. 26-35). The articulation of this theory was grounded in the use of several testing instruments and inquiry methods in Meier's research and that of his graduate students over a 40-year period. This text also provides for informative backgrounding and offers the reader a section with dialogue among the authors regarding contemporary issues about testing and children's art abilities.

Gardner and Grunbaum (1986) included a listing of art tests in their report on the "assessment of artistic thinking" (pp. 20-24). They list the test title, certain dates of publication, and phrases that characterize the aim of the test, as they interpreted the test relative to their values and descriptions of "artistic thinking" (pp. 8-11). The listing includes 22 instruments (many of which have appeared in previously cited listings) grouped into tests of perception, knowledge, comprehension, appreciation, and production. The listing continues with a section on qualitative methods of assessment that notes (a) portrayal and responsive evaluation, (b) connoisseurship, (c) critique, and (d) portfolio. The list closes with the NAEP in the arts and includes critical commentary (i. e., "very good," "excellent," does not adequately judge") with reference to various subtests or stated items of the NAEP. The NAEP is treated in much greater depth both descriptively and critically within the text of the article. However, the main thrust of the article is the consideration of artistic thinking and its nonverbal qualities, with substantial support for the assessment practice that values practice, including production, perception, and reflection, and has qualities of being "intelligence-fair."

Another documentation of groups of visual arts assessment instruments is my

186

thesis, "A Critical Description of Selected State Level Visual Arts Assessment Instruments" (Finlayson, 1989a). The Council of Chief State School Officers (CCSSO) (1985) and the *NAEA News* (1986) reported that 12 states and the District of Columbia were conducting state-level visual arts assessments. I decided that it would be meaningful to critically review the testing instuments using Anastasi's "Suggested Outline for Test Evaluation" as a format.

The tests or responses that were gathered fell into three groups. In the first group, seven states were *not* conducting the reported state-level visual arts assessment (Delaware, Louisiana, Maryland, Missouri, South Carolina, and Wisconsin) or had visual arts assessment in the form of three or four questions included in a fine arts assessment (Pennsylvania).

The second group consisted of three states and the District of Columbia that showed more involvement with assessment but did not have tests. Indiana and Washington, D.C., indicated that they were in the process of developing an assessment instrument to pilot; Indiana has subsequently done so. Michigan was the first state to have researched art questions in 1977-1978 and had a report on a set of art-related questions, Hawaii had a comprehensive, qualitative model for art program evaluation (Lai & Shishido, 1987).

The third group consisted of three states that had actually conducted state-level visual arts assessments constructed from the Released Exercise Set of NAEP (Connecticut and Minnesota) or that had tests constructed by an independent research group and referenced to a particular curriculum (Utah). These tests were critically reviewed using Anastasi's outline for test evaluation, which required information about test publication, administration, type, purpose, standardization and norming procedures, presentation, scoring, reliability, and validity.

Altogether, over half of the states reported by CCSSO to be included in this "trend" toward state-level standardized assessment in the visual arts simply had been misrepresented somewhere in the survey process. Also, as was noted about the previously reviewed lists, there was a scarcity of evidence about the validity and reliability of the tests; one would have expected to find such evidence had there been accompanying technical manuals.

An understanding of test purpose, validity, and reliability is invaluable in determining the appropriateness and worth of the outcome of any evaluative approach or test. Art learners, teachers, specialists, and administrators benefit from a greater awareness of these test and measurement elements and principles.

Meanings of Test Purpose, Validity, and Reliability

Test purpose, validity, and reliability have been mentioned above. Although an explanation of the standards, theories, and vocabulary of the test and measurement field could be extensive (Anastasi, 1982; Linn, 1989), this article will contain only a brief section about test purpose, validity, and reliability. For the person seriously working with evaluation of student learning, further reading is recommended. Numerous test and measurement tests, are available, as well as a standards manual published and updated by the American Psychological Association (1974).

Test purpose. With regard to test purpose:

> *Anastasi noted in her chapter on educational testing that tests may be loosely categorized on the basis of the measurement of developed abilities. "All ability tests — whether they be designed as general intelligence tests, multiple aptitude batteries, special aptitude tests, or achievement tests — measure the level of development attained by the individual in one or more abilities," (1982, p. 394). Anastasi suggested that types of tests could be ordered along a continuum in terms of the degree of specificity of background experience that they presuppose. Course oriented and teacher made achievement tests would be considered to have the most specific information focus. Next would come broadly oriented achievement tests; then, verbal type intelligence and aptitude tests followed by non-language and performance tests; and, finally, "culture-fair" tests designed for use with persons of widely varied backgrounds.*
>
> *After a review of lists of art tests, it was found that tests existed at most of the points along the continuum [representing various purposes]. There were interest inventories, tests of creativity, occupational competency tests, attitude scales, cognitive assessments, nonverbal ability tests, diagnostic achievement tests, assessments of aesthetic judgement and perception, item banks, and measurable objectives pools.* (Finlayson, 1989a, pp. 21-22)

Being aware of the stated purpose of the test, methodology, or way of questioning is important in order to be able to consider whether validity is present and whether the information revealed is that which is desired or specified.

Validity. Validity is a dynamic. It's a manner of thinking about how "true" to one's purpose a particular way of questioning may be. May meaning and inference be appropriately drawn from the outcome of a question? What inferences about visual/ kinesthetic ways may be made from verbal questioning that is mathematically manipulated? Does that which is disclosed, revealed, shown, and recorded in the response match the purpose of the questioner? Does the questioner understand the nature of the construct/domain/paradigm/discipline profoundly enough to pose questions that reveal process or ways of thinking and knowing associated with the construct/domain/paradigm/discipline?

What are potential moral and ethical problems in the interpretations and use of outcomes? How will being asked these questions affect the respondent? Does the respondent want to be asked the questions? Will limitations unknown to the respondent be placed on the respondent based on the quality and characteristics of responses to questions that may or may not be suited to the respondent's abilities, experience, development, personality, or philosophy? Is the respondent respected? Validity signifies integrity.

Evaluative techniques and tests that have undergone a validation process will have an accompanying "technical manual" with a rationale statement, a description of evaluation/test purpose, questioning approaches, and descriptions of item structure relative to the desired response and underlying process. This information should be critically analyzed in light of the reviewer's or user's (both administrator and examinee) purposes and philosophy/bias. Different validation procedures are suited to different philosophies and biases (Messick, 1989; Wainer & Braun, 1988).

For instance, from my perspective, people who are considering using a particular way of questioning must also consider the respondent's rights in order for the validation dynamic to be other than disempowering. My primary concern with regard to questioning, evaluation, and testing within the learning setting is the learner's rights to continued enthusiasm and confidence about learning. If an evaluative instrument strips the learner of those rights, I would consider that instrument to be invalid. "Tests that impinge on the rights and life chances of individuals are inherently disputable" (Cronbach, 1988).

Another example may be the matching of Hausman's (1988) concern for the continuance of expressive objectives in the teaching of art with the theory of "systemic validity" (Frederiksen & Collins, 1989). Hausman wrote,

> ... Our approaches to evaluating educational outcomes need to be designed for and responsive to a wide range of educational objectives. What I fear is happening is that the apparent ease and objectivity in measuring instructional objectives is fostering learning activities that would elicit such outcomes; conversely, the more openended nature of expressive objectives and the unavailability of tests to evaluate such outcomes is discouraging learning activities to meet expressive objectives. (p. 40)

A systemically valid test or evaluative approach would promote a learning environment with an accompanying sense of integrity toward curricular rationale. For instance, if an instructional purpose were to foster expressive objectives and student design capability through the creation of an interlocking pattern for a textile, a written vocabulary quiz on the elements and principles of design would not be

189

systemically valid and could misdirect instructional and learning energies. The learner — the examinee — may develop abilities to define terms but lack the skills of sketching, layout, planning the repeat, considering composition, visualizing positive and negative space, processing through trial and error, or developing visual concepts. In other words, the higher level processing skills of visual concept development may be sacrificed to more efficiently counted verbal recall skills. When an unintended evolution in curricular content occurs because of an evaluative tool, the tool is not systemically valid.

Reliability. Reliability is presented as a measure indicating the extent to which individual differences in test scores are attributable to "true" differences in the characteristics under consideration and the extent to which score differences are attributable to chance errors. If similar individuals had similar scores on a given test, if an individual had similar scores on the same test after having been retested, or if an individual had similar scores on two different tests that purport to measure the same construct, score correlations could indicate test reliability (Anastasi, 1982).

When considering the reliability of testing instruments relative to the art learning construct, we encounter a dilemma. Those traits that contribute most dramatically to score unreliability or error variance are traits that have been and are considered highly valuable by artists and art educators. As Greer and Hoepfner (1986) stated in reference to the tests used to disclose the achievement of program objectives in a discipline-based project, "The test types discussed ... have been selected by the authors for discussion because they have been shown to be *effective and efficient,* and they minimize dependence on unwanted variables, such as *creative expression, interests, attitudes, and values"* (p. 47).

Reliability theories have been intrinsically rooted in the statistical practices of ordering and comparison. One may manipulate the configuration of item types during the standardization process of test production in order to create a more robust numerical representation of reliability — in other words, throw out items that elicit erratic responses or individual differences. Hence, we read of suggestions of eliminating creative expression, interests, attitudes, and values from the educational outcome in order to facilitate a mathematical/statistical outcome. It is possible to artistically rethink appropriate reliability theory.

One other very important point: It is entirely possible for a test or questioning approach to be "reliable" without being valid. Reliability can be manipulated, mathematically extrapolated, and numerically represented, whereas validity addresses whether or not the test meets its stated purpose with integrity. Validity requires conscious deliberation, passion, awareness, and communication between and among assessment specialists and content area specialists. Beware the test or evaluative approach that substantiates its reliability effusively and makes scant

190

mention of the validation process.

Trends, Research, and Recommendations

An administrator or supervisor in the educational field, needs to keep informed of trends, research, and recommendations that may bear on the issues at hand. Given the topic of the evaluation of the art student's learning, three topic areas come to mind. The first is the topic of trends affecting general education that directly or indirectly relate to evaluation of art student learning. The second is research within the field of art education regarding evaluation and/or assessment of student learning. The third is the area of issues shaping recommendations when considerations of the meaning of artful learning adjoin evaluative practice.

Trends Affecting General Education

Although there are numerous trends or movements that affect general education, for the purposes of this paper two will be mentioned that seem to have strengthened my position on evaluating art learning. The first topic is the critical thinking skills movement; the second topic is public controversy about standardized testing.

Critical thinking skills movement. Developing Minds: A Resource Book for Teaching Thinking, edited by Costa, was chosen as a resource representing aspects of the thinking skills movement. Several comments arose.

The text contains articles with models of ways of thinking about thinking or teaching thinking, both theoretical and practical, as well as reviews of numerous packaged curricular approaches. I was constantly reminded of art criticism models and theories, and the critical exchanges that occur on a regular basis when the less experienced person and the more experienced person are working together on idea development.

It's refreshing to see a focus on *how,* rather than *what,* people think. A paradox: The critical thinking skills movement is, in part, in response to planetary accountability issues, national and international assessments, and governmental edicts. How can this country's students be prepared as competitive citizens of the world? The learning environments in which the quality of each learner's thought is developed and explored tend to be more cooperative and participatory than competitive.

There are tremendous parallels between this "new" emphasis and description of transferable "thinking skills" and characteristics of the development of artistic competencies, aesthetic awareness, and critical skills. One has only to compare

Costa's (1985) "indicators of intellectual growth" (pp. 289-290) and Norman C. Meier's "interlinkage theory of special ability" (Clark, Zimmerman, & Zurmuehlen, 1987, pp. 26-35). Toss in a little "artistic thinking" (Gardner & Grunbaum, 1986), and one begins to see commonalities such as the desirability of perseverance, idea development, creative imagination, perceptual skills, and aesthetic experiencing as means and end.

Another major commonality is that it is no easier to disclose, record, and assign numerical values to critical thinking skills than to artful learning. In discussing limitations concerning the development of standardizable testing to disclose critical thinking, Kneedler notes: "Recall questions are easy to write and can be made more difficult by focusing on esoteric aspects of subject material. If what is tested is what is taught, teachers may then address trivial aspects of the content area in the classroom" (1985, p. 279). This concern is not unlike that voiced by Hamblen in "If It Is to be Tested It Will Be Taught: A Rationale Worthy of Examination" (1988). Both authors voice concern for what may be remedied by systemic validity (Frederiksen & Collins, 1989), as noted in the validity section.

Public controversy about standardized testing. Systemic validity is a fairly new term, but the concern that it addresses is an old and widespread issue: Tests drive the curriculum. Shanker expressed concern for "curriculum alignment" of "content, textbooks, lesson plans ... geared to items that will be on the test" (1988); Quellmalz called for better methods for testing higher-order thinking skills (1985), and Koretz asked whether standardized tests are exaggerating achievement and distorting instruction (1988).

We not only have plenty of room for controversy regarding the impact of testing on curricular quality and content, we have massive numbers of people involved and we have big business. It's "estimated that elementary and high school students take more than 100 million standardized tests a year" (Fiske, 1988). *One hundred million* tests are purchased, administered, and scored with scores left open to interpretation.

I would suggest that the field of art education has been able to maintain a much higher level of teacher authenticity and learner and curricular integrity partly because of our lack of involvement with the testing "industry". I would go further to suggest that is a good time for us to clearly articulate appropriate evaluative instruments and approaches. We have an opportunity to learn from others' mistakes and provide leadership for those fields that are beginning to place higher value on revealing process, idea development, and the aesthetic of learning. Anachronistic evaluative practice may be avoided through careful review of the outcomes of contemporary research in the evaluation of art learning.

Research Regarding Evaluation of Art Learning

Six projects were chosen in the area of research in the field of art education that have as a primary component the evaluation or assessment of student learning. The projects reflect a variety of sponsorships, with national, university, private, and individual initiation. Brief descriptions and critical commentary will be given regarding the National Assessment of Educational Progress in Art (NAEP), standardized test promotion and development related to a discipline-based art education institution, a proposed National Endowment for the Arts achievement test development project at the University of Illinois at Champaign-Urbana, Beattie's research on the Dutch model of production assessment, Mac Gregor's review of art assessment in Britain, and evaluation related to the collaborative effort Arts Propel.

National Assessment of Educational Progress in Arts.

One of the largest research projects in the evaluation of art learning through standardized techniques has been the National Assessment of Educational Progress in Art, which was administered in 1974-1975 and again in 1978-1979. During the first assessment a sample of 9-, 13-, and 17-year-olds were tested and questioned to reveal knowledge of traditional forms of Western art, art production skills, sex differences in artistic achievement, and the relationship of achieving cognitive or affective objectives and to experiences with art. The emphasis was somewhat different in the second assessment, with categories of valuing art, knowledge of art history, responding to art (perceiving, describing, analyzing, and judging), and design/drawing skills. Experiential questions regarding visits to museums, numbers and types of art classes, and materials that the learner had used were also included (Finlayson, 1989a).

The test content and style reflects a behavioralist orientation with no unspecified/ open-ended objectives or attention to the ongoing expressive capabilities of the learner. The performance/drawing items were time limited, and, to my knowledge, the scoring procedures did not take into account differentiating levels of the young person's experience (information that had been gathered through other questions).

One fundamental question to be asked about item content and scoring within the NAEP would be "What philosophical orientation toward valuing art was represented or considered to be correct?" For example, in one item, if a young person chose one of two drawings as being "better" on the basis its realistic qualities, item constructors considered this to be the use of an unacceptable "mimetic standard" (Ward, 1982, p. 15). The artistic philosophy of the examinee and, possibly, the artistic philosophy of the public school art educator would have been discounted because of values inherent in item content, response specification, and scoring.

Some suggestion has been made about statistically reprocessing the data gathering by the NAEP in art; however, given a 12-year time lag and the impossibility of establishing content validity relative to a correlating sample of 1978 art curricula, it may not be advisable. Today's student population is not a replication of yesterday's standardization sample, and ongoing studio production was not touched upon with either of the two assessment instruments. Much would depend on the rationale for reprocessing. The NAEP in art may best be considered as experimental and as an example of a past approach to the possible assessment of art learning.

Standardized test promotion and development related to a discipline-based art education orientation. The disciplines of art history and art criticism may lend a broader integrity and motivation for studio production or stand alone, and an increased awareness of aesthetic experiencing holds great promise for enhanced life qualities. A structured, discipline-based orientation to art education is supported by some as a potential provider of an articulated, sequential curriculum that could be standardized and highly verbal, thereby easing the evaluation of student learning through testing. The four disciplines commonly cited in this movement are studio production, aesthetics, art criticism, and art history.

A test was written and piloted through sponsorship from the Getty Center for Education in the Arts with the express purpose "to assess the growth of students in the four disciplines of DBAE" (Greer & Hoepfner, 1986, p. 47). The test was to be used primarily as a tool in evaluating the effectiveness of instructional approaches and content rather than student achievement per se. At last report, it was due for revisions but considered by Greer and Hoepfner to have revealed "issues which were critical to the institute" (p. 47). I have not seen the instrument and do not know what specifications were given to the art learning constructs or disciplines. As previously mentioned, the reliability methodology required a minimized sensitivity to "creative expression, interests, attitudes, and values" (p. 47).

A proposed achievement test development project. One proposed research component of the politically and financially sanctioned National Arts Education Research Center (so stated because funding came from the National Endowment for the Arts and the U. S. Department of Education) at the University of Illinois at Urbana-Champaign involved the development of an achievement test in the visual arts. It was planned to develop four specific prototype tests in the areas of (a) critical processes and judgment, (b) organizational elements and principles, (c) history of art, and (d) art techniques and processes. Taxonomies of standards and performance objectives, along with sets of annotated objectives, were to be written as a part of the test specification process (Leonard, 1989).

194

The project began in 1988 and was originally scheduled for completion in the fall of 1990. NEA funding ceased after the first year. There had been an opportunity to develop a rationale for testing and to collect data on art testing within the United States, Holland, and England. However, the project did not continue to include articulation of an art learning construct or specification of taxonomies (T. Zernich, personal communication, May 1, 1990).

Beattie's research on the Dutch model of production assessment. Beattie conducted an on-site ethnographic study of the art assessment process in Holland. Her work has descriptively and critically reviewed the standardized assessment of art production (Beattie, 1989), history of art, and analysis of art (Beattie, 1990) as content areas. The assessment of studio production included the posing of thematic questions with the "student artist" responding with artwork and artist's statements in a portfolio presentation. Several weeks were given for portfolio development. Portfolios were reviewed and marked by both a visiting teacher and the classroom teacher.

Beattie states that the history of art and analysis of art assessment components belong to what is termed the "reflective domain" in Holland. A thematic and contextual understanding of art history is desired, and the examinee's critical skills of description, analysis, and interpretation are considered fundamental to the analysis of art. Classroom teachers work in committees to develop exams structured around themes that embrace a variety of art forms. Again, two teachers are involved in marking the exams, which serve as a summative evaluation as well as a didactic tool.

Critical commentary about the Dutch program included observations about the lack of multicultural visual content, the lack of an evaluative component that addresses aesthetics, and the lack of tables of specifications (generally found in a technical manual) that would lead to more proportional representation of actual learned content and behaviors within the tests (content validity).

MacGregor's review of art assessment in Britain. MacGregor's study of art assessment in Britain provides an informative report and analysis of a system-wide art learning assessment. Uniformity of practice is encouraged within regional examining boards that service area schools. The boards include examiners who work with committees to develop examination papers, moderators who ensure equity through comparison of grading outcomes, and assessors who validate marks given by classroom teachers.

Mac Gregor also reports regionally varying content, and the paper is rich with descriptions of possible art learning outcomes, evaluative criteria, and commentary

195

on cooperation and communication between and among examination board members and teachers. Varying administrative structures provide examples of how personnel are organized within particular regions or political entities.

Two policies may be of particular value given our current considerations of assessment issues. One is the principle of differentiation (pp. 12-13), through which the range of student capabilities and experiences is accommodated equitably in the evaluation process. A positive emphasis is placed on what the student knows, does, and understands rather than a negative emphasis on what the student does not know, does not do, or does not understand. A second policy of interest was related to the international baccalaureate in which the visiting examiner is explicitly instructed to become familiar with the teacher's philosophy and engage in dialogue with the student prior to marking the student's work.

The paper is a solid and articulate report. Mac Gregor's curiosity has evidenced equity and an impeccable sense of timing.

Arts Propel. The arts propel project is a collaborative effort with support from the Arts and Humanities Division of the Rockefeller Foundation, Harvard Project Zero, the Educational Testing Service, and the Pittsburgh Public Schools. Assessment tools were developed that sought to reveal learning and growth in the artistic competencies of production, perception, and reflection (Gardner, 1989).

Let me clearly state that I support this orientation toward valuing aspects of the artistic process and feel that it is of great benefit in strengthening the learner. However, I found myself reacting to parodoxical difficulties in the validity of three specific evaluative procedures reportedly in use within the Arts Propel field project (Gitomer, Sims-Gunzenhauser, Wolf, & Dobbs, 1989). First, it was stated that Arts Propel philosophically supported an orientation promoting an awareness of artistic development and the use of formative evaluation. However, rating scales had been introduced as an evaluative technique with the potential consequence that some learners would be recorded as being less capable than others without regard to development or experience. When the stated technique of an evaluation does not match the stated philosophy of a program, a validity problem is created. Second, learners had been asked to write about their process in the reflection component. This writing was scored on the basis of the sophistication and articulation of verbal skills and the student's linguistic and verbal narrative capabilities were revealed. Those less skilled in writing and verbal expression were downgraded. When the stated goal of a program is the development of visual artistic competencies through production, perception, and reflection, a literary evaluation would not be valid. Finally, there was an example of numerically rating student artwork based on visual content. A work that expressed the theme of drug- and alochol- related social problems was rated as less valuable than a "pretty picture." There appeared to be a

196

lack of valuing or understanding of instrumentalism, expressivism, or artwork as socially revelant on the part of the "item" constructor or interpreter. Evaluative techniques that are responsive to or respectful of the range of possible artistic styles, philosophies, or expressions create validity problems.

I asked Gitomer about my criticisms, and he commented that the rating scales were used in self-assessment as well as teacher assessment, with the goal being student understanding of criteria in relationship to personal artwork. He stated that the written reflection gave the learner an opportunity to provide context, show understanding of concepts, and describe personal artistic decisions. He indicated that Arts Propel hopes to broaden the student's awareness of stylistic variations in artwork. He agreed that there were difficulties in the validation process and expressed concern for the increase in art educators' dependence on numerical ratings (D. Gitomer, personal communication, July 3, 1990).

The aforementioned evaluative techniques could be considered to be reliable. They work consistently. Interrater reliability would be easy enough to facilitate. However, in my opinion, these evaluative procedures are not as positively representative of the "intelligence-fair" ideal put forth by Gardner and Hatch (1989) as would be possible. Intelligence-fairness as an ideal means revealing the learning through the modality in which it was learned. For instance, I can't talk to you about my dance; I can perform my dance, motion and physicality being the modality. The modality is the vehicle that reveals a particular capability, competency, or intelligence (Gardner & Hatch, 1989).

Recommendations

Many, positive outcomes have been forthcoming from the programs and areas of research featured in the preceding sections. Many young people are benefiting from more active involvement in the development of their artistry, critical articulation, knowledge about art, aesthetic growth, and ability to develop visual themes and in the strengths of their perceptions. In part, this is a result of changes in evaluative practice. More art educators are becoming aware of assessment issues and traditions.

As an art educator having been involved in a lengthy period of studies of art assessments, and techniques and theories of educational measurement, I've formed several recommendations regarding issues of evaluating art learning. I'll try to be brief and to the point. However, I am under no illusion that any of these recommendations will be easily actualized. Synthesis, theoretical reformulation, communication, and integrity are time-consuming endeavors.

The following recommendations are respectfully submitted to the reader. In keeping with the tone of the first sentence of this chapter, the recommendations are written in the form of objectives for the insightful leader/participant. The recommendations are also written in such a way that they may serve as topics for discussion during the process of developing evaluative approaches or affirmations for advocacy of art education.

1. Foster an Awareness of Teachers' and Learners' Artistic Philosophies While Planning Assessment Approaches. Chapman's work on "The Bearing of Artistic and Educational Commitments on the Teaching of Art" (1979) can serve as a basis for explorations of varying belief systems and their implications for learner/ teacher relationships and learner outcomes. Chapman's metatheoretical descriptions (1988) of the realist, idealist, existentialist, and experimentalist orientations provide further assistance for the leader who wishes to promote explicit recognition of artistic values relative to curricular content.

Jones's research (1988), based on assiduous studies of the interconnectedness of historical and contemporary schools of philosophy, can aid us in discerning theoretical underpinnings of current art education practice. Jones advocates the empowerment of a position valuing multiple perspectives through respect for the philosophical grounding of all participants in educational settings.

Maitland-Gholson's practice and writings (1988, 1989) provide creative and practical advice to design and implement an art learner assessment with teachers. A first step is to "identify and describe participants' (teachers') attitudes and beliefs about art, art curriculum, assessing student performance and outcomes in art" (1989, p. 1).

2. Promote Communicative, Equitable, and Participatory Work Settings. Planning and implementing assessment orientations at the local, regional, state, or national levels benefit from the recognition and participation of all parties affected (Jones, 1988; Mac Gregor, 1990; Maitland-Gholson, 1988, 1989). Also, the recognition of art education as a discipline (Ewens, 1988) and a genuine respect and appreciation for classroom art teachers and learners further strengthen one's position as an advocate for artistic learning.

3. Promote the Writing of Assessment Rationales and Specifications by Those Familiar With Both Validation Process and Artistic Learning. One may not assume that assessment specialists have a grounding in what it means to learn and develop artistically. And, conversely, one may not assume that art educators put in the position of working with evaluation of art learning are versant with the techniques and theories of educational measurement. Communication and learning advance the development of cross-disciplinary integrity.

Also, it helps to be acutely aware that the assessment specialist frequently operates from principles and assumptions suitable to a numerical/mathematical/

statistical paradigm, whereas the art educator and art learner frequently operate from principles and assumptions suitable to the visual/expressive/aesthetic paradigm; somehow, we attempt to reach one another through and between the principles of a verbal/financial/political paradigm. Dorn (1990) has done substantive work on the gathering and review of resources of import to the art educator involved in "solving significant evaluative problems". (p.41)

4. Stimulate Further Articulation of the Art Learning Construct. What does it mean to learn and develop artistry? Imagine the essence of mind and spirit in one's own personal artistry, and you may begin to consider the primary issues of articulating an art learning construct. This learning may manifest itself in imagery; it may be internal, as the unseen aesthetic of process as one works with motion, senses, media, and self or others; or it may be evident in endless other ways.

Resources abound that can aid us in naming this learning/development of artistry to provide clarification for those who have not experienced it. One may look to those who conceive of *cognition* as an umbrella term that "subsumes various modes of knowing — conceptual, perceptual, affective, metaphoric, intuitive, and kinesthetic" (Hamblen, 1983, p. 177), or those who lean heavily on resources that link the arts and cognition (Crozier & Chapman, 1984; Madeja, 1978; Perkins & Leondar, 1977; Sommerville & Hartley, 1986; Washburn, 1983). Meier's aesthetic intelligence (Clark, Zimmerman, & Zurmuehlen, 1987), Gardner and Grunbaum's artistic thinking (1986), and Arnheim's *Visual Thinking* (1969) are all resources that could serve us in specifying what art learning may be.

Ultimately, we need articulate aspects of a learning construct of artistry in the interest of the learner and in the interest of our personal artistry, both visual and pedagogical.

5. Rethink Reliability Theory and Consider Self- and Group-Generated Criteria for Evaluation. It is possible to artistically rethink appropriate reliability theory. Most precepts of traditional reliability theory do not work when the unexpected, individualized, or unspecified outcome is desired.

The individual learner or group of learners is capable of generating criteria or standards for the completed work while a course of study is in process. I refer to this as self-generated or group-generated criteria and have had wonderful results in learner outcomes and increased sense of learner competence. In general, after becoming familiar with curricular content, people know what they want or need to learn, and they want to live up to their potential. Perhaps a new reliability could be interpreted, in part, as a steadfastness toward one's self or one's colleagues' sensibilities.

Good luck with your work in disclosing art learning. When in doubt as to an

199

appropriate direction, bring your artistic self to the question and remember the students who have touched your heart.

References

American Psychological Association. (1974). *Standards for educational and psychological tests*. Washington, DC: Author

Anastasi, A. (1982). *Psychological testing*. New York: Macmillan.

Arnheim, R. (1969). *Visual thinking*. Berkeley and Los Angeles, CA: University of California Press.

Beattie, D. K. (1989, April). *Standardized assessment of art production: Lessons from the Dutch model*. Paper presented at the National Art Education Association annual conference, Washington, DC.

Beattie, D. K. (1990, April). *Development and implementation of a standardized theoretical examination at the secondary level: Lessons from the Dutch model*. Paper presented at the National Art Education Association annual conference, Kansas City, MO.

Bloom, B. S. (Ed.). (1956). Taxonomy of educational objectives. The classification of educational goals. *Handbook I: Cognitive Domain*. New York: David McKay.

Bowers, C. A. (1988). *The cultural dimensions of educational computing. Understanding the non-neutrality of technology*. New York: Teachers College Press.

Chapman, L. (1979). The bearing of artistic and educational commitments on the teaching of art. In G. L. Knieter & J. Stallings, (Eds.), *TheTeaching Process & Arts and Aesthetic*. St. Louis: CEMREL.

Chapman, L. (1978). *Approaches to art in education*. New York: Harcourt Brace Jovanovich.

Chapman, L. (1988, April). Meta-theoretical basis for themes in *"Approaches to Art in Educacation."* Chart prepared for Theoretical Concepts Session, National Art Education Association conference, Los Angeles.

Clark, G., Zimmerman, E., & Zurmuehlen, M. (1987). *Understanding art testing*. Reston, VA: National Art Education Association.

Clark, G. A., Day, M. D., & Greer, W. D. (1987). Discipline-based art education: Becoming students of art. *Journal of Aesthetic Education, 21* (2), 129-193.

Costa, A. L. (Ed.). (1985). *Developing minds: A resource book for teaching thinking*. Alexandria, VA: Association for Supervision and Curriculum Development.

Council of Chief State School Officers. (1985). *Arts, education and the states, a survey of state education policies,* Washington, DC: Author.

Cronbach, L. J. (1988). Five perspectives on the validity argument. In H. Wainer & H. I. Braun, (Eds.), *Test Validity* (pp. 3-18). Hillsdale, NJ: Erlbaum.

Crozier, W. R., & Chapman, A. J. (1984). *Cognitive processes in the perception of art*. Amsterdam, the Netherlands: Elsevier Science Publishing Company.

Day, M. D. (1985). Evaluating student achievement in discipline-based art programs. *Studies in Art Education,* 26 (4), 232-240.

Dorn, C. M. (1990). An annotated bibliography on evaluation and testing in visual arts education. *Design for Arts in Education, 91* (3), 34-41.

Educational Testing Service. (1987). ETS test collection. *Annotated bibliography of tests: Art.* Princeton, NJ: Author.

Eisner, E. W. (1972). *Educating artistic vision*. New York: Macmillan.

Ewens, T. (1988). In art education, more DBAE equals less art. *Design for Arts in Education, 89* (4), 35-42.

Finlayson, S. J. (1988). Can we speak the language? Toward an understanding of standardized testing techniques with an examination of states' approaches to assessment of the visual art student. *In Working papers in art education*. Iowa City: University of Iowa.

Finlayson, S. J. (1989a). A critical description of selected state level visual arts assessment instruments (Master's thesis, University of Oregon, 1988). *Masters Abstracts International,* 2702

Finlayson, S. J. (1989b, April). *Standardized testing in art education, structures and meanings: Fostering an awareness of possibilities and limitations*. Paper presented at the National Art Education Association annual convention, Washington, D. C.

Fiske, E. B. (1988, May 1). Testing has become an educational mania. *The New York Times,* p. 2E.

Frederiksen, J. R., & Collins, A. (1989). A systems approach to educational testing. *Educational Researcher, 18*(9), 27-32.

Gaitskell, C. D., Hurwitz, A., & Day, M. (1982) *Children and their art* (4th ed.). New York: Harcourt Brace Jovanovich.

Gardner, H. (1988, May). *Assessment in context: The alternative to standardized testing*. Cambridge, MA.: Harvard Project Zero.

Gardner, H. (1989). Zero-based arts education: An introduction to Arts Propel. *Studies in Art Education, 30*(2), 71-83.

Gardner, H., & Grunbaum, J. (1986). *The assessment of artistic thinking: Comments on the National Assessment of Educational Progress in the Arts*. Paper commissioned by the Study Group on the National Assessment of Student Achievement. (ERIC Document Reproduction Service No. ED 279 677.

Gardner, H., & Hatch, T. (1989). Multiple intelligences to to school: Educational implications of the theory of multiple intelligences. *Educational Researcher, 18*(8), 4-10.

Gerhart, G. (1986). Effects of evaluative statements on artistic performance and motivation. *Studies in Art Education, 27*(2), 61-72.

Gitomer, D., Sims-Gunzenhauser, A., Wolf, D., & Dobbs, S. (1989, April). *Arts PROPEL; A progress review*. Paper presented at the National Art Education Association annual convention, Washington, DC.

Greer, W. D., Hoepfner, R. (1986). Achievement testing in the visual arts. *Design for Arts in Education, 88*(1), 43-47.

Hamblen, K. S. (1983). The cognitive umbrella. *Studies in Art Education, 24*(3), 177-183.

Hamblen, K. A. (1988). If it is to be tested, it will be taught: A rationale worthy of examination. *Art Education, 41*(5), 59-62.

Hausman, J. J. (1988). Back to the future: Reflections on present-day emphasis in curriculum and evaluation. *Art Education, 41*(2), 37-41.

Hoepfner, R. (1984). Measuring student achievement in art. *Studies in Art Education, 25*(4), 251-258.

Hull, C. (1984). Marking: A critical alternative. *Journal of Curriculum Studies, 16*(2), 155-164.

Jones, B. J. (1988). Art education in context. *Journal of Multi-Cultural and Cross-Cultural Research in Art Education, 6*(1), 38-54.

Johnson, T. J. & Hess, R. J. (Eds.). (1971). *Test in the arts*. St. Louis: CEMREL.

Kneedler, P. (1985). California assesses critical thinking. In A. L. Costa (Ed.), *Developing Minds: A Resource Book For Teaching Thinking*. Alexandria, VA: Association for Supervision and Curriculum Development.

Koretz, E. (1988). Arriving in Lake Wobegon: Are standardized tests exaggerating achievement and distorting instruction. *American Educator, 12*(2), 8-15.

Lai, M. K. & Shishido, J. (1987, April). *A model for evaluating art education programs*. Paper presented at the annual meeting of the American Educational Research Association.

Lakoff, G., & Johnson, M. (1980). *Metaphors we live by*. Chicago: University of Chicago Press.

Leonard, C. (1989, April). *The National Arts Education Research Center: University of Illinois*. Paper presented at the National Art Education Association annual convention. Washington, DC.

Linn, R. L. (Ed.). (1989). *Educational measurement* (3rd ed.). New York: Macmillan.

Lowenfeld, V. (1957). *Creative and mental growth* (3rd ed.). New York: Macmillan.

Lowenfeld, V., & Brittain, W. L. (1987). *Creative and mental growth* (7th ed.) New York: Macmillan.

Mac Gregor, R. (1990, April). *Art assessment in Britain: Structure, content, and administration*. Paper presented at the National Art Education Association annual conference, Kansas City, MO.

Madeja, S. S. (Ed.). (1978). *The arts, cognitive, and basic skills*. St. Louis: CEMREL.

Maitland-Gholson, J. (1988). *Research and development of student assessment instruments and strategies: 1987-1988 year end report*. Eugene, OR: 4J School District.

Maitland-Gholson, J. (1989, November). *Research in evaluation: Assessment models*. (Presentation in a research methodology course). Eugene: University of Oregon.

Messick, S. (1989). Validity. In R. L. Linn (Ed.), *Educational measurement*. (pp. 13-104). New York: Macmillan.

National Art Education Association. (1986, December). *NAEA News*, pp. 1-28.

Perkins, D., & Leondar, B. (1977). *The arts and cognition*. Baltimore: Johns Hopkins University Press.

Quellmalz, E. S. (1985). Needed: Better methods for testing higher-order thinking skills. *Educational Leadership*. pp. 29-35.

Shanker, A. (1988, April 24). Where we stand: Exams fail the test. *The New York Times*, p. E7.

Sommerville, S. C., & Hartley, J. L. (1986). Art. In R. F. Dillon & R. J. Sternberg, *Cognition and instruction*. New York: Harcourt Brace Jovanovich.

Ward, B. J. (1982). A look at students' art achievement: Result from the National Assessment of Educational Progress. *Visual Arts Research, 16*, 12-18.

Washburn, D. K. (1983). *Structure and cognition in art: New directions in archeology*. Cambridge, England: Press Syndicate of the University of Cambridge.

Wilson, B. (1971). Evaluation of learning in art education. In B. Bloom, T. Hastings, & G. Madaus, *Handbook on formative and summative evaluation of student learning*. New York: McGraw-Hill.

17

A Status Report of the Art Program: Anchorage School District, Alaska

MYRNA CLARK

Anchorage, Alaska, School District

Background

An art evaluator from outside the state was contracted through the school district Curriculum and Instructional Services Division to examine the art and photography programs of the Anchorage School District's junior and senior high schools. The purpose of the study was to compile information and make recommendations in a report for use by the art education staff, building administrators, and the districtwide administration. This 6-month-long study was conducted by Anne Taylor of School Zone North, Inc.

The primary objective was to develop an in-depth written document reflecting the evaluated operation, achievements, and problems that could be used by individual units and the district art office for long-range planning in the overall program and facilities. The program was considered in relationship to the environment in which it operates; also, however, an experienced art educator objectively evaluated the program with an eye for change, synergism, and the future. A summary of the evaluation process and recommendations of general interest are included here to promote ideas that might be adapted in a districtwide art program for any school district.

Description of the District

Despite a decline in Anchorage's population from 259,000 in 1985 at the peak of the oil boom to the current 225,000, school enrollment is down a mere 500 students. The population decline was due in large to a young, unmarried population of male construction-related employees who were forced to leave the state for economic reasons. A state department of education mandate for changing the minimum age for students entering kindergarten reduced the school enrollment in 1986. The next school year the enrollment increased with an influx of eligible kindergarten-aged students.

The Anchorage School District is managed by a seven-member elected school board that hires the superintendent. The district supports a "community" school concept, allowing students to attend schools in the community they inhabit. Local school autonomy is encouraged through unit building managers, and community involvement by parents is widely supported. There are 37 advisory boards in the district, one of which is a 35-member Art Curriculum Committee. The primary function of the committee is to monitor and approve changes in the K-12 art program. Of the total of 40,884 students currently enrolled, over 24,500 receive art instruction in either the elementary or secondary art program.

The major art education program of higher learning in the state is conducted by the Fine Arts Department of the University of Alaska Anchorage. A close working relationship has been established between the university art staff and public school art departments. Several references are made here to activities conducted in collaboration with the university; these activities may not be available in other districts.

Introduction to the Study

After a culture dies or centuries pass, art and architecture are all that usually remain, yet in classes of history and literature the arts are seldom addressed. It is through the arts that cultures can be preserved. No student is fully educated or adequately prepared to live in an increasingly technological world or contribute significantly to our culture without understanding the meaning, mystery, and beauty transmitted by the arts. Yet the schools of America, for the most part — and Anchorage is no exception — persist in a model visual arts program that fosters technique and skills primarily in drawing, painting, and sculpture. The practice of teaching students to value, analyze, and interpret artworks and to develop a sensitivity to the world around them has been virtually excluded, along with the teaching of cultures and historical contributions to art.

It is clear that the arts, particularly the visual arts, are not on equal footing with the rest of the curriculum in schools, nor has art been considered a discipline worthy of study. If art is to move from the sidelines of instruction to a more central position in a balanced school curriculum, it is necessary to look at ways in which the art program can be strengthened as a discipline and curriculum offerings developed with continuity and consistency for future producers and consumers of art.

Conducting the Survey

The evaluation process, designed to strengthen the Anchorage School District's secondary visual arts program, was conducted during the 1986-1987 school year. The study was initiated by sending questionnaires to all art and photography teachers and unit principals, including the curriculum principals. The questionnaires were structured by the evaluator and reviewed by the members of the district Assessment and Evaluation Division before they were distributed to appropriate participants. Three visits were made to all schools. The first visit served as an introduction to the survey. The purpose of the second visit was to evaluate the learning environment. During the third, art teachers were interviewed, and teaching strategies and student learning were observed. All art teachers were interviewed by the evaluator to discern job satisfaction and to solicit suggestions for professional growth opportunities and program concerns. Principals were interviewed to determine their knowledge of the arts and art learning behaviors as well as the extent of support to art programs. Administrators from the central district office, the superintendent, two school board members, representatives of the community, and selected students were also interviewed. The art supervisor was the last person to be interviewed. This process allowed the art evaluator to assess all aspects of the program openly without predetermined conclusions.

Information collected from the evaluation resulted in recommendations for the following study categories: (a) organization and supervison, (b) curriculum and instruction, (c) personnel and professionalism, (d) time and scheduling, (e) facilities, (f) student evaluation, (g) community resources, (h) the art budget , and (i) the fine arts school.

RECOMMENDATIONS

As the relationship of parts to any whole entity is related to larger issues, the reader will find that some recommendations go beyond the art program because, in part, the district and its management directly affect the program being studied.

Organization and Administration

1. There must be stated goals and a written commitment, supported by the superintendent and endorsed by the school board, to require the study of art by *all* students. The study of art must include more than art production course offerings; it must include art history, culture, criticism (valuing), and aesthetics. A sign of commitment to support preparations for the future would be the inclusion of computer graphics, filmmaking, video, and design, with an awareness of related careers.

2. A sequential curriculum would include art history, criticism, and aesthetics with creative expression in a simple to complex form, with levels of achievements defined by length of the course.

3. The district must clearly articulate a set of goals and objectives in a long-range plan for art education.

4. The long-range plan for the visual arts should include strategies for program review and evaluation.

5. The district should study the availability of adequate instructional time, space, financial resources, and expert consultants in order to improve programs.

6. Provide in-service programs in art for all administrators in order to seek their commitment to a comprehensive quality art program.

7. The district should work with outside consultants and the university system to prepare an intensive, week-long retreat on the arts for administrators to better help them understand what art is and the value it has in educating the "whole" child.

8. Investigate ways to integrate and infuse arts into other subject matters areas.

9. Initiate collaborations with museums and other community resources for the enhancement of quality art programs.

10. The building principal, who may never have had any art training, should share this responsibility for the art program with the district art supervisor.

11. Counselors should not use art classes as a "dumping ground" for problem students or students who flunk out of other classes.

12. Schools should plan for special events in the arts where all students can experience and be exposed to diverse art media and perhaps participate in an in-depth art experience over a 3- to 5-day period.

The Art Supervisor

1. All art teachers and art supervisor job descriptions should be reviewed and rewritten to be compatible with and supportive of new long-range plans and goals of the art program. Job descriptions should include responsibilities for a teacher on a performance criteria basis, especially in the areas of curriculum development and responsibility for departmental and districtwide duties.

2. The art supervisor should work closely with the building principal to set evaluation expectations for the teacher appraisal system, because art teaching is different from other kinds of teaching. Most building principals do not understand that art demands another teaching mode.

3. As the art education program grows and includes a requirement for graduation from junior/senior high school, the supervisor should have two supervisor/teacher assistants. One would supervise the 55 elementary art teachers and the elementary art program, including in-service courses for elementary art and classroom teachers. The other could supervise and work closely with the junior and senior high schools. Both individuals would have a joint appointment with the University of Alaska Anchorage (Figure 17.1).

4. The art supervisor should be given a university status appointment as a lecturer at the university in order to train staff, give credit as a class for curriculum development and other art education courses and training. The art supervisor would work

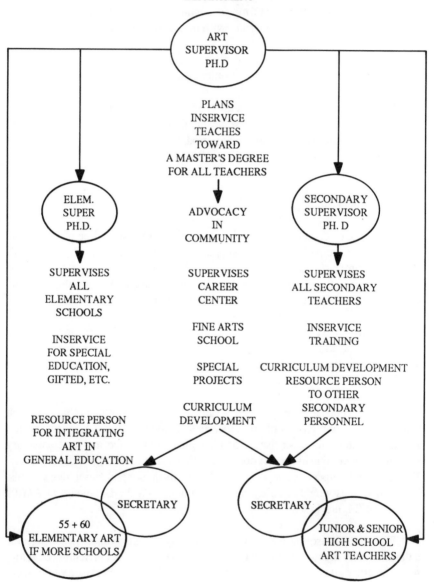

Figure 17.1 Year 2000
**ART DEPARTMENT
SUPERVISION MODEL
ANCHORAGE SCHOOL DISTRICT**

DEPARTMENT

ART
SUPERVISOR
PH.D

PLANS
INSERVICE
TEACHES
TOWARD
A MASTER'S DEGREE
FOR ALL TEACHERS

ELEM.
SUPER
PH.D.

ADVOCACY
IN
COMMUNITY

SECONDARY
SUPERVISOR
PH. D

SUPERVISES
ALL
ELEMENTARY
SCHOOLS

SUPERVISES
CAREER
CENTER

SUPERVISES
ALL SECONDARY
TEACHERS

INSERVICE
FOR SPECIAL
EDUCATION,
GIFTED, ETC.

FINE ARTS
SCHOOL

SPECIAL
PROJECTS

INSERVICE
TRAINING

CURRICULUM DEVELOPMENT
RESOURCE PERSON
TO OTHER
SECONDARY
PERSONNEL

RESOURCE PERSON
FOR INTEGRATING
ART IN
GENERAL EDUCATION

CURRICULUM
DEVELOPMENT

SECRETARY

SECRETARY

55 + 60
ELEMENTARY ART
IF MORE SCHOOLS

JUNIOR & SENIOR
HIGH SCHOOL
ART TEACHERS

with the university to develop courses to meet the staff retraining needs leading to an MA or MFA in art, as well as retraining for regular classroom teachers.

5. The art supervisor should be encouraged to take an administrative intern interested in the arts from the university administration program.

6. The district art program needs to be housed in the same building with other curriculum coordinators.

7. A community group, "Friends of Arts Education," should be established. This could be a combined effort with other arts support groups.

8. The art supervisor should administer the total districtwide art budget.

Curriculum and Instruction

1. Art teachers need several in-service sessions or a course on theories of curriculum and instruction to understand the philosophy and construction of curriculum.

2. Each art teacher should be made responsible for the development of one curriculum theme each year, have the rest of the staff use it after a demonstration, and give feedback for revision. This could be a basis for field testing and for a continual regenerative library of field-tested materials and activities.

3. Integrated art curriculum materials should be expanded and adapted for secondary art history, criticism, aesthetics, and creative expression in arts education.

4. Linkages to other art forms taught in the schools should be offered, as well as linkages to related courses, such as programs for gifted and talented students and multicultural programs.

5. An intensive program in drawing should be offered to all students in the junior and senior high schools.

6. Teachers need in-service training and they need to continually update the skills they use to teach art. Example: if a *media exploration* (techniques, tools, equipment, elements of design) studio format is used, teachers should be trained in other ways

to motivate art expression, such as fantasy, direct observation of events, projected image, relationship to art forms in other cultures, design problems, reassembling of materials/order, and use of symbolism and its meaning. Teachers need to have magic to put magic into their teaching.

7. Career education in the arts should be developed and emphasized.

Personnel and Professionalism

1. All art teachers at the junior and senior high levels should be full-time art teachers with at least a master's degree in art education or a master of fine arts.

2. If art teachers are to be assigned to teach non art courses, such as social studies or business finance, the building principal must seek the approval of the art supervisor.

3. Art teachers should collaborate with other teachers in peer coaching and team teaching.

Time and Scheduling

1. Flexible scheduling would aid in providing quality and in-depth time for students to pursue art activities.

2. Scheduling should permit a talented student to work in the community with a mentor.

Materials, Equipment, and Supplies

1. The system for ordering art supplies should be computerized.

2. Equipment needs for art classes should be identified, and equipment should be purchased over the next 5 years in order to update and infuse quality into the program.

Facilities

1. A committee of art teachers should be formed to assess the physical facilities of all art rooms in the district and to make recommendations to the administration for retrofitting and remodeling where needed and appropriate over the next 5 years. This should become an official part of the capital improvement program.

2. All junior and senior high schools should spend time redesigning their entry ways as a compelling and aesthetically beautiful statement about the school.

3. All schools should find a space (an unused classroom) and remodel it as an art gallery.

Community Resources

1. A "Friends of Art Education" community group should be formed to help operationalize the status report and provide support for the arts to the school board.

Budget for Art

1. The budget for art should be administered directly by the art supervisor.

2. The budget of each art teacher should reflect allocations for repair, replacement, and additions of materials, furniture, and equipment on an ongoing basis.

3. The budget should provide incentives for extraordinary enterprises, for new ideas, and for curriculum development or research.

Fine Arts School

1. The Anchorage School District should investigate the feasibility of a joint appointment with the university within the School of Arts and Science. In this way a summer school for the arts could be devised for high school students.

2. The district should support and build on an already-existing program of placing talented art students with art mentors in the community.

3. The district should prepare a feasibility study for a fine arts school. A community needs assessment would add strength to the proposal.

Summary

The data collected and recommendations made were based on a model of evaluation that focused on documents through observations, interviews, questionnaires, and in-house records. The final evaluation form was descriptive and interpretive rather than measured with predictions.

The recommendations were not radical. Some ideas were implemented immediately while others will require funding and revision of long-range planning.

Changes are difficult and slow in coming to fruition, especially without substantial evidence to merit movement in a new direction. The status report provided the needs assessment necessary to progress with long-range planning and a system to develop the secondary art program into a full-blown model of art education including aesthetics, criticism, and art heritage with creative expression.

Long-range planning over the first 5 years, along with further planning over the next 10-15 years, was outlined in the document. Details for facility changes (e.g., ventilation) were outlined by unit and reviewed with principals. A copy of The Art Learning Environment was provided for the director of operations. This provides support for principals requesting facility improvements needed to ensure a safe, hazard-free learning environment for students. Documentation and information compiled in the status report has served as a vehicle for making positive changes in the Anchorage School District secondary art program.

The process of long-range planning involves the implementation of goals and objectives. It looks at the whole. It is also a process that slowly and persistently discovers ways to bring bits and parts together to complete the whole of the original objectives. Change is a slow process. For example, a major change will occur districtwide during October of the 1990-1991 school year. All K-12 art teachers, will be involved in a full-day in-service program provided by a Getty Center for Education in the Arts consultant, followed by two credit courses in discipline-based art education. All art teachers will function with the same level of information, emphasizing art history, art criticism, aesthetics, and art production.

The results outlined the status report serve as a catalyst for continuing changes in the secondary art program and significant implications for the districtwide art education progress in the Anchorage School District. The report presents a common language for administrators to begin to understand art education program needs and to understand the value of the visual arts in a balanced education for all students.

212

References

Taylor, A. (1986). *The status of the art and photography programs in the junior and senior high Anchorage school district, Anchorage, Alaska. 1986.*

Contributors

Placed in order of their articles

E. Andrew Mills before taking an early retirement in 1989, was Chief of the Bureau of Arts, Music and Humanities for the New York State Education Department. In this administrative post he worked closely with art, music, dance, theater, and humanities programs in the New York State public and nonpublic schools and universities, as well as with arts councils, museums, and performing arts groups.

He has been active with NAEA for more than 30 years, has held many leadership positions, and has been the recipient of numerous awards. He is a past member of the NAEA Board, was National Art Educator of the Year in 1985, and was Supervision and Administration Art Educator of the Year in 1988. He chaired the Super Sessions for the 1990 NAEA Convention in Kansas City, is on the Editorial Board of *Art Education,* and is a member of the Standards for Teacher Preparation Committee. He is also a Special Life Member of the New York State Art Teachers Association.

Mills received his BFA and MS degrees in art education at Syracuse University. He is an exhibiting artist, an arts consultant, and, with his wife, Virginia Ward Mills, is proprietor of the Mills Studio and Gallery, Wellfleet (Cape Cod), Massachusetts. In addition to his involvement with the visual arts, he has long been active as a performer and soloist in musical organizations and community theater.

Gene C. Wenner is an experienced arts consultant, author, and keynote speaker who is currently President of Arts Education Consultants, Inc. of Reston, Virginia. He has held such positions as Special Assistant for the Arts to U.S. Commissioner of Education Ernest Boyer, Associate Director for the John D. Rockefeller III Fund's Arts in Education Program, Vice President of the National Foundation for Advancement in the Arts, and Arts Consultant for the Pennsylvania Department of Education. In 1988 he was Project Coordinator for National Public Radio's Arts History and Criticism Project. Mr. Wenner has taught music in the Philadelphia Public Schools and was Professor of Music and Choral and Orchestral Conductor at Kutztown State University, Kutztown, Pennsylvania.

Laura J. Magee is Director of Arts Education for the Pittsburgh Public Schools, Pittsburgh, Pennsylvania. Her responsibilities include the areas of visual arts, music, theatre, dance, and media arts. Previously she held a similar position as Arts Consultant with the Iowa Department of Education. Her academic preparation includes an Ed. D. from Arizona State University, an MA from Louisiana State University, and a BFA from Newcomb College of Tulane University, New Orleans, Louisiana. She taught art education, design, and ceramics to undergraduate and graduate students at Drake University, Des Moines, Iowa; Arizona State University, Tempe, Arizona; and Louisiana State University, Baton Rouge, Louisiana. At Delgado College in New Orleans, she taught commercial art. In rural Mississippi and urban New Orleans she taught art in elementary and secondary public schools. She has been involved with numerous local and state arts organizations.

Gretchen A. Boyer is the Fine Arts Specialist for Visual Arts for the Arizona Department of Education. She received her BFA and MA in Art Education/Studio Art from Michigan State University. Ms. Boyer has taught or directed kindergarten through university visual arts programs for the past 17 years in both Michigan and Arizona. She has been an active member of the Arizona Art Education Association, serving as State Youth Art Month Chairperson, Newsletter Editor, Secretary, and President. Boyer was NAEA Pacific Region Art Educator of the Year in 1986 and Arizona Art Educator of the Year in 1987. She is currently on the Editorial Board of *Art Education*. She has organized a variety of state and regional conferences in Arizona, including Building Relationships: Symposium in Arts Education Management and the Mountain States Art Education Consortium.

Boyer is an exhibiting fiber artist working in weaving, felt, and hand-made paper.

Robert Eaker is the Dean of the School of Education at Middle Tennessee State University. He has written widely on the issues of effective teaching and effective schools. His latest book, coauthored with Richard DuFour, is *Fulfilling the Promise of Excellence: Practical Strategies for School Improvement.* He has been the invited speaker at numerous state and national meetings and regularly consults with school districts throughout the nation regarding school improvement issues.

Mary Ann Ranells is the Director of Curriculum and Instruction for the Nampa School District in Nampa, Idaho. For 12 years she taught English, reading, and Spanish at the secondary level. Since 1985 she has assisted several districts in the implementation of the school improvement process based on the effective schools research.

Nan Yoshida is the District Specialist for Elementary Art Instruction for the Los Angeles Unified School District, where she was previously classroom teacher, art resource teacher, Gifted Programs Coordinator, and Area Fine Arts Advisor. She is the author and co-author of many district art publications. In the commercial field she has coauthored *Discover Art — Art Print Guides,* published by Davis Publications, Inc. She is a consultant to the California Commission on Teacher Credentialing and serves on the Advisory panel for the Elementary Subject Matter Assessment.

Yoshida is active in both the NAEA and the California Art Education Association (CAEA), and currently serves as CAEA Membership Chair. She was recognized in 1990 by CAEA as Elementary Art Educator of the Year.

Yoshida received her BA from the University of California at Los Angeles and her MA from California Lutheran University.

Ronald J. Topping earned his EdD at Teachers College, Columbia University, in New York City. He is K-12 Program Coordinator and High School Chairman of Art, Music, Arts in General Education, the Gifted and Talented Program, and Home Economics for the White Plains, New York, School District. He has been an art teacher; he was district Art Supervisor for 10 years, and at one time he was K-12 Program Coordinator for five different curricular areas.

Topping was the first president of the Council of Administrators of Art Education in New York State. He has written a number of articles for professional publications on topics such as architecture and the schools, art and zoology, and art and humanistic education. He has made numerous presentations at NAEA Conventions; and in 1990 was named New York State and NAEA Eastern Regional Supervision and Administration Art Educator of the Year.

Katherine O'Donnell, EdD, is on the faculty of the Graduate School of Education at Bank Street College in New York City. She teaches courses in foundations of administration and instructional supervision and directs the Leadership in Museum Education program. The developmental stages of transition from teaching to administration are of special interest to her.

Gary M. Crow is on the graduate faculty in educational leadership at the Bank Street College of Education. Part of his responsibility includes instruction in school administration in the Bank Street College/Parsons School of Design Master's program. He received his PhD in Educational Administration from the University of Chicago. His areas of specialization are the sociology of work and occupations and the school principalship. In addition to his research on art teachers moving into administration, he is currently involved in a study of the development of administrative identification from a career perspective.

Billie McKindra Phillips is Supervisor of Art Education for the St. Louis, Missouri, City Schools. She received her Bachelor of Arts Degree from Stowe Teachers College and her Master's in Teaching Aesthetic Education from Webster University, St. Louis.

Her past educational experiences include early childhood teaching; K-12 Art Specialist; Art Department Head, Sumner High School; and Art Area Head, Visual and Performing Arts High School. Phillips continues conducting workshops and seminars, including demonstrations for teachers, in Gross Pointe, Michigan. She is the coauthor of several books and published poet, and she currently coedits the *Green Pages for Teaching K-8* magazine (Allen Raymond, Publisher).

Ms. Phillips's article, *An Infinity of Space Within the Frame* (Concordia College), expresses her belief that art provides opportunities for reinforcing the education of the whole person. All educational thrusts should encompass creative growth so that "the imagination grows wings for soaring."

Richard R. Doornek is the Curriculum Specialist in Art for the Milwaukee Public Schools. He coordinates the K-12 Art Education Program for 150 schools. He has taught art at all levels since 1965, when he received a Bachelor's Degree in Art Education from the University of Wisconsin — Milwaukee. He began teaching art in the Milwaukee Public Schools in 1965. He received an Experienced Teacher Fellowship to attend Arizona State University, where he was awarded a Master's Degree in 1968. After 5 years as a high school Art Department Chair, he was appointed as Supervisor of Art Education for the district. In 1975 he received a doctoral fellowship at Ball State University. He was awarded the doctorate in 1978.

Doornek has held leadership positions in art education locally and nationally. He has been President of the Milwaukee Area Teachers of Art, the Wisconsin Art Education Association, and the Milwaukee Art Commission, and Chairman of the Very Special Arts, Milwaukee Imagination Celebration, and State Conference Committees. He has served as Director of the Supervision and Administration Division on the NAEA Board.

He has been a regular presenter at national conferences and has written five articles for *School Arts*. He has been honored by his colleagues as Wisconsin's Outstanding Art Educator in 1983 and Outstanding Supervisor in 1987.

Martin Rayala is the Art Consultant for the Wisconsin Department of Public Instruction. He is President-Elect of the National Association of State Directors of Art Education and National Director-Elect of the Division of Supervision and Administration of NAEA. He received his doctorate from the University of Oregon — Eugene. As a teacher in the Wisconsin public schools, he helped start the Fine Arts Elementary School in Racine.

In his position with the state, Rayala has developed conferences on such topics as architecture, assessment, and aesthetics and has developed curriculum guides for art education and arts for students with exceptional needs. He has published articles on computers in art education and the role of art in general education. He is currently doing research in the area of urban aesthetics.

Larry N. Peeno is Supervisor of Fine Arts for the Missouri State Department of Education. He earned his Bachelor's and Master's degrees from Western Kentucky University, and his EdD from the University of Missouri. Prior to his position with the state, he was District Coordinator of Art for the Normandy School District, St. Louis, Missouri. It was in that capacity that he authored the article in this publication.

Peeno has served on local, state, and national committees, as well as on art museum advisory boards. He has been on the Editorial Board of *Art Education*, and in 1990 he coordinated the Supervision and Administration Division's Leadership Workshop prior to the NAEA Convention in Kansas City.

Carolyn White-Travanti is a K-12 Supervisor of Art Education for the Milwaukee Public Schools. After receiving a Bachelor's degree in Art Education from the University of Wisconsin — Milwaukee in 1969, she taught secondary art for the Milwaukee Public Schools. In 1974 she completed a Master of Science in Art (Painting) from the University of Wisconsin — Milwaukee. In 1976 she was appointed director/teacher of a new cooperative Art Satellite Program for Milwaukee Public Schools at the Milwaukee Art Museum. This unique program is a daily one-semester accredited high school class for city and suburban students meeting at the Milwaukee Art Museum. In 1981 she was awarded a Master of Fine Arts Degree from the University of Wisconsin — Milwaukee. She exhibits specific installations, environments, and small assemblages.

White-Travanti has held office in the Wisconsin Art Education Association and local artists' organizations, and has been a guest lecturer on art education and artists. She has published articles in NAEA publications and was cited in the 1984 *Art History, Art Criticism, and Art Production* Getty Report published in 1984. In 1985 she was named Wisconsin Art Educator of the Year and Outstanding High School Teacher of Art by the Rhode Island School of Arts and Design.

Mac Arthur Goodwin is the Art Consultant for the South Carolina Department of Education. He received his BA degree from Claflin College and an MAT from the University of South Carolina. Goodwin is Chair of the South Carolina Alliance and has been appointed to the National Arts Education Outcome Goals Committee. He was the Convention Program Chair for the 1990 NAEA Convention in Kansas City. In 1989 he won the NAEA Southeastern Regional Art Educator of the Year Award, and in 1990 he was the NAEA Supervision and Administration Art Educator of the Year. He received the South Carolina Governor's Award in Art Education, the Elizabeth O'Neill Verner Award, in 1990.

As a producing artist, Goodwin maintains an exhibition schedule throughout the Southeast. He was recently awarded the Purchase Prize in the Atlanta Ninth Annual National Art Exhibition and Competition.

220

Paul M. Patterson is Coordinator of Fine Arts for Illinois' second largest school district, District U-2 in Elgin. For 17 years prior to this appointment he was a music teacher.

As Coordinator of Fine Arts, he is responsible for the administration of all aspects of dance, drama, visual arts, and music K-12. He has written and administered three competitive arts in education grants from the Illinois State Arts Council. He is currently Chair of the Illinois State Board of Education Arts Advisory Committee, which is assisting in the implementation of state arts mandates. He is President-Elect of the Illinois Alliance for Arts Education and continues to be a guest conductor in Illinois.

Sandra Finlayson holds a BA in French from the University of Idaho and an MA in Art Education from the University of Oregon. Through her sense of enjoyment and enthusiasm for the development of learner capabilities, she has had a variety of teaching experiences. She has spent the past 4 years as a graduate teaching fellow in the Art Education Department at the University of Oregon, where she works with preservice teachers.

Her doctoral research is a study of traditional and contemporary validity theories juxtaposed against a possible articulation of the art learning construct. The hoped-for outcome is a more appropriate validation process with regard to evaluation and disclosure of art learning.

In addition to her visual arts expressions, Finlayson's interests include interpretive dance, writing, teaching, domestic arts, and conversational French.

Myrna B. Clark is Supervisor of Visual Arts for the Anchorage, Alaska School District, a position she has held for the past 9 years. Previously she was Assistant Visual Arts Director for School District #2, Billings, Montana. Her art teaching experiences include elementary, junior, and senior high school levels in Iowa, Ohio, Montana, and Wyoming.

Clark earned a BFA in Graphic Arts Design and Education from the University of South Dakota, and an MEd degree in Educational Administration from Montana State University. In 1989 Myrna was the recipient of the NAEA Pacific Region Supervision and Administration Award. She received national recognition from NAEA for award-winning Youth Art Month Celebrations in Montana while serving as YAM chairperson.

Clark is a trained IVAE (Improving Visual Arts Education) consultant for the Getty Center for Education in the Arts.